The Scottish Country Miller
1700-1900

MERRY THE MAID BE

Merry the maid be
That marries the miller
For foul day, and fair day,
He's aye bringing till her;
Has aye a penny in his purse
For dinner and for supper;
And, gin she please, a good fat cheese,
And lumps of yellow butter.

When Jamie first did woo me,
I speer'd what was his calling;
Fair maid, said he, O come and see,
You're welcome to my dwelling;
Though I was shy, yet I cou'd spy
The truth of what he told me,
And that his house was warm and couth,
And room in it to hold me.

Behind the door a bag of meal,
And in the kist was plenty
Of good hard cakes his mother bakes,
And bannocks werena scanty;
A good fat sow, a sleeky cow
Was standing in the byre;
Whilst lazy puss, with mealy mouse,
Was playing at the fire.

Good signs are these, my mither says,
And bids me tak the miller;
For foul day, and fair day,
He's aye bringing till her;
For meal and malt she doesna want,
Nor ony thing that's dainty;
And now and then a keckling hen,
To lay her eggs in plenty.

In winter when the win' and rain
Bla's o'er the barn and byre,
The miller on a good hearth-stane,
Before a ranting fire,
He sits, and cracks, and tells his tale,
O'er ale that is right nappy;
Who'd be Queen, that gaudy thing,
When a miller's wife's sae happy.

From *The Goldfinch, or New Modern Songster,* Glasgow, 1783, Song LXXV, p. 63.

The Scottish Country Miller 1700-1900

A History of Water-powered Meal Milling in Scotland

ENID GAULDIE

JOHN DONALD PUBLISHERS LTD
EDINBURGH

Published by
John Donald Publishers
an imprint of Birlinn Limited
Unit 8
Canongate Venture
5 New Street
Edinburgh EH8 8BH

Reprinted 1999

Printed in Great Britain by Bell & Bain Ltd, Glasgow

Preface

The history of Scotland has been too often the history of its aristocracy, its lawyers and its clergy. But recent years have brought growing interest in the lives of the anonymous, the country people, the domestic craftsmen and the rural workers. One possible way to make their acquaintance is to single out a class of men whose character, whose circumstances and whose occupation already distinguish them to some extent from their fellows. Study of such a class is made possible partly because their distinguishing characteristics make them noticeable and liable to be commented on by their contemporaries and partly because their importance to the community meant that their presence or absence, their efficiency or lack of it, their congeniality or surliness, their enterprise or passivity could not fail to affect that community's progress.

Such an importance can be claimed for the miller. Of course, with minister, doctor and dominie, with brewer, baker and weaver, with blacksmith, wright, mason and shoemaker, he is only one of the men important to small town and village life. The difference is that until the industrialisation of the towns and the depopulation of the countryside — and these changes took place at widely differing pace in different regions of Scotland — there had to be a miller even in settlements where very few of the others existed. His product was the chief element of the diet of the whole Scottish people until Victorian times and of important sections of the population until the First World War. Before the expansion of retail trade the mill was shop as well as manufacturer, the only source of what most people ate most of the time.

There are three main sources of information about mills and millers. One is field study, and I have done my share of walking river banks and poking among nettles for clogged lades and broken sluices, of gingerly treading over rotting floors and dodging swinging pieces of broken machinery. I have been fortunate in finding a very few old water-powered mills still working and in having their beautiful operation shown to me by men who take pride in their possession. In other countries corn mills have been preserved either by government funds or enlightened private patronage. In Scotland it is already too late to save or even to record most of the hundreds of mill sites which existed even ten years ago. The spread of industrialisation has erased many of them, farming of marginal land has filled in dams and lades and accounted for the pulling down of walls and buildings, neglect has allowed the crumbling of many others. How much longer the privilege of seeing a water-powered meal mill in action in Scotland will exist depends very much on popular concern for their survival.

Written information about mills occurs both in printed and in manuscript form. Because the system of thirlage tied farms to mills, estate records show many transactions, especially complaints about the amount of mill dues exacted from tenants and about the state of repair of mills. Thirlage again accounts for the frequent occurrence of reference to mills and millers in legal records. And the late eighteenth century agricultural writers' dislike of thirlage meant that, in their advocacy of land improvement, they invariably discussed corn mills and the farmers' dependence on them. The amalgamation of many small mills under the control of a few large milling companies has sometimes resulted in the preservation of mill records. Parish histories and the autobiographies of men with rural backgrounds often describe both mill and miller as an important part of a remembered past. The lives of the great engineers and technical works about early engineering give accounts of mill machinery, of improvements to it, and sometimes of the millers who used it.

The third source of information is the memory of elderly people who once worked, or whose families worked, as millers in the days when mills were still of central importance to the rural economy. There are many things which would have remained mysterious to me if my curiosity had not been met by patient kindliness from the millers I have encountered on my way.

In balancing the kind of information which emerges from these three sources I have attempted to present as true a picture as possible of mills and millers and to place them in the context of the Scotland of the not so distant past.

As a suburban dweller, if a reluctant one, all my life, my interest in country mills needs perhaps some explanation. It was awakened in the first place by my study of bleachfields in Scotland because, in studying any particular bleachfield, I was interested to find that, in almost every case, it had been, before the growth of the linen industry, a much more ancient corn mill. A little further research showed that the same applied to many spinning mills. Corn millers had been, in fact, the first selectors of industrial sites, the first harnessers of power, all over the country. This seemed to make them, in themselves, worth some further thought.

There were other spurs to my interest. One is a thirty years' acquaintance with one of the last country mills, the Mill of Benholm, the other is the fact that my husband's great grandfather, the William Gaudy who appears in this book, was miller of Lunan, and some of his records survive.

I have been extraordinarily lucky in the help I have been given and the friendships I have made in the course of my work. There are very many people whose advice I should acknowledge, industrial archaeologists, and in particular my distinguished friends Rex Wailes and Anders Jespersen, architects and architectural historians, and in particular my husband Sinclair Gauldie, Bruce Walker of the Department of Architecture, Duncan of Jordanstone College of Art, Dundee, and David Walker of the Historic Buildings Council for Scotland, historians and lawyers and, in particular, Alexander Fenton of the National Museum of Antiquities in Edinburgh and James Robertson of the Department of Scots Law, Dundee University. Of the millers who have helped me I must single out Mr Lindsay Watson of Benholm, Mr William Gavin of Peterculter and Mr James Dallas of Benvie. I have also been helped immeasurably by a retired millwright, Mr George Davidson, and a miller's daughter, Mrs Williams, both of Aberdeen. To all these I owe my grateful thanks. Any qualities the book has it owes to them but its failings are my own.

I must also thank, for their kindness in making milling records available to me, Arthur Young M'Clelland Moores and Company of Perth and the Hamlyn/Angus Milling Company of Kirriemuir.

Enid Gauldie

Contents

Abbreviations

Ag. Hist. Rev.	*Agricultural History Review*
E.H.R.	*Economic History Review*
Ind. Arch.	*Industrial Archaeology*
Inst. Brit. Geog.	Institute of British Geographers
N.R.A.(S)	National Register of Archives (Scotland)
N.S.A.	*New Statistical Account of Scotland*
O.S.A.	*Old Statistical Account of Scotland*
P.P.	*Parliamentary Papers*
P.S.A.S.	*Proceedings of the Society of Antiquaries of Scotland*
Roy. Scot. Geog. Soc.	Royal Scottish Geographical Society
Scot. Arch. Forum.	*Scottish Archaeological Forum*
Scot. Geog. Mag.	*Scottish Geographical Magazine*
S.H.R.	*Scottish Historical Review*
S.H.S.	Scottish History Society
S.R.O.	Scottish Record Office
T.H.A.S.S.	*Transactions of the Highland and Agricultural Society of Scotland*

1
Diet — The Product of the Mill

The central importance of the corn mill to the traditional Scots community is not easily grasped until it is understood that the mill used to be the supplier of almost every mouthful of food. A wholly admirable wish to upgrade the quality and variety of food in Scottish restaurants has resulted in recent years in a seeking out of old Scots recipes and an interesting reconstruction of a tradition based on venison, salmon, excellent beef and lamb.

But cookery books played no part at all in the kitchen management of the Scots peasantry, and until at least the second half of the nineteenth century the Scottish population was predominantly agricultural, living for the most part on what it could produce. Edinburgh middle class families and country lairds might enjoy a richer diet, Highlanders — where they lived under the protection of a benevolent chieftain — had fish and game to eat. Along the coast and as far into the hinterland as the fish cadgers travelled with their creels there might be fresh sea food or salt herring. For most people, however, food was meal, ground from their own grains and pulses.

Accounts of the dietary habits of the Scots people range from those which linger over the luxurious providing of the prosperous lairds to those which emphasise the near-famine subsistence of the poor. The first describe the abundance of game, the salmon-packed rivers, the splendid cattle, the imported clarets and brandies. The second write of a people grubbing for a diet of husks and diseased mutton. Truth lies, as ever, between the two extremes. There is little that is precise that can be said about the whole country or the whole of our period, the food available varying from region to region, from generation to generation and from one social class to another. A few certainties, however, emerge. Until potato farming was perfected in the early nineteenth century, cereals were the mainstay of the Scottish people, for many not just the main ingredient of their diet but the whole of their diet, the only variation lying in the form of their preparation. And for some, for farm servants for instance, diet deteriorated rather than improved in the nineteenth century. Whatever the variations which might be added to their basic diet, the whole of the population of Scotland remained throughout our period very dependent upon the products of the corn mill.

Oats are always thought of as the chief element in the Scotsman's diet, but, in fact, at the beginning of the eighteenth century a mixture of barley, peas and beans was the most common food. Although oats were grown, a large proportion was not available to the grower as food for his family. Oats made the rent-paying crop, rent being paid in meal to the landlord, and the proportion of the crop accounted for in this way has been estimated at 30%.[1] To ensure that next year's crop would allow the payment of the high fixed rents endured by tenant farmers during the seventeenth and eighteenth centuries, another 25% of the crop had to be retained as seed corn. In good years the remaining 45% of the corn, after the deduction of mill dues, could be eaten by the farmer's dependents or sold to purchase other requirements. In years of bad harvests, rent and seed corn exhausted the stock, leaving no surplus for the farmer's own consumption, and there were many instances of the landlord having to forego his rents to prevent widespread starvation among his tenants. Even on the Sutherland estates, not famed for their generous treatment of tenants at that period, the factor wrote of the need to import oatmeal if the people were 'to be got brought to meet a new crop . . . I have great reason to believe that 900 to 1000 bolls of oatmeal and perhaps 400 bolls of seed oats with a few bolls of pease if they can be got and a little seed potatoes (which will be a great consideration as a change at any rate) will be a supply if cautiously dealt out which will bring the people to the first of a new crop . . . tho' were they readily to get it they would consume twice or thrice that quantity of meal. But, as public roads and other improvements will be going on in the Country this summer these will not fare worse that the inhabitants should experience a certain degree of hardship to lead them to seek after more active scenes than they have hitherto been accustomed to.'[2]

There were large areas of Scotland where oats were grown by the tenant farmers for the subsistence not of themselves but of their baronial landlords. Landowners, after deducting what was required for their own use, exported the corn paid to them in rents. Smout and Fenton reckon that, after 1660, 'There was hardly a considerable family on such lands (the coastal estates) north of the Tay which was not shipping grain or meal either coastwise or abroad.'[3] An indication that oats was a cash crop rather than for domestic consumption is that during the very bad years of 1782/3 farmers were able to make high profits by selling corn.[4]

This accounts for the dependence of a large part of the population on pulses which were grown specifically for their own consumption, and explains why, even in periods of dearth, large quantities of corn could be exported. At Peterhead, for instance, even in the years 1789 to 1794, 9216 bolls were exported annually.[5]

It was, of course, all grist to the mill, whether the product reached the bellies of the farmers or not. 'Every pea, every barley corn, every grain of oats'[6] had to go to the hopper. Mills were adapted not only for oats but to the grinding of bere and the pulses either separately or as a mixture. Sometimes the seeds were sown in separate fields and the grain mixed after it was harvested, but sometimes patches of ground were sown by the cottar folk themselves, or by the farmer for the use of his servants, with a mixture of seeds. The resultant meal could be made into a coarse bread, flat and unleavened, or into porridge, and it could be used for thickening kail. Barley which had been 'knockit', that is rubbed and beaten free of its husks and left whole rather than ground, was used for barley broth. The Forfeited Estates Commissioners found, in Auchterarder, 'A few tenants excepted, no family had oatmeal in their houses, nor could they get any. They eat nothing better than bear meal and a few greens boiled together at mid-day and bear-meal porridge evening and morning.'[7]

What is thought of, in fact, as the traditional Scots diet has not such a long tradition. Until agricultural improvements had brought about the enclosing, draining and fertilising of fields, and the scientific selection of seed, the kind of good milleable oats which bred late Victorian Scotsmen for the Metropolitan Police and the Scots Guards hardly existed. Bere, the primitive indigenous form of one-sided barley, was preferred as a food crop partly because its yield on poor soil was higher[8] and its straw, on which farmers depended for thatching, was longer and stronger. So oatmeal porridge and bannocks are not so much the traditional food of the Scots peasantry as the improved food of that section of the agricultural population which remained on the land after improved farming methods had begun the movement towards the towns.

Similarly mealie puddings, while having a long enough history in the homes of the well to do, were not common fare for the eighteenth century country dweller, although town dwellers could buy them at market stalls such as Pudden Lizzie's in Edinburgh.[9] Puddings are made of oatmeal, seasoning and herbs stuffed into the cleaned and emptied entrails of the pig. But the keeping of pigs is dependent upon a steady supply of surplus from kitchen and dairy. Until the establishment of potato farming, which was far from general throughout Scotland until the second quarter of the nineteenth century, pig keeping was beyond the means of most agricultural workers.[10]

Cock-a-leekie, extolled by all who like to write about the Scots cuisine and given pride of place in those restaurants which claim a rich tradition of cooking in Scotland, was never a common dish except at the laird's table. Grain was not abundant enough to be scattered for poultry. Many farms forbade the keeping of fowls to those who lived on the place.[11] Where it was common to pay 'kaim' or poultry as part of the rent in kind the rents were raised as a cash crop due to the landlord rather than a source of food, although there is no doubt a hen found its way to the cottar's table occasionally.

As everywhere else, at every period, the food of the common people was bread, made of the kind of meal available in their own region. But whereas in England 'maslin', bread made from a mixture of wheat and rye, began to be uncommon after the seventeenth century,[12] the Scottish 'mashlum', a mixture of peas, beans, bere or oats, was still generally eaten by all classes until the end of the eighteenth century and by working people after that except in some Lowland areas.[13] Jamieson's *Dictionary* gives *mashlach, mashlich, mashlie, mashloch, mashlock* and *mashlum* as variations for mixed grain, generally, he says, peas or oats, and the bread made from it. The word survives in the *mash* given to horses and derives from Old English *masc,* to mix. A mixture of pease and barley meal was known as 'bread-meal' and was still 'a profitable article with us' in Perth as late as 1837.[14] There was, until 1976, one water mill in Scotland still equipped for making pease meal. Dripps Mill at Waterfoot, East Kilbride, built in 1761, has a pair of stones set for pea grinding and a girdle for roasting the peas to prepare them for grinding.[15] In Arran as late as 1818 a report said, 'Peas are to be met with everywhere and everywhere good. The people use them as much as bread corn.'[16]

The backwardness of farming in most areas until the last quarter of the eighteenth century meant that wheat was seldom or ineffectively grown. With efficient drainage and proper soil management good selected wheat seed can flourish in parts of Scotland where the climate is moderately kind; but boggy ground, starved soil and poor seed added to long winters and late springs made wheat a chancy crop even for those eighteenth century landlords with the initiative to try it. It was grown with some success in South-East Scotland, the Carse of Gowrie, Moray, Fife and some parts of Easter Ross in the late eighteenth century but was regarded not as a food but as a cash crop.[17] Bread from wheat flour was made occasionally for the gentry but not eaten by those who laboured to grow it. Jerry Melford, in *Humphrey Clinker*, journeying through Scotland in the 1760s, found in the lunch basket provided by his hosts 'a bushel of oatmeal, made in thin cakes and bannocks, with a small wheaten loaf in the middle for the strangers'.[18] By the end of the eighteenth century lawyers were beginning to experience some difficulty in that the law of Scotland, insofar as it placed limitations upon tenant farmers, had been drawn up in an era which did not envisage the growing of wheat. Some tenants were finding it possible to evade taxation by stressing that their tenancy agreements did not apply to wheat.[19] Millers in some areas began to find their income reduced because wheat had replaced oats as the chief crop in their area. Robert Henry, the miller of Ussie, wrote to J. A. Stewart Mackenzie, Esq., in 1821, complaining of the decrease in mill dues 'as the greatest part of the property is laid out in large farms and the most of the produce of them being wheat, turnips and grass, consequently very little corn comes to this mill'.[20] There were two reasons why the wheat grown in the area round Mill of Ussie was not being brought to the mill as oats would have been. Wheat in the main was stored and exported as grain, not as flour. Its primary use was not for the food of the neighbourhood, and so there was no need to grind it into flour for local use and more danger of deterioration during transit if it was exported as flour. But even if the wheat had been intended for local consumption the local farmers, because they could not be forced to bring wheat to their landlord's mill, as they were bound to do with their oats, might have chosen to have their grain ground elsewhere. This area was one of those in which wheat was supplanting bere as the main crop.

The spread of wheat as farming methods improved is generally known and accepted. What is perhaps less well known is that oats as a crop was only slightly better established in the earlier part of the eighteenth century and that it was spreading concurrently with wheat as agricultural science made it possible. Oats has not been immemorially the food of the Scots as is popularly imagined and in fact it replaced bere as the main food crop only gradually. Wheat, then, did not supplant oats in the Scottish diet, or rather it did not do so until the end of the nineteenth century. What happened was that, slowly during the eighteenth century, and much more rapidly from the late eighteenth until the middle of the nineteenth century, wheat and oats together began to spread across all the arable lands capable of being improved, ousting the old crops of bere, peas and beans as they went, wheat taking the lower-lying areas of temperate climate, oats the higher, colder and later ground. But whereas wheat reached a peak of production by the middle of the nineteenth century of 1,000,000 acres in 1857, falling away to 58,000 in 1928, oats continued to increase its acreage.[21] More importantly for our present study, the vastly increased production of wheat between 1780 and 1850 made very little difference indeed to the diet of the population, very fortunately for the Scots considering the relative purity of oatmeal compared to the state of adulteration of Victorian wheat flour which was commonly filled with plaster of Paris, alum, sulphate of copper, rice flour and potato starch.

Authorities are inclined to differ on the importance of wheat to the Scottish population. Fairlie asserts that wheat consumption in Scotland was 'still probably negligible' in 1870.[22] But Collins shows figures for wheat consumption in Scotland increasing from 10% in 1800 to 84% in 1900.[23] If it is realised, however, that these figures show the use of *some* wheat flour rather than the inclusion of wheat as a major part of the diet, they seem less important. Collins also quotes figures of 'less than 1½lb of oatmeal per head per week' in 1904 as indicative of a small consumption of meal. One is forced to wonder if he had ever tried consuming 1½lbs of oatmeal. One ounce of meal makes porridge for one person; 1½lbs of oatmeal, then, allows 24 portions of porridge per person per week, which means either porridge twice a day or porridge in the morning and a large portion of oatcakes every evening — hardly a negligible proportion of the diet.[24] It is, however, extremely small compared with the figure of 10-16 ounces of oatmeal consumed as a normal portion at each meal by Scottish labourers in the 1860s which is given by Dr Edward Smith.[25] Accounts of contemporaries about how much oatmeal was necessary for each person's healthy survival are inclined to be affected by the writer's own viewpoint. For instance, a Mr Parish, of Montrose, claimed in 1800, in a report which was used as evidence by the parliamentary 'Committee to consider the High Price of Provisions', that a labouring man required two pecks of oatmeal a week at a cost of 48 pence; but Mr Parish was in the business of selling rice, which he liked to claim could fill a man more cheaply than his native oats.[26]

There were two good additional reasons why the growing of oats was increasing in many districts at the end of the eighteenth and in the early nineteenth century. While the Malt Tax remained moderate, farmers got good prices for bere from local distilleries and breweries and from many illicit stills. 'Bear is cultivated everywhere; and, being the basis of the whisky manufacture, the people have a warm side to it and give it a great proportion of good land.'[27] When tax was raised and licensing laws tightened they found bere less profitable and oats more worthwhile.[28] And in some districts where bere had been excluded from the multures exacted on oats, as in Peeblesshire, farmers had been inclined to 'the preposterous sowing of bere, where oats would have been more profitable',[29] simply to evade the mill multures. The removal of thirlage clauses from their leases in the nineteenth century, then, encouraged the growing of oats.

The fact that white flour was made up only in 20-stone bags until the 1870s shows how seldom it was sold for ordinary domestic use.[30] But oatmeal during the same period established for itself the main place in the Scottish diet, so that by 1869 the *Report on the Dietaries of Scottish Agricultural Labourers* noted that it was the main article of daily subsistence of working class families in Scotland.[31] The *Cyclopedia of Agriculture* in 1855 said oatmeal was then 'the principal food of that proportion of the mechanic class whose employment was not of a sedentary nature'.[32] Edward Smith found in 1863 that oatmeal was the principal food of 90% of all Scots families, although 62% ate some wheat and 20% some barley meal and pease meal.[33] Even the potato had not displaced it and white bread had made no real impact at all. The place of oatmeal was by then so secure that it has become part of the folk tradition of Scotland, the older traditions which it supplanted quite forgotten and the powers of oatmeal to nourish and strengthen extolled with romantic nostalgia.

The oats grown in Scotland until the end of the eighteenth century was a poor crop, with a low yield, lower even than the common bere, with a small flat seed and short straw. 'What shall we think of the situation of that land and those who labour it from which an increase in the proportion of three to one is reckoned an excellent crop? The inferiority of the oats and barley produced on such ground is experienced both at the mill and at the market.'[34]

There were three main types of oat. The Small or Grey Oat, which gave a very poor return for labour of only three grains for each seed planted, had the one advantage that it would grow on poor soil even when planted year after year without intermediate crops. By the end of the eighteenth century it had been given up everywhere except in the Highlands and Islands although it was still grown in parts of the Western Isles in the middle of the twentieth century, and in the Northern Isles until the present time.[35]

The Great or White Corn was grown during the eighteenth century on the better, lower ground and in those areas where landlords insisted on a proper rotation of crops with not more than two 'white' crops grown in successive years. It was not strictly a variety in the sense that agricultural scientists would define it today. 'The Great Corn included all the diversities of the Common Oat generally cultivated throughout this Island,' James Anderson wrote in his *General View of the Agriculture of the County of Aberdeen* in 1794.[36] It included, in fact, not only a mixture of varieties but also a large quantity of weed seeds, as there was no means of cleaning and grading beyond what hand, eye and patience could achieve.

The third quality was Brocked Oats, a mixture of grey and white seed commonly sown on soils better than those customary for Small Corn, but not fertile enough to justify expenditure on Great Corn.[37] 'If soil be clay, put white oats into it, if mixed, use mixed seeds, if light and dry sow it with small corn.'[38]

All of these produced a flattish seed, not easily milled, especially by millers whose techniques were adapted to the softer and rounder seeds of pea and bean. The difficulty of producing good meal from these early oat varieties may have been one additional reason for the very general use of pease and barley meal. It is possible that the Great Corn was even harder to grind than the Small. At any rate millers were paid more for the labour of grinding Great Oats than Small. This might, of course, reflect not so much difficulty in grinding as value of end product.[39]

In 1782 and again in 1799 harvests were disastrously bad. Landlords and tenants alike were moved away from their conservative paths towards experiments with new seed in the hope of advancing harvests and so avoiding early frosts. The oat crops of eighteenth century Scotland were frequently still in the fields in November. Farmers were reduced almost to starvation. Landlords, forced either to forego the rents due to them, or to see their tenants eat seed corn, were ready to try new ways.

The problem was to find a variety able to withstand frost both at the beginning and the end of the growing season. As one farmer wrote, 'Oats are no doubt a hardy kind of grain, as nature has furnished it with a *great coat* to defend it from the inclemency of the weather; but it is when the plant is in flower and before this great coat can be buttoned closely, if I may use the expression, that its powers of vegetation are most easily and most deeply wounded.'[40]

General interest in agricultural science had, by the end of the eighteenth century, resulted in the breeding of several named varieties of oats. The draining and enclosing of fields, the proper understanding of soil management which had caused clauses about manuring and liming of ground and the proper rotation of crops to be written into new, longer leases, meant that fertile ground was ready for the reception of the new varieties. Their successful cultivation meant that they quickly spread throughout the arable areas of Scotland. The three main varieties were Kildrummy, Naked Oats and the Potato Oat. Kildrummy was most popular in Aberdeenshire. It gave an early crop suited to poor soil in regions where harvests were late. It yielded a low bushel weight but made a good quality oatmeal. These were characteristics which made it preferred in counties where the crop was grown for home consumption rather than as a cash crop. The Naked Oat, so called because it grew without husks, was liked for poultry and was grown, therefore, in areas where hen-keeping was encouraged. The Potato Oat was, however, much the most popular variety, so successful that within a few years of its introduction at the end of the eighteenth century it was known and cultivated in all parts of Scotland and in the North of England in spite of a tendency, remarked on by Sir James Mackenzie, to 'shake' in Highland areas.[41] It is said to have been given its name because it originated in a single plant growing alone in a potato plot and spotted by an astute farmer as having qualities then unknown in the oatfields. It was found much the best variety for good soil although less well adapted than Kildrummy to the colder areas and poorer soils of northern Scotland. The extra quantity of meal produced from a bushel of grain accounts for the variety's immediate popularity.[42]

With the introduction of these new, reliable varieties of oat the population's taste for oatmeal products was developed. Oatmeal had, of course, always been a part of the Scottish diet. Porridge, however, now thought of as exclusively made of oats, was in the past a dish made of whatever meal was most readily available. Sir Walter Scott, in a letter to his son-in-law, J. G. Lockhart, wrote, 'What meal does Johnnie want for his porridge? I will send it up from Abbotsford. I think it will agree with him better than the southern food for horses.'[43] Scott alluded, of course, to Dr Johnson's famous definition of oats — 'a grain generally given to horses'[44] — but seems to be suggesting a meal made from grain other than oats as preferable. The change towards oatmeal made during Scott's lifetime may have left him with that common nostalgic liking for the diet of his childhood which almost certainly included bere-meal porridge.

The eighteenth century had seen some general trend towards variety in diet. As well as the introduction of imported luxuries such as tea and sugar, so often commented on and so much deplored by the parish ministers who wrote the *First Statistical Account,* the more settled state of the country after the suppression of the Jacobite Rebellions had allowed a new commerce in foodstuffs. Communities, at least in the more agriculturally advanced areas, were becoming slightly less dependent on the products of their own immediate area and slightly more able, at least in good years, to produce a better diet on their own ground. The introduction of root crops to eke out the traditional greens, the improvement of quality and yield of grains, the insistence by landlords on the rotation of crops, the institution of new weekly markets in many areas, all strengthened the trend towards greater variety in diet. In Edinburgh a new meal market was built 'eastward of the Back Stairs' after a fire had destroyed remnants of the old market in 1700.[45] In 1794 Cupar provided the only weekly corn market in Fife, but there was a reported need for others.[46] In 1827 one was erected in Kirkcaldy.[47] Glasgow was complaining at the end of the eighteenth century at the removal of the old market to make room for a Bridewell, and in 1800 a new one was opened.[48] In Nairn a weekly corn market was first established in 1832.[49] The Border Country was served by a meal market at Dalkeith, of which the only survival is the Old Meal Market Inn.

Improved roads and the decreased risk of meeting trouble on the journey encouraged the travelling from district to district of fishwives with salt herring, as well as egg hawkers and meal-mongers.[50] Within the next generation bakers began to appear in the smaller towns and villages. In Leuchars, Fife, in the 1840s it was reported that 'you find the cottager enjoying a loaf from the baker which he accompanies with beer, milk or tea.'[51] In Dunbartonshire at the same time the 'usual food of the peasantry' was oatmeal, potatoes, milk, cheese and barley broth, but in the villages wheaten bread, butter, tea and even coffee were beginning to be used.[52] Perthshire was beginning to see more common use of wheaten bread and tea but 'their bread is commonly of oat or barley meal' and 'potatoes, pork and the produce of the dairy constitute a very considerable portion of their ordinary food.'[53] In Lanarkshire, 'Oatmeal porridge for breakfast and supper, potatoes with herrings for dinner was the usual diet of the labouring classes.'[54]

The potato was spreading across the country. Potatoes were first heard of in Scotland in 1701 when the Duchess of Buccleuch recorded in her household book the purchase of a peck at 2/6d. In 1733 it was occasionally served at supper at the Earl of Eglinton's table, and the Grahams of Fintry had eggs and potatoes for supper three days a week in October 1739. About 1740 'it was beginning to be cultivated in gardens but still with a hesitation about it's moral character.'[55] Fenton, assessing the victory of the potato, quotes the Famine Relief Committee's report in 1846 that it then formed 75-88% of the Highlander's diet and 25% of the Lowlander's.[56] In the Lowlands it became a valuable addition to the table, a useful source of vitamins, a food with some welcome bulk to it, and it made the rearing of pigs possible. In the Highlands it brought the population dangerously close to complete dependence on one crop whose failure could cause famine and starvation. In the towns, especially after the influx of Irish families and Highlanders who had already grown accustomed to it, the potato became the most important part of the diet of a substantial part of the population. Dundonians ate potatoes mashed with a spoonful of grated beef suet in them and sometimes took large potatoes to the mills with them, where they were baked in the steam engine furnace, providing a welcome midday meal and hand-warmer combined. A number of mills attempted the production of potato flour, so that even the switch from grain to root crops could provide some work for the miller. There were, among other places, farina mills at Errol, Monikie, Pitlochry, Dunkeld, and Bendochy of which mill it was said 'nothing can be finer than the flour here manufactured'.[57]

At all times, even into the twentieth century, the diet of the Scots was limited not only by the harshness of their climate and the resultant limitation on their food products, but also by the extreme poverty of their housing and the consequent lack of cooking facilities. The house of the Scots peasant until the end of the eighteenth century was in all parts of the country a comfortless hovel. It is sufficient to look at the countryside today to see how few cottages, how few even of farmhouses, survive from the period before about 1840. Picturesque villages of pretty eighteenth century cottages are not a common feature of the Scottish landscape. The form of construction of cottages before the middle of the nineteenth century was not one to survive time and the weather.[58] Certainly it was not able to survive the gradual growth of conscience about the living conditions of the poor which culminated in the Report of the Royal Commission on the Housing of the Industrial Population of Scotland, Rural and Urban, in 1917.[59] The usual Scots kitchen of the nineteenth century, an open fire with a *swey* (hook and chain) above it, allowed the boiling or toasting of food but not the baking or roasting of it. There is no evidence that I know of of the brick oven built into the wall which was common in English farm kitchens. The eighteenth century had commonly not even the facility of the chimneyed fire but had to make do with a fire in the middle of the floor and such pots as could be made to balance on it or hang on tripods above it. Only after the introduction of the iron range with its side ovens and polished top plate did the Scots win their reputation for good baking. Scones, pancakes and sponge cakes as common articles of diet date only from the end of the nineteenth century, the installation of the cast iron oven and the adoption of imported white flour.

Oatcakes, and before them flat cakes of bere or pease meal, were made by mixing meal, salt and water and patting them gently, almost with reverence, into shape. They were then dried, rather than baked, by toasting slowly before the fire.[60] Oats were, until the nineteenth century, as we have seen, a food eaten a step further up the social scale than the bottom, where mixed grains and pulses were the rule. Oats before the nineteenth century seem, in fact, to have had attached to them some ritual significance, being the food for special occasions and festivals. The *New Statistical Account* describes the making of Rutherglen sour cakes for St Luke's Fair:

> Each of them is provided with a bake-board, about two feet square, which they hold on their knees. The woman who roasts the cakes, which is done on a girdle before the fire, is called the Queen or Bride, and the rest her maidens. These are distinguished from one another by names given them for the occasion. She who sits next the fire towards the east is called the Todler; her companion on the left hand is called the Hodler, and the rest have arbitrary names given them by the Bride, as Mrs. Baker, best &

> worst maids, etc. The operation is begun by the Todler, who takes a ball of the dough, forms it into a small cake, & then casts it on the bake-board of the Hodler, who beats it out a little thinner. This being done, she in her turn throws it on the board of her neighbour, and thus it goes round from east to west, in the direction of the course of the sun, until it comes to the toaster, by which time it is as thin and smooth as a sheet of paper . . . As the baking is wholly performed by hand a great deal of noise is the consequence. The beats, however, are not irregular, nor destitute of an agreeable harmony, espec. when they are accom. by vocal music, which is freq. the case. Great dexterity is reqd. not only to beat out the cakes with no other instrument than the hand so that no part of them shall be thicker than another, but espec. to cast them from one board to another, without ruffling or breaking them . . . The whole is a scene of activity, mirth & diversion & might afford an excellent subj. for a pict. There is no account of the origin of this custom. The bread thus baked was doubtless never intend. for common use.[61]

Another example is the Festy Cock, a ball of new-ground meal baked in the mill's kiln at Shrovetide and eaten as a feast day celebration.[62]

As better farming made better oats available and as more prosperous town dwellers and farmers took to the occasional use of white bread, wheat took the place oats had once had on the social scale, bere meal and mashlum disappeared gradually from the diet except in Orkney and Shetland and remote areas of the mainland, and oats became the common food of the ordinary family. It was still, however, one food among a variety available. The first half of the nineteenth century saw a change, which was only accentuated in the second half, towards a much more limited diet for the agricultural worker, a diet in which oatmeal played not only a dominant but almost the only part.

The agricultural improvements of the eighteenth century had seen at first an increased need for farm workers to perform the many tasks of threshing and barn work, stone clearing, ditching and draining, intaking of marginal land, fence building and tree planting which were then undertaken. Farm servants in such demand lived, as they had traditionally always done, in the farmer's own house and ate at his own table, sharing a diet which, as we have seen, was becoming increasingly varied and nutritious with the addition of meat, dairy products and vegetables to the basic cereals.

After the first mammoth tasks of farm improvement had been accomplished, fewer men were needed. At the same time the enlarging of farms and enclosing of fields had left a smaller acreage on which the cottar could support himself and his family. During the same period the employers, that is, in this case, the tenant farmers and small proprietors, developed social ambitions and became less willing to share their homes with their servants, although the habit was very slow to disappear in some districts and was still common enough on small farms in the North-East up to the Second World War. In Fife, by 1893, 'The custom of feeding farm servants in the master's kitchen occurs only in small places, where the farmers themselves do not object to take their meals at the same table with their employees. The custom is rapidly dying out. It is stated that the men are difficult to please and prone to complain of the quality of the food provided. Furthermore, that their presence keeps the house servants in an unsettled condition, often resulting in breaches of morality.'[63] Only too often, in fact, ploughmen in the kitchen brought about the situation described by Helen Cruikshank:

> Up the Noran Water,
> Doon by Inglismaldie,
> Annie's got a bairnie
> That hasna got a daddie.

So unmarried farm servants, who had once lived as 'family', were relegated to quarters in the farmyard. If they were lucky it would be a bothy specially built for their accommodation, if less lucky they would bed themselves down in the loft above byre or stables. Married workers lived in cottages on the farm where cottages were provided, but many, both married and unmarried, finding their services less wanted and cottages unavailable, moved away from the country and into the towns. Those who remained found their social status and their buying power diminished.

The old, integrated 'ferm toun' became a more segregated place, the farmers' wives, daughters and serving maidies cloistered, however unsuccessfully, from the bothy men who, cooking their own food in their own rough quarters, became coarser and therefore less welcome in the farmhouse with every generation.[64] Farm life had changed from the primitive but shared domesticity of Scott to the harsher world of Lewis Grassic Gibbon. The lad with the 'nickie tams' was often enough successful in courting 'Old Mains' kitchie deem' and no doubt often wheedled from her 'a muckle piece wi' different kinds o' jams', but his bed was dirty and unmade and he possessed little more than the brose caup and horn spoon with which he supped his porridge. In the farm kitchen the long tradition of Scots baking and jam making had begun. In the bothies it was oatmeal for breakfast, dinner and supper.

Farmers still accepted their responsibility for feeding their servants — an indication, perhaps, not so much of paternal care as of the hard fact that no other means of acquiring food was available to the worker on farms at a distance from shops and grocers' carts, and of the fact that he was deprived of the piece of land which might once have made him more self-sufficient. But while farmers admitted the need to provide food, they no longer felt it necessary to feed their workers as well as they fed themselves. It had been difficult to eat meat at the same table as the men without sharing it, although there were farmers whose sensitivities allowed it. Once the men were removed to the bothy it became easier for the farmer's family to enjoy delicacies not thought necessary for the men. From this period dates the dependence upon oatmeal, because the farm worker, after his exile from the farmhouse, was paid with a yearly ration of meal and a daily pint of milk, and on this diet he lived. There were, of course, regional variations in the diet. By 1893 the Lothians, for instance, had 'discontinued meal and milk'.[65] But the standard payment for farm workers throughout the nineteenth century was 6½ bolls of oatmeal and a daily delivery of milk. In the northern arable areas milk and meal constituted the whole diet of the bothy man, dairy cows being kept on the farm solely for the feeding of the men.[66] In pastoral areas, where dairy cows were kept for the production of butter, cheese and milk to be sold in the towns, workers were less likely to be paid in meal. An oatmeal diet is not palatable without the addition of milk, and even the increasingly depressed agricultural worker was liable to rebel at porridge without milk. Workers in the prosperous Lothians came to expect broth with meat in it and white bread to eat with it, but the bothy men of Angus and the Mearns, of Aberdeenshire and the Moray Firth, lived almost exclusively on oatmeal and milk.

Farmers sent a *melder* (one milling) of oats to the local mill every three months for the use of their own household and of their servants.[67] Although the meal constituted their wages, the men were supplied with it not by the farmer but by the miller who kept a list of each farm's employees and delivered their bolls of meal in his cart to the bothies and the farm cottages. The farm servant then told the miller how much of his allowance he wanted and took it as he needed it. By the 1920s some of the ploughmen's wives were asking the miller to give them part of their allowance in white flour, and most of the mills kept a pair of stones which could grind wheat, as well as the regular meal stones. But the majority took all their bolls of meal.

Each worker in the bothy had his own 'kists' (chests), one for his few clothes and other possessions, one for his meal. The meal kist was his seat in the bothy, his platform when moved to sing and his drum on which he played 'the spoons'. The meal supplied to the farms was of a grade known to the miller as 'ploughman's meal', the bothy men, whose diet was so exclusive, having become very discriminating in their taste for it and insisting on the highest quality. One farmer claimed that if the men had been paid in money and bought meal for themselves 'they would not get such good oatmeal as they got from him, as he sent his oats to the miller to be ground into good meal irrespective of quantity'.[68] The inference is clearly that the miller had ways of producing greater bulk at the expense of quality for customers of less discernment. A boll is a measure of volume, not of weight, and meal ground into dust-like fineness can be made to occupy more space than the coarser ground and more flavoursome meal.

Tastes in oatmeal varied from region to region and it was perhaps the high proportion of boll wages that made the North-East demand a finer cut of meal from its millers than did the Lothians and the Border Country. Bothy dwellers, perhaps because they fell into bed at night without forethought for the morning, despised the habit, common in southern Scotland, of putting porridge meal to soak overnight. So, if they were not to spend too long with the spurtle in the morning, the meal had to be ground into particles small enough to cook quickly. The coarser Midlothian cut was thought to require soaking if it were not to have a very long cooking and, as porridge must be stirred all the time it is cooking, the time willingly spent on it varied with the patience of its cook — and patience was not a virtue much come by in bothies before dawn on a winter's morning.

In answer to the differing regional requirements, the millers of the main oatmeal-producing regions began to produce patented oat products and to advertise them under trade names. The type of meal manufactured in southern Scotland was affected partly by a demand from English wholesalers. For instance, Edington Mills produced, and still produce, *white groats* which the black pudding makers of Lancashire prefer to all other types of meal.[69] The new nineteenth century interest in child diet and invalid foods produced a demand for bland products such as Grant's Oat Flour, milled at Craig Mills, Strathmartine. But in the North-East it was porridge for men that kept the mills busy.

In many districts it was customary for the men to sell a proportion of their meal. Sometimes they left a proportion of the meal to which they were entitled at the mill and the miller paid them in cash for it.[70] Sometimes they sold it to cottars, blacksmiths and the other country tradesmen not supplied with meal as part of their wages.[71] The proportion sold varied from region to region. On Balboughty, Lord Mansfield's farm near Perth, the men were accustomed by the end of the century to sell half their meal.[72] Some men in Fife sold as much as two-thirds of theirs, but more usually one-third was sold and two-thirds eaten. In Aberdeenshire and Kincardineshire only a very small amount was ever sold. The money was used partly to augment the diet. In Argyll the habit was deplored: 'It is bad that they part with good meal for tea and baker's bread.'[73] In Fife there were places where 'jam, cheese and rice puddings are observed on the table any day of the year'.[74] In Aberdeenshire even the table would have been an unknown luxury in some parts, and where money was got from the miller it was more than likely to be spent on a twice-yearly spree at the feeing mercat.[75]

Payment at least partly in kind continued throughout our period in all parts of Scotland, and meal made up a large proportion of the payment of all farm servants in every county except Lanark, Wigton, Kirkcudbright and Dumfries.[76] The first substitution of money for perquisites appears to have been six shillings a year in Haddington in 1855 in place of the liberty to keep hens. 'The ice once broken the boll wage grew steadily in disfavour.'[77] But it was very slow in disappearing, nevertheless, and remained common in the eastern half of Scotland until the 1950s, when mills such as Kirriemuir's had long lists of farm cottages to call on with the ploughman's bolls.

The mills, in fact, always of central importance, had become during the nineteenth century even more important as almost the sole provider of food for large parts of the country. It is this difference between eastern and western regions of Scotland, between the regions where oatmeal formed the major part of the diet and those dairying and city-bordering counties where variations in diet were possible, which accounts for the larger number of mill sites in the North-East and for their later survival. But even in the Lowlands meal was an essential ingredient of the daily diet. The miller was the chief processor of food when bakers, grocers and butchers served only the towns and the greater part of the population still lived on the land. After the shift of population towards the towns those workers left in rural employment remained so heavily dependent upon the products of the mill that the miller was not at first much affected by the decline in their numbers.

NOTES

1. Smout and Fenton, 'Scottish agriculture before the improvers', 73
2. Adam, *Sutherland Estate Management*, vol. 2, 13
3. Smout and Fenton, 80
4. *O.S.A.* 1, 35-6
5. *N.S.A.*, XXII, 357
6. *O.S.A.* 4, 244
7. *N.S.A.* X, 289
8. Fenton, *Scottish Country Life*, 167-8; see also Collins, 'Dietary change and cereal consumption in Britain in the 19th century', 97-8
9. McNeill, *The Scots Kitchen*, 217
10. See also pp. 183-5 below
11. Royal Commission on Labour, *The Agricultural Labourer, III*, Scotland, Part 1, Reports, London 1893, c.6894 xv, *passim* (henceforth *Agricultural Labourer*)
12. David, Elizabeth, *English Bread and Yeast Cookery*, London 1977, 53; Hartley, Dorothy, *Food in England*, London 1962, 508; Smith, Edward, *Foods*, 196
13. Fenton, *Scottish Country Life*, 166-7, 172
14. M'Dougall, Alex, tacksman of the Perth Meal and Barley Mills, sederunt books 1828-46, Minutes of Trustees, 14 July, 1837 (NRA(S) 1510)
15. Hume, *Industrial Archaeology of Scotland: the Lowlands and Borders*, 14-17; see also Collins, 100
16. *Farmers Magazine*, 1818, LXXIII, 8
17. Fenton, *Scottish Country Life*, 163-4
18. Smollet, Tobias, *Humphrey Clinker*, Everyman edition, 1945, 231
19. Hunter, *Treatise on the Law of Landlord and Tenant*, 1, 260; see also Morison, ed., *Decisions of the Court of Session*, 16074, M. Abercorn v Mags. of Paisley, 1798 and 16057, Wright v Rannie, 1768
20. SRO, GD 46/17/591
21. Oats acreage continued to increase until it reached 3,253,000 at the end of the century. It fell slightly until the First World War but reached a height of 4,024,000 in 1918 from which, again, it fell only slowly until 1941. Mitchell, B. R. and Deane, Phyllis, *Abstract of British Historical Statistics*, London 1962, 78-81
22. Fairlie, 'The corn laws and British wheat production, 1829-76'
23. Collins, Dietary change . . .', 97-8

24. McNeill, *The Scots Kitchen*, 210
25. Smith, Dr Edward, *Reports of the Medical Officer of the Privy Council*, 5th Report 1863, P.P. XXVIII, 347
26. P.P. XXVIII, 1799/1800, 104, Appendix D, letter from Mr Parish of Mountboy Cottage, near Montrose
27. *Farmers Magazine*, LXXIII, 1818, 8
28. Keith, *General View of the Agriculture of the County of Aberdeen*, 527
29. Findlater, *General View of the Agriculture of the County of Peebles*, 20
30. Dundee Public Libraries, Lamb Collection, 196 (47)
31. Quoted Fenton, *Scottish Country Life*
32. Morton, *Cyclopedia of Agriculture*, 1, 191
33. Smith, *op. cit.*, 345; see also Smith, *Foods*
34. *O.S.A.*, 18, 348
35. Fenton, *The Northern Isles* is essential reading for anyone interested in this subject; also Fenton, 'Traditional elements in the diet of the Northern Isles of Scotland'
36. Anderson, *General View of the Agriculture of the County of Aberdeen*, 48-9
37. Findlay, *Oats*, 17-18; Handley, *Scottish Farming in the 18th Century*, 251
38. Arbuthnot, 'A true method of treating light hazelly ground'
39. Barron, ed., *Court Book of the Barony of Urie*, xlvii
40. *Farmers Magazine*, 1800, 1, 217
41. Mackenzie, *Hints for the use of Highland tenants and cottagers, by a proprietor*, 100
42. Findlay, *Oats*, 22-31; Fenton, *Scottish Country Life*, 166-7
43. Quoted McNeill, *The Scots Kitchen, 210*
44. *Dictionary*, 10th ed., London 1762
45. Grant, *Old and New Edinburgh*, III, 248
46. Beatson, *General View of the Agriculture of the County of Fife*, 34
47. *N.S.A.*, IX, 757
48. Marwick and Renwick, *Extracts from the Records of the Burgh of Glasgow*, IX, 1796-1808, 1916, 235
49. Bain, George, *History of Nairnshire*, Nairn, 1928, 469
50. Fenton, *Scottish Country Life*, 176
51. *N.S.A.*, IX, 224
52. *N.S.A.*, VIII, 8
53. *N.S.A.*, X, 276
54. *N.S.A.*, VI, 20
55. University of Dundee MS 15/7; Chambers, *Domestic Annals of Scotland*, 404
56. Fenton, *Scottish Country Life*, 118-123
57. *N.S.A.*, X, 998, 1195; see also Missive offer for Farina Mill near

Pitlochry, 5 Feb. 1860, held by Arthur Young McLelland Moores and Company of Perth, 22/1

58. Walker, Bruce, 'Clay buildings in North East Scotland', Scottish Vernacular Buildings Working Group, Dundee and Edinburgh, 1977

59. Royal Commission on the Housing of the Industrial Population of Scotland, Rural and Urban (Edinburgh 1917), vol. 13, 358ff

60. McNeill, *The Scots Kitchen* describes the varieties of oatcake in detail, 184-6

61. *N.S.A.*, VI, 384

62. Jamieson, *Dictionary*, *q.v.*

63. *Agricultural Labourer*, Part 1, 56

64. *Ibid.*, Part 1, 135; see also *Journal of Agriculture*, 'Report by a Committee of the Synod of Angus and Mearns as to Agricultural Labourers, 1856', March 1861, 729

65. *Agricultural Labourer*, Part 2, 20

66. *Ibid.*, Part 1, 25

67. Findlay, *Oats*, 6

68. *Agricultural Labourer*, Part 1, 149, 162; Part 2, 156

69. Information kindly supplied by Mr Alexander Graham of R. F. Bell and Son Ltd, Edington Mills, Chirnside

70. *Agricultural Labourer*, Part 1, 135

71. *Ibid.*, Part 1, 162

72. *Ibid.*, Part 1, 162

73. *Ibid.*, Part 2, 56

74. *Ibid.*, Part 2, 57

75. *Ibid.*, Part 2, 67

76. *Ibid.*, Analytical Index, 26

77. *Ibid.*, Part 2, 104

2
Abbey, Town and Barony — The Origins of the Mill

The corn mills, then, were traditionally the providers of food. Those which best survived the changes in society and agricultural methods without entirely changing their own character, those, that is, which remained water-powered meal mills without turning to steam and the production of roller-milled white flour, were, as we have seen, the country mills serving the farmers.

Mills in England have been variously divided by modern authors into *toll* and *merchant* mills[1] or into *upland* and *lowland* mills.[2] In Scotland, because of the later break-up of the feudal system and later commercialisation of milling, and because of the different organisation of agricultural society, these categories are not satisfactory. The influence of the baronial courts on Scottish mills was still apparent until at least the end of the eighteenth century, and the biggest difference in mills was between those experiencing that influence and those separately evolving. This is not to say that Scottish mills could not be divided into Highland and Lowland types but that it would not be particularly useful to do so; and to use *upland* and *lowland* as main categories would be to risk confusion, because the Scottish lowland mill is most like the English upland mill and the English lowland mill would have few representatives in Scotland. Similarly the toll system in England, although similar to the thirlage system in Scotland, is not exactly the same, so to use *toll* to describe astricted mills would be confusing. Virtually all Scottish mills were *toll* mills in this sense until after the end of the eighteenth century and therefore require further categorisation. From the nineteenth century onwards they are probably better divided quite simply into town and country mills, distinguished more by their products and their customers than by their situations, but traditionally mills showed four different kinds of ownership and organisation. There were the *Abbey* mills, the *King's* mills, the *Towns'* mills, and the *Baronial* mills.

The first water mills, at least of any size and appreciable importance, were built by the abbeys and monasteries for their own use. As centres of knowledge, in correspondence with religious communities on the continent of Europe, they alone had the technical knowledge to build and operate what were, for their time, examples of advanced mechanical engineering. Their interest in and knowledge of the best agricultural methods and their extensive holdings of land made it worthwhile for them to introduce faster and more efficient methods of processing the grain they grew, faster, that is, than the hand mills of their tenants. It might seem, at first, that the Church was successful in acquiring all the best farming land at an early date in Scottish history, but it is perhaps truer to say that those lands which were in the hands of the monks have a longer history of intelligent husbandry than others and show to this day the advantages of early improvement and the application of agricultural knowledge. The first mill sites were chosen with care by the abbeys to provide a regular and smooth-flowing water supply, but the streams which supplied them were dammed and governed with foreknowledge of the effects of that control upon the working of the mill. For instance, the monks of Newbattle obtained from the proprietors of the lands of Morham and Hales the liberty of making mill dams and water courses in the eleventh century.[3] Some of these sites carried working water mills until recent times, the names Abbey Mill, Bishop's Mill and Dean's Mill indicating their continued use for three or four hundred years. There were Abbey mills in St Andrews, in Kilwinning and in Paisley, Bishop mills in Cadder in Lanarkshire and in Glasgow, and there were mills at Abbothall in Fife. The mills of Fearn, in Ross-shire, once belonged to the Bishop of Ross and the Abbot of Fearn. The mills of Linlithgow belonged to the Priory of Manuel. Balbirnie Mill, still in operation in Angus as a water-powered oatmeal mill, was built in the fifteenth century by and for the use of the Bishops of Brechin. The Cupar meal mills belonged to the monks of St Andrews and still pay an annual feu duty of £30 to the University of St Andrews.[4] George Shaw, abbot of the monastery of Paisley, granted a charter in 1490 in favour of the magistrates and community erecting Paisley into a burgh of barony and providing that the inhabitants should bring all their grain to 'our mill of Paisley'.[5]

The very great age of the monastic mills was acknowledged as giving them a special position in law. These mills had 'a more ancient existence than the feus' in that they were built before the letting of land by feu charter, and lawyers noted 'a very remarkable distinction between mills lately erected and those which have been of old standing . . . not only time out of mind, but as far back as the title deeds go'.[6] The early ecclesiastical ownership of the mills may account in part for the reluctance to change any part of their operations which was reported in some districts as late as the eighteenth century: 'The ancient mills for grinding oats, it was believed, had been piously placed by their forefathers where they could be worked according to God's order, without artificially embanking the water or turning it from its natural course, which would be sinful.'[7]

It is the great age of the monastic mills, also, which causes some confusion about their first ownership. Some of their feu charters show mills as having been given *to* an abbey by the King. Alexander II, for instance, gave the mills of Linlithgow to the Priory of Manuel.[8] David I granted to the monks of Holyrood 'one of my mills of Dene, a tithe of the mill of Libertun and of Dene and of the new mill of Edinburgh' in 1143.[9] And it was not uncommon for kings to reward priests who had done some service with the grant of a piece of land with a mill on it. It is unlikely, however, that the mills were built at that time and for that purpose. More likely the King, in issuing a charter, was recognising an existing state of affairs, and graciously consenting, because the abbey was at that time in his favour, to legitimise the holding of land which had been in the abbey's possession before the feuing of land had been instituted.[10]

The abbeys themselves began to feu some of their lands and to let some of their mills during the sixteenth century. Walter Reid, abbot of Kinloss Abbey, began the setting of the abbey lands of Strathisla in feu ferme from 1558. Lord Saltoun feued Overmill from the Abbey in 1569, George Adamson, son of a prominent Edinburgh burgess, feued Nethermill in 1570.[11] By this means abbey mills began to pass into the hands of the landowning classes even before the dissolution of the monasteries. One or two remained in church hands long afterwards, perhaps due to the protection of a devout baron. The Miln of Dunblane was still, in 1756, the property of the Bishop of St Asaph.[12]

After the forfeiture of the great land holdings of the Roman Catholic Church the mills reverted to the property of the King or of the barons upon whom the lands were conferred. Although the Kings of Scotland made a practice of giving mills and mill lands to those in their favour, a number seems to have remained in royal hands. At any rate the law lords found it necessary to consider the special position of the King's mills when they were discussing the question of thirlage to mills,[13] as they were forced to do at intervals during the eighteenth century: 'Thirlage of lands to mills of the King's property is sufficiently instructed by use of coming to the mill and paying the insucken multures though the thirlage be not founded upon writ, which is a royal prerogative necessary for the King, because he is not prejudged by the neglect of his officers in keeping any writs.'[14]

Some few of the mills known as King's mills were indeed built especially for the supply of the King's own household, and sited near the various palaces to which the early kings of Scotland found it expedient to withdraw their courts during more troubled periods. That these were, like the abbey mills, slightly better constructed and organised than the ordinary run of mills then existing is suggested by the injunction that baronial mills should emulate them in employing a miller and two servants.[15] But the majority came into the king's hands from the abbeys at the time of Scotland's Reformation. Some of the resultant transactions were complicated in the extreme and the degree of their political motivation hard to assess. They were, however, only a continuation of the process whereby kings had immemorially honoured their loyal dependants with gifts of a mill or sometimes of 'half the mill', meaning half the proceeds of the mill. Robert I granted Lord Grey half the mill of Pitkerro for his services at the Battle of Bannockburn, and Robert II gave the same mill to Walter Oliphant.[16] In 1566 Elizabeth Lundy, wife of Robert Keith, son of William, Earl Marischal, resigned the lands and mill of Benholm 'into the hands of Queen Mary in favour of her spouse and herself'. But in the same year a charter by Henry and Mary, King and Queen of Scots, granted Robert Keith and Elizabeth Lundy the same lands and mill and erected Benholm into a free barony.[17] The Mill of Milnab was given by James IV to John Drummond of Auchterarder who was the King's Master of Works.[18]

The royal household found less and less use for the large number of mills it owned throughout the country after the court settled in Edinburgh. Then, after the Union of the Crowns, the King's mills were needed neither to supply the royal table nor for the income derived from them which must have seemed derisory beside the greatly increased revenues of the United Kingdom. The mills were disposed of either to the towns which they already served and whose indwellers were already thirled to them, or to neighbouring gentlemen from whom they passed to the town when the monetary needs of the landowners dictated the transaction.

By these means most mills had come into the possession of the towns or baronies before our period begins, some of them even using the very sticks and stones of the abbeys for their own rebuilding. The mill of Dunino on the estate of Stravithie in Fife had a roof supported by rafters from Cardinal Beaton's castle in St Andrews.[19]

By the eighteenth century, then, mills have passed from king and abbey into the hands of town and baron. There was no great difference between the way town and baronial mills were administered. In the towns the mills formed part of the common good, their rents a useful source of income to the town. The magistrates, as proprietors, set up, where necessary, mill committees to see to their letting and repairing and the mills were let to tacksmen millers just as were the baronial mills. The town's inhabitants paid multures to the mill multurer just as did the Baron's tenants. Because the burgh mills had access to the town's meal markets and served a larger population they could, if efficiently run, deal with a large volume of trade and bring in a considerable income. They seem, nevertheless, to have become more of a burden and a source of trouble to the magistrates than an asset to the towns.

During the eighteenth century most towns found the ancient mills to which they had fallen heir inadequate to meet the new demands made upon them. The growth in numbers of town dwellers demanded in some places an increased output from the town mills. In others the improvement in the agriculture of the hinterland and the better organisation of the weekly rural markets meant a decreased demand for oatmeal from the local mills as the importation of grain and meal increased in volume and efficiency. The upheaval caused by the Rebellions of 1715 and 1745 had left Glasgow poor and ill-organised. Dundee had still not recovered from General Monk's sacking of the town. The burgh mills were run down and in need of repair and the income from them not high enough to justify expenditure from the inadequate resources of the towns' purses. To raise revenues from the mills town councils gradually, if reluctantly, faced the need to make repairs to the old mills and to grant longer leases to the new tenants as encouragement to them to make improvements to the mills. No tenant was going to spend much money or labour on improvements while his lease ran only from year to year and might not be renewed. The hope was that, if the magistrates first put the mills into good repair, they might then be let to new and enterprising tacksmen at higher rents. Glasgow magistrates, noting in 1769 that the mill leases had nearly expired, appointed a committee to consider 'what improvements can be made upon these milns and what will be the proper mode and terms of setting them at the expiration of the said tacks'.[20] Like the farms of the customs and the tolls of the turnpikes, the multure of the mills was let out to the highest bidder.

Glasgow owned three mills on the Molendinar[21] burn, Partick, Provan and the Sub-dean's Mill. Provan Mill came into the hands of the Town in 1667 when the magistrates acquired the lands of Provan, with the mill thereof, from Sir Robert Hamilton of Silverton. Partick came to the town by Royal charter. Subdean, the most ancient of the three, was, as its name shows, originally a church property. The town at first attempted to raise the rents of their mills prior to making improvements, but failing to do so, the chamberlain was authorised to reset the tacks to the same tenants on the same terms for another year 'if higher could not be obtained'.[22] The committee recommended that 'A report should be obtained from a competent millwright as to any suitable improvements and that the mills should be forthwith let for 19 years.' They had difficulty in finding a taker for the most decrepit of the mills, Subdean. In 1798 they received a written offer from William Meek, then the tenant of Jinkabout Milns, for a lease of 19 years of the town's Subdean Mill, provided that the magistrates first spent £600 sterling on repairs to the mill. The magistrates refused to treat with Mr Meek and decided to spend a tenth of the sum suggested by him. They were unwise, however, because instead of the £100 yearly rent offered by Meek for the mill after repairs they were able only to get £15 a year from the tenant they finally found to take the unimproved mill.[23]

Partick Mills were said in the 1790s to be 'very extensive . . . well constructed and much machinery introduced for the abridgement of labour'.[24] Between 1786 and 1790, 36,113 bolls of wheat were milled annually. By 1798 the town was having difficulty in finding a tenant because of their poor state of repair and the mill committee ordered 'such repairs as may appear to be necessary for rendering them tenantable'.[25] In 1805 they were let to Smithfield and Company.

In 1802 coal was found on the lands of Provan Mill and Matthew Liddell and Company were given a lease to work it. The mill was now let separately from its lands and thereafter suffered from problems over water supplies, as did the neighbouring Subdean Mill.[26] Glasgow's burgh mills ceased profitable working as a result firstly of competition from other, newer industries and secondly from greatly increased importation of flour. The importation of wheat as flour was relatively short-lived and when the shipping companies began to offer lower rates for transporting grain than flour the occasion arose for large milling concerns at the ports in Scotland to process the imported grain. But it was not the burgh but private individuals within it who were ready to benefit from this change. Flour milling was left to private enterprise.[27]

In Edinburgh the pattern was very similar, mediaeval royal charters giving the town ownership of the mills on the Dean Water and the right to exact multures, a long history of complaints from the bakers and brewers who were the town mills' largest customers, failure to modernise the mills and keep them in good repair, and the eventual emergence in the nineteenth century of private enterprise to answer the demand for white flour milling.

Dundee's position was different. Because of her desperate lack of water the three town mills were situated on the river Dighty at a considerable distance from the town. The burgh's slow path to economic recovery, followed by the swallowing up of all available capital by the textile industries, left those mills vulnerable and they were quickly converted into bleachfields to serve the spinning mills.[28] Backward-looking harbour trustees who imposed high duties on corn discouraged the imports of wheat grain and there was therefore little scope for private enterprise flour mill building. Leith and Aberdeen captured between them the east coast import of wheat and Dundee became dependent for its flour upon the mills of those towns.

An attempt by the working men of Dundee to form a co-operative venture into flour milling is of some interest here. They were, it was reported, 'impressed with the idea that were they to take the means into their own hands they would be more certain of obtaining pure and unadulterated flour'.[29] They equipped a steam-powered flour mill at the Stannergate and raised capital for it by the issue of small-value shares. This seems unfortunately to have been no more of a success than the other flour mills in Dundee, which gradually disappeared from sight, sometimes having been advertised for sale in the local papers for a number of years without finding a purchaser. In 1874, when John F. White's steam-powered flour mill was opened in Dock Street, it was said that it 're-established an industry in town which had been for many years discontinued'.[30]

There was a variety of reasons for the lack of success of flour milling in Dundee. One was the extremely low purchasing power of the working population of the city with a strong influx of potato-eating Irish immigrants. Another was the influence of the jute industry, which acted like a vacuum, sucking capital from all other possible industries in the town. When Dundee's first successful flour mill was eventually opened it was by an Aberdeen miller with an extensive business long established in that town.

If things were different for the old mills in the smaller provincial towns it was because they still served an agricultural hinterland. They remained at least as dependent on the surrounding farms for custom as on the local bakers and they therefore in most cases continued as oatmeal millers for at least another half century, the addition of wheat stones and white flour production making another branch to their business rather than completely replacing the old trade.

Lanark was one town prepared to spend some money on the upkeep of its burgh mill. In 1795 they consulted Meikle the millwright about what would be required to bring it up to date. He suggested adding a storey to the mill to accommodate new machinery for wheat and corn. Tenders were advertised for in the *Glasgow Courier* and the *Edinburgh Advertiser* but no one offered to do the work for less than Meikle's estimate of £230. A barley mill and a new kiln were added later and, in 1808, the mill was insured with Glasgow Fire Office for £250.[31]

In St Andrews the Town Council sold their Abbey Mill to the Incorporation of Bakers in 1808 on terms which must reflect the Trade's optimistic forecast of their own future at a time when bread prices were rising rapidly. The bakers agreed to pay the town in feu duty £50 sterling for the first eleven and a half years 'and the sum of £75 for all time coming thereafter and doubling said feu duty of £75 the first year after the expiry of every 40 years'. But the highest price for bread was reached in 1817 when the price was 14/3d per quarter. Thus the bakers' expenses for the mill were rising while their profits were falling. In November 1861 they sold the mill to John Hutton, farmer, West Newhall in the parish of Crail.[32] Here, as in other small towns, 'the traditional agricultural background has reasserted itself'.[33]

In Perth the city mills, although at the end of the eighteenth century they were manufacturing about 60 bolls of flour each day,[34] never gave up the processing of oats and barley and were therefore in a better position to withstand the drop in wheat prices which put out of business town mills who had converted from oats to wheat in answer to the bakers' enthusiasm for white flour. In 1833 the mills were feued to Alex. M'Dougall, a merchant in Perth, as 'meal and barley mills'.[35]

M'Dougall put in a manager and continued to draw customers from the farmers of the Carse. The Perth bakers, instead of taking over the city mills as did the bakers of many other towns, took a tack of the old mill at Pitcairnfield, a village nearby, from Robert Sutherland, owner of the adjoining land. This had been a wheat flour mill since at least the end of the eighteenth century when the *Old Statistical Account* reported it as let by the then landowner, Lord Methven, to Mr James Ray, who manufactured there 5,000 bolls of wheat into flour annually.[36] By 1845, however, the bakers were in trouble. They had only seven years of their lease to run and Sutherland, interested as were most of the neighbouring landowners in the profits to be made from textiles, was obviously easing them out. He built a new flax mill, to be turned by the same fall of water as the flour mill, allowing the bakers use of the fall only at night. The mill which had up till then ground 200 quarters per week[37] would be restricted to only 50 quarters.

In Cupar, the ancient mills, whose origin was said to be 'lost in antiquity', were improved before the end of the eighteenth century, not by the town but by the tacksman to whom they were let, who added flour-bolting equipment to the old machinery.[38] The next tacksman, a baker, who feued the mills in 1792 for £105 yearly and £1.015 of *grassum*, improved the mills even further. He remained in possession until the mid-nineteenth century and this long uninterrupted tack allowed him to bring the town's mills to the state of prosperity in which they were 'celebrated the best in Fife and employed by bakers and meal dealers from a great distance'.[39] Inglis, however, did not change their character sufficiently to put them at too much risk after that flush of prosperity had passed. They were still, in 1929, described as doing 'the business of a country miller, supplying farmers, grocers and others in Fife with meal, flour and feeding stuffs'.[40]

It would appear, then, that the towns only reluctantly accepted responsibility for the mills which had come into town ownership almost fortuitously as inheritance from king or abbey. The burgh mills were always sublet to tenants or feued outright, never managed by the town. Where the tacksmen were able, because of demand for the product from the town's population, to make profits large enough to maintain, adapt and rebuild the mills, the mills kept pace with changing demands and prospered, or at least survived. Where enterprising tenants, or those with sufficient capital, were not forthcoming the mills dwindled away. The town mills of small communities — Pittenweem is an example of the smallest — were an exception, but their small scale gave them more in common with the farm mills in spite of their town ownership. Town mills, because of the increased demand for wheaten bread, became tied up with the fluctuating fortunes of the baker trade to an extent which left them very vulnerable. The bakers were the only large-scale buyers from the mills. Other individual customers had not the corporate punch to influence development. The late eighteenth and early nineteenth century demand for wheaten bread brought profitability to the mills because the baker incorporations wanted them for grinding locally produced wheat. But as the bakers began to prefer the whiter flour which could be ground from English wheat in the large English mills and, later, American flour, they became less anxious to take tacks of the old burgh mills. By the time the new importation of American wheat as grain had produced a new need for milling facilities at the ports the old mills were useless and that need could be filled by large steam-powered roller mills backed by large amounts of capital from private enterprise. Only those mills which had kept their country connections and still ground oatmeal for the farming communities could survive such competition.

Of the baronial mills some were ancient foundations built for the use of abbot or monarch in times beyond memory while others, often in districts remote from the jurisdiction of church and crown, had been built by the gentlemen landowners for the use of their tenants. The purpose of the baron in wishing to have a mill on his land was essentially different from that of the owners of the king's and abbey mills. While these latter did derive revenue from their mills, this was not their primary purpose. For the barons, while there was some element of altruism in their provision of a mill, it was a small ingredient. They had a pressing need to raise money from their estates, a need which increased with the eighteenth century as their awareness of the advantages enjoyed by more progressive landowners increased. In districts where the only products were cereal and pulse crops the only way to increase productivity and to make the product more saleable was to improve and speed their processing. That the water mills were not provided at the tenants' wish is shown by the difficulty landlords had in suppressing the use of hand querns. 'By the custom of baronies, house-mills and querns are always broke.'[41] Where the crop was used only to support the tenant's family, the quern was found sufficient. It was the landlord's anxiety to have a quantity of meal to sell for cash which made him build a mill and force its use upon his tenants.

'Victual then is all the Product of this Country and when it giveth a good price, then it goeth well with the Masters Heritours, but when it is otherwise they are ordinarily much straitened for money.'[42]

By building a mill and *astricting* his tenants to it the baron could not only control to some extent the quality of meal processed on his estate, more importantly he could derive more from the rents, keep check of the quantities grown, and be sure that the proper proportion reached the estate girnal. *Thirlage,* the institution which forced those living on an estate to bring all their corn to the landlord's mill and to pay a substantial part of their crop as mill *multures* was by no means new to the eighteenth century. But it seems, from the last quarter of the seventeenth century, to have become institutionalised more formally and to have been more vigorously applied than it had previously been. The law lords thought that thirlage was not of the immemorial age of the mills themselves: 'Mills *at first* were built, as sometimes they are yet, without any astriction or thirlage but only to gain by the work thereof the equivalent hire . . . but now most lands are astricted to certain mills for a certain quantity of multure, far beyond the value of the work of grinding the corns . . . whereby it is a part of the rent of the lands.'[43] Landlords extended their power by imposing thirlage which did not always co-originate with the baronies. It was undoubtedly a new way of raising rents.

The building and repair of baronial mills which became fairly common during the eighteenth century was probably the direct result of the period of good corn harvests experienced during the period 1707 to 1760 and the stable prices derived from them.[44] The accumulation of a certain amount of profit in the barons' purses, resulting from the accumulation of grain from victual rents in their girnals, was necessary to allow the expenditure.

A good mill, well furnished and well run, was an asset to the estate, both because of the relatively high and steady rent paid by the miller himself and because the miller took over some of the organisation of the rent-collecting of the estate. Of all the corn brought to his mill he was entitled by the baron to take from an eleventh to a twenty-first part for himself, and he was, therefore, the person best able to know just how much each farmer was growing and by deduction what rent he was able to pay. 'The tenants are liable to be called to give an account upon oath before the baron baillie what they have bought and sold for 3 years back; and if a man's memory, who cannot keep accounts, has failed him and he conscientiously refuse to take an oath, he is charged arbitrarily. Such a mode of proceeding is surely contrary to the essential principles of justice and very hurtful to morals as frequent oaths must often be, especially where the interest of the person taking the oath may be materially affected thereby,' wrote one parish minister,[45] perhaps not wholly unswayed by the fact that ministers had to pay multures on the product of their glebes. Where a landlord wanted to increase the rents on his estate he would sometimes consult the miller first and even leave it in the miller's hands to organise the volunteering of higher offers, a custom not endearing the miller to his neighbours.[46]

The very earliest millers had neither extra status nor any very unusual mechanical skill but were chosen by their fellow tenants at the baron-baillie's behest, the only requirement being that they be good and honest men. This may seem less singular when it is understood, first, how extremely simple was the construction of the early mills and, second, how varied were the skills taken for granted in every country dweller. 'The occupation of the Men, whether Gentry or Comons is labouring and Husbandry; other Trades, except what is simply necessary, are scarce plyed. And generally all are accustomed to learn and practise so much of these as serves their own turn, that there is little encouragement for Arts and Trades here.'[47] There was, in fact, no more need for a skilled and apprenticed miller than there was for a stone mason. People built their own houses and could all turn their hand to the operation of the estate mill. Its machinery was familiar to them and easily understood. Therefore any man within the barony might apply to take a tack of the mill and, if acceptable to the other tenants, would become, for that period, the miller.

But as the organisation of the estate became more formal, as the application of thirlage became more rigid and the construction of mills more complicated, the miller became distanced from the other tenants. Entrusted by the baron with 'power to poynd for all dissobedience thair miln service',[48] he was not unnaturally excluded from the trust of the farmers.

The barons gained financially by the exaction of thirlage and mill services but made for themselves thereby a constant source of trouble. The baronial court, where the baron exerted jurisdiction over those who lived within his barony, was constantly taken up with complaints from the tenants about what seemed to them to be unfair treatment by the miller and from millers who found tenants unwilling to pay their mill dues and perform the tasks asked of them. So the laird of Urie, for instance, had to insist 'that ewerie tennent and sub tennent, cotters and greasmen, sall answer and obey John Milne,[49] milner at the milne of

Montquheiche, as they salbe requyrit to cast the laids, fens the damis, and bring watter to the milne in stormes'.[50]

At Monymusk, as on most other estates where written leases were given, all leases contained a clause that tenants should 'doe dutie to kirk, school, miln and officer use and wont'.[51] But in 1715 the tenants refused to rebuild the wall at Monymusk Mill and the baillie threatened to fine them '3 pund Scots for their contumacie'; and again, in 1746, several of them appeared in court and unanimously refused to bear any part in building a dam for the new mill on the Don: 'They would renounce their tacks rather than build any part of the said dam.'[52] Tenants very much resented the fact that they had not only to pay to the miller a fairly large proportion of all they grew, a proportion seemingly bearing no relation to the labour performed in grinding it, but had also to keep his mill, dam and house in good repair. Sir Archibald Grant of Monymusk might be the instigator of the building of a new mill on his estate, or of the repair of an old one, but it was his tenants who quarried the stones for it, cut the turf for its roof or the heather for its thatch, felled and carried the timber for it, dug its dam, made its road, and fetched home the mill stones for it. All this being at the expense of their own field work, it would have been extraordinary if they had not resented it and disliked the miller for whom the work was done and who acted as overseer of their labours. Most landlords eventually found it expedient to convert to money rents to allow for cash expenditure on the mill or to empower the miller to exact a certain money sum from all those who used the mill to go towards upkeep and repair. The beginnings of this are seen in 1749 at Monymusk where Grant gave the miller power to sell the goods of a defaulter and hire labour with the proceeds.[53] And the end of the story is as late as 1901 when the Lord President of the Court of Session, providing an interpretation of the Thirlage Act of 1799, explained that it allowed for the substitution of a fixed annual payment in lieu of services.[54]

The quality of the service offered by the baronial mills showed marked regional variations. Lands held by the enlightened, improving landlords might be provided with newly built, or at least properly repaired, mills while estates neglected in other respects were neglected in this. Thus the mill of Phantassie in Midlothian became a model of its kind, a nursery for engineering genius.[55] Sir Archibald Grant built a new mill for his tenants and repaired the old, although he had to be prompted to it by his factor, Thomas Wilson: 'I have daily complaints from the tenants about the mills. You may remember I told you that as long as Robert Grant had any concern with them I would never be at ease . . . You know very well that the mill at Glenton, through his fault, is down; so that all the sucken is divided between the Mill of Monymusk and Ordmill and the Mill of Monymusk was not sufficient before then to serve the sucken and much less now. The Mill of Ord has been almost idle for want of a running stone . . . if there is no remedy you will have no peace from daily complaints.'[56] Mr Macleod of Geanies, in Ross-shire, whose lands lay in the same parish as the ancient abbey mills of Fearn, built new mills 'to accommodate himself and his people'. His rents were then paid partly in oatmeal, partly in barley and partly in that scarce commodity, money.[57] In Caithness Mr Traill of Hobbester, sheriff-depute of the county, erected in the 1780s a mill whose wheel turned machinery for lint-milling as well as a corn and barley mill.[58] The 'encouragements' given by the Board of Trustees for Manufactures for the improvement of flax culture meant that the building of lint mills was taken up with some zeal by landowners in the eighteenth century. Later on the installation of threshing machines became an infectious enthusiasm. Because these were new crazes they caught the imagination of a landowning class already fired by the new scientific thought on agriculture. The corn mills, which had always been there, and still worked with moderate and unexciting efficiency, were of less interest to them because they lacked novelty and so they were less often written about and less often boasted of at meetings of the agricultural improvers. But modernisation of the ancient mills did proceed in all the improving counties. Lord Banff's Mill of Ribra was well kept up and well operated.[59] Planned villages, such as Colonel Dirom's at Brideskirk and Robert Rennie's, showed new corn mills marked on their streams as a matter of course.[60] Sir James Agnew paid for 'a sufficient milne, new built in timber iron and new stones' on his estate as early as 1719.[61]

The fertile arable lands of the improving lairds repaid expenditure on mills. But it must be remembered that the Highlands of Scotland are not only those parts of the country lying north of Inverness. Not a county but has its upland areas, and in the eighteenth century these were neglected and barren, many of them the property of 'disaffected' gentlemen whose lands were milked dry of money before the Rebellion and forfeited after it. The Commissioners for the Annexed Estates reported broken and ruined and inefficient mills of great age and sad mismanagement. The family of the Dukes of Perth had built a mill to serve the barony of Callender in 1733 but it was badly sited. In New

Tarbet all the mills in the barony were 'in very bad repair'. The Miln of Monaltry in Aberdeenshire was 'always troublesome and seldome in good repair' and the Miln of Camaghouran was 'greatly in disrepair'.[62]

However, the Highland lairds can hardly be blamed for their failure to maintain good mills when their chances of deriving income from them were so small. Some of the small mills paid no rent at all and produced only trifling amounts in multures.[63]

One of the reasons for the weakening of baronial control was the growth in prosperity and status of the farmer tenants. One of the results was that farmers were forced to reassess their own relationship with the mill and its miller. While the mill belonged to the baron landlord and the miller exacted multures, the farmers, although to some extent dependent upon the mill and forced to share in its upkeep, felt no responsibility for it. In very many districts they had had their own arrangements for milling — the hand quern or the horizontal mill — and had gone only reluctantly to the estate mill. With the ending of astriction to the mill, however, many landlords, ceasing to derive much benefit from the system, ceased also to accept responsibility for the upkeep and repair of the mill. Some of them even continued to exact multures without keeping up the mill, as in the case of the Mill of Kinross, burnt down twenty years previously and not replaced, but on whose account the landowner continued to charge his tenant farmers a percentage of their crops; or the Mill of Torphichen where the mill had been in ruins for years. In the case of Forbes Trustees versus Davidson about the Mill of Nairn the Court decided it was a condition of the right to exact payments that the mill should be in working order, but cases concerning ruined mills on lands where the farmers were still paying multures recurred in the Court of Session during the nineteenth century.[64]

Landlords gave up the repair of mills when they ceased to derive an appreciable source of income from them and, perhaps more important, when it became impossible for them to put the labour of their tenants at the disposal of the miller. The period of expenditure on mills by landowners runs from the first period of agricultural improvement during the early eighteenth century until the end of that century. From then on the upkeep of country mills had to be the concern either of the millers themselves or of the farmers who used them.

The changes in conveyancing of land which took place concurrently with the rise in social and financial status of the tenant farmer from the end of the eighteenth century and the drawing up of formal leases in some cases for the first time meant that some tenant farmers found themselves with baronial mills left on the land they feued. They could choose either to maintain them or to let them fall into disuse. The question was resolved by the change in social patterns and dietary habits we have already observed. In counties where the people were less dependent on oatmeal not all, but the vast majority, of mills fell into disuse. In counties where farm servants were paid in oatmeal and it comprised their diet almost exclusively, it was necessary for the farmers to keep the mills in repair.

The process whereby old baronial mills were translated into farm mills is well illustrated by the history of Mill of Benholm. The first definite evidence of its existence comes in the fifteenth century when the lands and barony of Benhame, with the mill thereof, were granted by John Lundy of that ilk, knight, and Isabel his spouse, to their son Robert Lundy, to be held of the King.[65] It was not then a new mill and may have dated back to the twelfth century when the family de Benhame were first granted their charter of the lands. It passed by marriage from the Lundy family to the family of Keith, Earls Marischal, and remained in their hands until 1669 when James Scott of Logie bought it for his son Robert. During the eighteenth century the lands were divided between the sons of the Scott family so that by 1803 David Scott of the farm of Nether Benholm owned 'half the mill' and John Scott of Brotherton farm the other half. The lands of Over Knox of Benholm and Nether Knox of Benholm, along with the granary or girnal house called the White House of Gourdon, went to Margaret Scott who married Sir Alexander Gordon Lesmore.[66] Thus the estate had already been divided by marriage settlements and inheritance. In 1879 the estate of Benholm was bought by a William Smith (for £26,500) who improved and enlarged the house and estate to the tune of £30,000, but it fetched only £21,000 when sold again in 1905. The buyers were then the neighbouring tenant farmers who each bought their own piece of land, the mill going with the farm of Brotherton under whose management it remained until 1929 when it finally came into the hands of the miller whose family have operated it ever since.[67] Similarly Mill of Cowie, one of the baronial mills of Grant of Monymusk, ended up in farm ownership. Benvie Mill, once the property of the Abbey of Coupar Angus, was owned by the Gray estate and bought by the tenant farmer from the Earl of Moray in 1918.[68] The ancient families often continued as feudal superiors of the mills after the lands on which they stood had passed into farm ownership, and many mills reached the lesser gentry and so eventually the farming class through marriage settlement. Landowners were fond of giving the mill or 'half the mill' as a marriage settlement for wives and daughters. Lady Halliburton, for instance, was provided 'by her contract of marriage to the mains of Halliburton with the mill and pertinents and her precept of sasine bearing warrant to infeft her in the mains and mill, by earth and stone of the land and by the clap of the mill'.[69]

By these various ways the mills fell into farm ownership and became the responsibility of the farmers who used them. When the original transaction between estate and farmer was made, clauses about the upkeep of the mill were usually inserted but farmers found it difficult to hold the estate to its promises about expenditure. In 1848 the Duke of Hamilton gave Alexander Fleming lease of the farm of Rouseland with the mills and mill lands of Kinneil for nineteen years at a rent in victual and money of £500, the proprietor undertaking to spend not more than £380 within the first four years of the lease on building and repairing the houses. 'Further, in regard that the greater part of the machinery in the said mills is old, imperfectly constructed and not in good repair, therefore, in consideration of the lease hereby to be granted, the tenant obliges himself within the first 2 years of the lease to expend a sum of not less than £800 in repairing, renewing and making additions to the said machinery, according to such plan as may be approved by the proprietor and to produce vouchers for at least that expenditure and thereafter to keep all in good working order and repair . . . Further the tenant obliges himself . . . to have the whole houses and machinery constantly insured in some respectable insurance office to the extent of £1200 sterling.' Fleming kept his part of the bargain but when, in 1865, the mills were destroyed by fire the landlord took the insurance money but did not rebuild the mills.[70]

Apart from these inherited baronial mills, the first and earliest farm mills were those constructed for the domestic use of the farmer's family and housed either in the barn or close by. They were of two kinds, the quern, or hand mill, or the water-powered horizontal mill. Their technology will be discussed in another chapter, but to understand the prevalence of these little mills — and there were a hundred mills in Berwickshire alone[71] — it is necessary to understand something of the organisation of the typical small Scottish farm. The first task of the day was the threshing of corn in the barn. It was a weekly, in some touns even a daily, rather than a seasonal one, performed so often partly because the beasts were fed on straw (the straw being then considered to hold as much nutritive value as grain) and the straw had to be fresh and uncrushed,[72] and partly because many farms had no safe storage for grain, preferring therefore to keep corn in stack. This frequent threshing meant that there was always a stock of grain waiting to be milled.

In this, as in other respects, variation is regional rather than chronological, for while in the Northern Highlands and Islands the small mills and the old pattern of agriculture which they served lingered on almost to the present day, in the Lothians and in the hinterland of Glasgow the little mills and the hand-threshing had disappeared almost completely by the beginning of the nineteenth century. The same qualification must be applied to diet. While lowland areas near towns had become consumers of shop-bought white bread, remoter areas conformed to the old habits of food production. J. G. Mackay described a visit to an old woman on the heights of Assynt where the guest was pressed to stay for something to eat. 'The old matron went out to the barn, took in a sheaf of corn and in a minute whipped the oats off with her hand, winnowed it with a fan at the end of the house, then placed it in a pot on the fire to dry; after that it was ready to be ground, and then, being put through a sieve, was ready to bake. The whole thing was done in an hour, from the time she took in the sheaf of corn till the cakes were on the table.'[73] If eighteenth century farms were generally a little slower in transforming grain into food it was nevertheless a continual process, always being carried on, from threshing floor to drying kiln at the end of the barn, from kiln to mill, from mill to table. Although every farmhouse kitchen kept its meal kist, it was quickly emptied and had to be steadily replenished, and freshly ground oatmeal was preferred by those who, eating it every day, could discriminate between a good milling and a poor one. It was, therefore, in the farmer's interest to have his own mill, operated by his own farm servants, and making the 'ferm-toun' self-sufficient in food for man and beast. Certainly these little mills did co-exist with the baronial mills. Their presence preserved the tenant farmer from complete dependence on the landlord's mill, which might or might not be kept in good repair, and allowed him to dodge some degree of the thirlage dues exacted there. And it was this which kept the baron-baillie courts so occupied in forcing astriction.

But until 1799, a very powerful disincentive towards mill building on farms existed, at least in those areas where the baron baillie's power was effectively enforced. If the landowner found that a mill other than his own was operating 'within the sucken', he could apply to the courts for power to demolish it. There is little doubt his men often demolished without application to the courts. If the mill on the farm remained domestic in scale and did not set up to compete with the estate mill by attracting custom from other farms it must ordinarily have been tolerated except for sudden outbursts of enthusiastic quern-bashing and mill-demolishing by zealous factors. The risk of such treatment must certainly have deterred farmers from investing either capital or effort in ambitious ventures into mill-building, even had the capital and initiative been available on tenanted farms of the period.

There were other disincentives. Where the feeding of horses began to be better understood and farmers began to show a new ambition to own stronger and better bred animals, they began to feed them oats. 'Farmers, whether purely from the pride of seeing their horses make a better appearance or whether they find they enhance the value of the animal in the full proportion of the additional food given it, allow their horses more oats than formerly; and secondly the number of horses and the demand for oats to feed them having greatly increased in the country of late years, husbandmen frequently find it more advantageous to sell their oats unmanufactured than to make them into meal especially in backward seasons when the oats are less productive.'[74]

This was happening in the same regions and at the same time as a preference for white bread and a less pressing demand for oatmeal was bringing less custom to the local mills and a reduction of numbers working on the land was leaving farmers with less need to manufacture meal to feed their servants. In those areas, then, farmers were unlikely to build new mills or keep the old ones in repair and there came most often to be one sizeable independent mill serving the needs of a large area. But in the oat-growing uplands the case was different and many of the mills whose ruins can be seen on farms in the North owe their long-continued existence to the increased need for meal for farm servants which was experienced during the nineteenth century.

Thus, of the country mills surviving into the twentieth century, some had evolved from the barn mills of the early farms, having been gradually improved and brought up to date as the farmer found it worthwhile. Others, originally baronial mills, had a longer history. Some of them were still set in tack to individual millers by the estates but many had come, through the amalgamation of small farms into larger ones, through marriage settlements, or simply through the breaking up of the old estates, into the ownership of farmers.

Mills of this kind had always been situated in buildings separated from the farm and had always, or at least back to a time beyond written records, been powered by vertical water wheels. Under farm ownership they were either let to a miller tenant, who was then responsible for the maintenance or improvement of the machinery, or operated by a miller who was an employee of the farmer and was paid wages by him. In that case meal bought by country people from the mill would be paid for at the farm, the miller being simply an operative and having no part in the keeping of accounts.[75] But in most cases the miller was a tenant of one of the larger farmers and he himself ran the mill as a commercial undertaking, grinding meal and feedstuffs for 'the Mains', for his fellow tenants, and for any other customers who came his way.

Of the five categories of meal mill surviving from mediaeval times into the eighteenth century, abbey, crown, town and barony mill have all disappeared. Only the farm, or country mill, because it answered the real needs of the inhabitants, survived the changes in society which happened in the nineteenth century.

NOTES

1. *Transactions of the Second International Symposium on Molinology*, Brede, 1969, 304. Comments by Anders Jespersen on preceding paper
2. Jones, 'The water-powered corn mills of England, Wales, and the Isle of Man: a preliminary account of their development', 338
3. *Chartularies of the Abbey of Newbotle*, 95.6.7.103, quoted in Chalmers, *Caledonia*, I, 488n
4. Hamlyn/Angus Milling Co. records
5. Morison, *Decision of Court of Session*, 16074
6. *Ibid.*, 16029
7. Graham, *The social life of Scotland in the 18th century*, 160
8. *O.S.A.*, XIV, 557
9. Grant, *Old and New Edinburgh*, III, 64
10. Dalrymple, Sir James, Viscount Stair, *Principles of the Law of Scotland*, ed. Patrick Shaw (henceforth Shaw, *Stair*), 479-80
11. Sanderson, 'The feuing of Strathisla: a study in 16th century social history', 3
12. Wills, *Reports on the Annexed Estates, 1755-1769*, 15
13. See p. 43ff.
14. Morison, *Decisions of Court of Session*, 16034
15. Balfour, Sir James, of Pittendreich, *Practicks of Scots Law*, 1209

16. Dundee Public Libraries, Lamb Collection, 224 (25) 15
17. SRO, GD 4/63
18. MacPhail, *Papers from the collection of Sir William Fraser*, 222n
19. *N.S.A.*, 9, 367
20. Marwick and Renwick, *Extracts from the Records of the Burgh of Glasgow*, 26
21. Literally the 'millers' burn', from Latin *molendinarius*, miller
22. Marwick and Renwick, *Records of the Burgh of Glasgow*, 689
23. *Ibid.*, 116
24. *O.S.A.*, XII, 116n
25. Marwick and Renwick, *Records of the Burgh of Glasgow*, 131
26. *Ibid.*, 314; Court of Session, Magistrates of Glasgow v Miller, Feb. 11, 1813
27. See pp. 74, 142, 151
28. Gauldie, Enid, Scottish Bleachfields, St Andrews University B.Phil. thesis 1967, Appendix: Title deeds of Midmill bleachfield
29. Dundee Public Libraries, Lamb Collection, 196/47. See also pp. 6, 74
30. *Ibid.*
31. Robertson, *Lanark: the Burgh and its Councils, 1469-1880*, 161
32. Macadam, *The Baxter Books of St Andrews*, 223, 294ff.
33. Turner, 'The significance of water power in industrial location', 98-115
34. *N.S.A.*, X, 191
35. Alex M'Dougall's Trustees, Minutes 14, April 1837 (NRA[S] 1510)
36. *O.S.A.*, 18, 518
37. Note that this is already only half the quantity the mill had been producing at the end of the eighteenth century.
38. Instrument of sasine in favour of John Inglis, baker in Cupar, Feb. 2, 1792
39. *N.S.A.*, IX, 11
40. Particulars of sale of Cupar corn and flour mills, Jan. 10, 1929
41. Morison, *Decisions of Court of Session*, 8897
42. Macfarlane, Walter, *Geographical Collections*, S.H.S. Edinburgh, 1908, 3, 225
43. Shaw, *Stair*, 239, 479
44. Hamilton, Henry, ed., *Selections from the Monymusk Papers, 1713-1755*, 236 (henceforth Hamilton, *Monymusk*); Smout and Fenton, 'Scottish agriculture before the Improvers', 73-4
45. *O.S.A.*, 9, 578
46. S.R.O. GD 24/1/639
47. Macfarlane, *op. cit.*, 225
48. Barron, D. G., ed., *Court Book of the Barony of Urie, 1604-1747*, 29 (henceforth Barron, *Urie*)
49. See p. 189

50. Barron, *Urie*, 38
51. Hamilton, *Monymusk*, 197
52. *Ibid.*, 228
53. *Ibid.*, 238
54. Court of Session, Porteous v Haig, 1901; but see also p. 59 below
55. Boucher, *John Rennie*, 6
56. Hamilton, *Monymusk*, 128
57. *O.S.A.*, 6, 434
58. *O.S.A.*, 12, 158n
59. *O.S.A.*, 14, 537
60. *Prize Essays and Transactions of the Highland Society of Scotland*, 2, 1803, Robert Rennie, 'Plan of an Inland Village'; Matthew, Robert, *Two Villages*, Edinburgh, n.d; Wood, 'Regulating the settlers and establishing industry', 39
61. S.R.O. GD 154/460: Survey of milns in the parish of Leswalt
62. Wills, *Reports on the Annexed Estates*, 5, 38, 55
63. Adam, *Sutherland Estate Management*, 56-7, 67
64. Court of Session, Forbes Trustees v Davidson, 1901
65. S.R.O. GD 4/10
66. Registers of Sasine, Kincardineshire
67. I am grateful to Mr Lindsay Watson for his advice and kindness over the many years this book has been in preparation
68. S.R.O. GD 4/410. Information from the present owner, Mr Jack Thoms of Benvie, and the tenant of the mill, Mr James Dallas
69. Morison, *Decisions of Court of Session*, 8896
70. Court of Session, Duke of Hamilton's Trustees v Fleming, Dec. 23, 1870
71. Macfarlane, *op. cit.*, 184
72. Findlay, *Oats*, 178; Fenton, *Scottish Country Life*, 79; *Agricultural Labourer*, I, 56, 138; *ibid.*, III, 2, 49; *N.S.A.*, IX, 958; see also Cameron, *The Ballad and the Plough*, 37
73. McNeill, *The Scots Kitchen*, 12
74. *O.S.A.*, 7, 427
75. Mr Donald McBeath described to me how 'Geordie the Mill' used to deliver meal to his parents' home and how he himself as a small boy used to go up to the farm house to pay the farmer for it, being rewarded there with 'a huge chunk of sponge cake which I didn't quite know how to handle'

3
Thirlage — Service to the Mill

In any history of mills in Scotland the system of thirlage is bound to be discussed. For those unfamiliar with Scottish legal terms it may be useful to attempt a definition of thirlage and of a few other words attendant upon it.

The word *thirl* has the same root as *thrall*, 'thirlage' having much the same original meaning as *thraldom*. By the eighteenth century it had come to have the special meaning of bondage to a particular mill. Those tenants living on an estate, that is *within the thirl* of that estate, were *thirled* or, in the North-East, 'bunsucken', to the estate's mill, that is, they were bound to bring their corn to be ground to their landlord's mill and to no other. The tenants so thirled to the mill were known as *suckeners*, and the area over which the mill held this power was the *sucken*. *Sucken* and *thirl* are used with the same meaning, *sucken* being perhaps slightly more colloquial than *thirl*. In the higher courts the word *astricted* is more often used than *thirled* — tenants were *astricted* to their lord's mill. Their thirlage to the mill bound them to perform certain services for the miller and to pay *multures* and *sequels*. *Multure* or *moulter*, pronounced 'mooter', was a fixed proportion of the tenant's grain paid to the miller, who was also known as the *multurer*. *Insucken multures* were paid by the thirled tenants. *Outsucken multures* had to be paid by those who, living outside the sucken and so not bound to the mill, nevertheless found occasion to bring their grain to that mill for grinding. On some estates *dry multures* were exacted, which meant that tenants had to pay a proportion of all the grain they grew, whether it was ground into meal or not. When tenants failed to bring their corn to the mill of the thirl they could be sued for *abstracted multures*, or for *abstraction*. *Sequels* were the small amounts of meal paid to the miller's servants, over and above the amount owing to the miller himself as multurer, and these small amounts, usually accepted as the quantity which could be held heaped within two clasped hands, were variously known as *knaveship, bannock* or *the lick*, or *lock, of goodwill.*[1]

In England, similarly, a baron had *soke rights* over his tenants and bound them in the same way to use the mill built by him on his land. Bennett and Elton say that in Saxon times the system did not exist in England but that by the fourteenth century most tenants had become bound to their lord's mill. Tenants in England had the right to build a mill if they chose and, apparently, did so; but if the owner of the land built a mill he had the power to compel his tenants to grind there.[2] In Scotland it was David I who subjected the mills to tithes, a century before Henry III imposed the tythe system on mills in England.[3]

Some Scottish tenants did build the small Highland mills on their own initiative and at their own expense and would, in many cases, have preferred to be allowed to use them rather than pay multures at the larger mills of their landlords. Professor Bell and Lord Kames both supposed that thirlage was devised as a means of recompense to landowners who provided their tenants with mills. Professor Bell wrote, 'Thirlage was devised as an expedient for indemnifying the builder of a mill for extraordinary outlay in a rude age.'[4] Kames, in a well-known judgment, said, 'Of old, mills, being expensive, and of difficult construction, were justly favoured. It was thought to require the privilege of a monopoly to encourage men to lay out their money upon works so generally useful. And hence it came to be an established point that other mills could not be built within the thirle.'[5]

The monks, who built the mills to produce flour and meal for their own use, also thirled all tenants on the abbey lands to their mills. On the dissolution of the abbeys the mills passed into the hands of the baronial estates with the sytem of thirlage intact. Thirlage unquestionably originated in feudal principles. It had the twin purposes of raising revenue and exerting a form of control over the tenants, both of which it served admirably. The monks had derived large revenues from their mills.[6] Baronial estates found them equally valuable. But it would appear that the system had been applied with some leniency until the eighteenth century and that the tenants' habit of grinding their grain in their own mills was very often winked at. Only occasional bursts of activity on the baron baillie's part, usually occasioned by complaints from a miller whose income was dropping, compelled backsliders to attend the mill and pay multures, until his attention wandered again. One factor wrote to his employer, 'the miller thinks himself injured and apply *(sic)* to me for redress' because 'the tenants are sending little or none to the mill . . . I suspect the miller will require all the assistance the law of equity can give him.'[7]

The fact of the matter was that, especially on a laxly run estate, there was no great advantage to the landlord in enforcing astriction to the mill. The multures were the property of the miller, not that of the owner of the mill, a fact emphasised in a Court of Session judgment in 1785.[8] The landlord's benefit came from the high rent he could charge his miller-tacksman in expectation of the amount coming to him by way of multures. Having leased the mill and set the rent, the landlord was understandably less anxious than the miller about the enforcement of the conditions. This situation changed during the eighteenth century. A course of events was set in train which culminated in the Thirlage Act of 1799, a statute removing one, but not the last, vestige of the feudal system from Scots law.

As with many reforms, the campaign to achieve the abolition of thirlage began with a period of extra severity in its application. Those baronial estates beginning to be affected by the spirit of improvement put some energy both into the repair and rebuilding of mills and into the tidying up and stricter enforcement of estate administration. The greater interest taken in their estates by some landlords had revealed very often a situation in which the mill of the thirl crumbled into desuetude while the tenants resorted to the primitive mills of their own construction. Unwilling to spend money on the repair of mills unless they were used to the full, landlords setting about reconstruction were more likely to enforce attendance upon the estate mill. During the same period, perhaps because by the eighteenth century the ancient mills had been allowed for too long to crumble and decay, millers more and more often complained in the baronial courts of the difficulty of making the tenants come to them, and there were large numbers of cases of suing for abstracted multures. The Courts of Session, too, saw an increasing number of cases in which one landowner sued another for abstraction of multures because the tenants of one estate, with an ill-kept or inconveniently situated mill, were resorting to the mill of another. In these cases the owner of the neglected mill was sometimes entitled to charge dry multures, even when his mill was not used, while the owner of the mill to which the suckeners chose to come could charge them outsucken multures. Protesting tenants were thus subjected to double multures, an inequity naturally not accepted with any degree of equanimity.[9]

As with every law requiring change, firstly, test cases were being brought to court decades before there was any suggestion of parliamentary action, and, secondly, the law lords were not unanimous in their support for the laws and precedents which maintained the system. Conflicting decisions had been given sufficiently often by 1752 to stir the law lords to draw up a short history of thirlage and to define their own position. By 1757 Lord Kames was openly disagreeing with precedent and with decisions made by his noble colleagues on the bench. 'Mills,' he said, 'at present require no extra-ordinary encouragement, because they may be erected at a very small expense; and therefore it is full time that this monopoly were at an end. The more rivalship the better for the lieges.' Thirlage and multures were 'only so many vestiges of the tyranny of the Popish clergy'.[10]

This last was a view taken up, not perhaps surprisingly, with great enthusiasm by the Presbyterian clergy and, by the last decade of the century, when the statistical accounts of the parishes of Scotland were drawn up by the parish ministers, they were almost unanimous in decrying the system of thirlage.

The factors which had brought about this questioning of a long tradition were many and complicated. Perhaps the first and most important was the agricultural revolution and the upheaval it occasioned in patterns of land use and the organisation of society. In some cases improved methods of cultivation increased grain production and consequently increased the multures due to the miller. Tenants objected to the miller's benefiting, without much effort on his part, from their expenditure of energy on increased production. In other districts changes from cereals to root crops or to pasture resulted in a drastic reduction of multures, and in this case it was the miller who complained or who failed to pay his rent. Some regions saw shifts of population as a result of estate improvements which made the situation of the old mills inconvenient. The new relocation of tenants required the building of new mills, and the question arose of whether new mills could be built within the thirl. This was a very frequent occasion for lawsuits and one of the reasons why Kames and the more open-minded of the judges felt that the system required review. As the law stood, anyone building a new mill in a district where the tenants were already thirled to an existing mill could be forced to demolish it, the question of its usefulness to the neighbourhood being quite irrelevant.

In 1752 it was stated categorically that 'a corn mill cannot be erected, upon any pretext, within the thirle of another mill'.[11] In 1760 John

Miller, miller of Millheugh, Blantyre, complained to the Sheriff that Alexander Corse had erected a new mill within his thirlage, and Corse was ordered, after a considerable amount of debate, to demolish his new mill.[12]

Another aspect of the problem appeared in 1781 when the old Mill of Redgodens, which had fallen into ruin, was demolished and a new one built in a different place more convenient to the tenants. David Balhardie, tacksman of the old, demolished mill, took a lease of the new mill at Ledcarsie, and attempted to enforce those once astricted to him to come to his new mill. The Lords ruled that 'to oblige the possessors of the land thirled to one mill to go to another mill was imposing a new servitude . . . which could not be.'[13] An opposing view seems to have been taken in the case of Sir William Jardine versus Lady Douglas in 1793, where servitude to the mill was insisted on although the lands of the barony of Sibbaldie had been redistributed for the convenience of their administration.[14] Conflicting decisions of this kind struck at the certainty which had been the basis for tenants' ancient unquestioning acceptance of their thirlage. In such ways the consequences of agricultural reform encouraged new thinking on the question.

Similarly the breaking up and feuing off of ancient estates caused some tenant opposition to thirlage, especially where new landlords attempted, as they sometimes did, to extend the thirl or more strictly to insist on the performance of mill services. Tenants, willing out of habit and custom to accept the domination of ancient landlords, were not necessarily willing to accept the same style from newcomers. Rebellious mutterings were given form as the habit of giving written contracts of tenure increased. Until the eighteenth century written leases had been relatively uncommon and tenants had habitually accepted the conditions of their tenancy, thirlage to the mill among others, as laid down to them verbally by the baron baillie. They were not, however, always so willing to accept the strict clause in a written contract which laid such an obligation upon them. There were many cases in which landlords asked the courts to support them in insisting on astriction to the estate mills on lands where the tenants had, in practice, always been thirled to the mill and had paid multures there but were now rebellious. But the courts did not uphold them. A test case established that 'there is no principle of law more firmly settled than that the use of grinding at a mill, however constant and uniform and for whatever length of time it may have taken place, will not of itself constitute a thirlage and make that *necessitatis* which more naturally is *volun-*

tatis.'[15] This seemed to overturn an earlier view that the tenants of a baron should be considered thirled to his mill if they had been accustomed to pay multures there by *use and wont*.[16]

The law lords, faced with a flood of cases seeming to suggest an inequity in the application of the old laws and a doubt about the principles underlying them, found themselves, as the century progressed, out of sympathy with the idea of thirlage. Yet, at the same time, on the old baronial estates, the feudal barons were attempting to tighten rather than slacken the ties of the system. At Monymusk, for instance, it was not until 1749 that the thirlage of the estate, although accepted by use and wont for centuries, was clearly defined and its stricter enforcement attempted. This was made necessary, as in so many cases, both by an increased unwillingness to pay multures on the tenants' part and a more vigorous prosecution of their own claims by the millers: 'Whereas many disputes have arose betwixt the millers and tenants in this Barony to the great hurt of both about what corns are subject to multure, the millars for many years past having been negligent in prosecuting their claims though they have always made a claim to multure for all that grew, except the seed; and whereas upon inquiry into the practice of all the neighbourhood it is found to be agreeable to what is hereafter enacted and that by the constant claim of the millars, the reason of the thing and the almost general practice of the whole country and that upon inquiry it has been found that many even upon this Barony have conformed thereto it is justly presumeable it was the establishment and practice of this Barrony. It is hereby enacted in this General Court of the Barony that for the future after Whitsunday next all corns or bear or other grain growing within the Barony shall be subject to pay one and a half pecks shilling in the four bolls.'[17]

After the Rebellions the administration of forfeited estates by the crown brought to the attention of the law lords and the Edinburgh gentry the circumstances of some of the old baronies far removed from the enlightened views of the capital. The Commissioners of the estates annexed to the Crown, left with the problem of dragging neglected estates into a semblance of modern improved agriculture, became convinced that the ancient feudal burdens were contributing to the backwardness of the land. In the plan drawn up for the improvement of farms on the estates under their care the very first rule, given priority in the list of instructions, reads: 'That the tenants, whose leases shall bear relation to these articles, shall continue astricted to the mills of the annexed estates to which they are now severally thirled, and shall pay and perform the multures and mill services use and wont. But, because the Commissioners intend, as soon as may be, to abolish (or at least greatly to abate) the burden of thirlage in the annexed estates; therefore, as soon as they shall accomplish that intention, by granting new leases of the mills without astricted multures (or with an abatement thereof) then the said tenants shall not only pay whatever diminution the mill rents shall suffer thereby, in proportion to the rents of their several astricted lands, but shall also continue to perform such of the present mill-services as shall be reserved in the said leases of the several mills.'[18]

Even where, as here, there was a definite commitment towards the abolition of thirlage it could not happen overnight because of the fact that mills had commonly longer and more precisely drawn leases than farms of that period and their leases entitled them to multures and mill services. But the information about mills and the supposed effect of thirlage upon their efficiency gathered during their period of service as Commissioners for the forfeited estates certainly formed the opinions of those gentlemen involved. Whether they were right in believing that the abolition of thirlage would in itself make a material difference to the efficiency of milling is another question. There were, in fact, other forces at work during the period before abolition which had at least as much effect as their conversion.

Especially after the quashing of the Rebellions of 1715 and 1745, the possibility of freer travelling about the country inevitably spread knowledge about the best existing practice even into the more backward areas. Technological improvements pioneered in the Lothians were soon talked about in the West and north of the Tay, and alongside the improvements in machinery there came as a natural result more rational organisation of the mills. At the same time, as farming was put on a more efficient footing, men from the farms had less time to spare for waiting at the mill. The miller's natural reluctance to allow customers to 'mistemper'[19] his new machinery and the customers' new awareness of the importance of time meant that the miller was more likely to have the whole business of processing grain, from barn to meal girnal, under his own control, a system which, in the proper hands, made, in itself, for greater efficiency.

But there was a side effect of the technological revolution which boosted the campaign for abolition. The invention of new mill machinery proved an incentive to build different kinds of mills to satisfy new markets. The pot barley mill, for instance, was installed very widely throughout the Lowlands, either within the old mills or on adjacent sites. Lint mills, for preparing field flax for the linen industry, became very popular, especially as they were given financial encouragement by the Board of Trustees for the Encouragement of the Linen Industry. This was a body of Edinburgh gentlemen set up after the Union of the Parliaments to administer a fund for the improvement of manufacturing industry, many of whom also sat among the Commissioners for the forfeited estates. Lint mills, like barley mills, were often set up within the old mill buildings, or close to them. The question then arose of whether lint seed and barley for pot barley could be said to be subject to thirlage. Millers naturally hoped that they would be, thus increasing both their multures and their influence. Landowners were torn between the wish to encourage the new industries to settle on their land and an equally strong wish to keep them under their own feudal control. Many cases came into the courts, although almost certainly an even larger number of disputes on the subject were settled amicably outside. At first the law lords took the view that these lint and barley mills could not be allowed to be erected within the thirl because 'it would open a door to daily fraud'.[20] They meant that a farmer taking his barley to a mill where he would not have to pay multures might take his other corns there to be ground at the same time, so dodging the dues that should have been paid to the mill of the thirl. But Lord Kames, a leading figure on the Board of Trustees, came out strongly in favour of allowing the new constructions. In 1748 a lint mill was built at Sir Archibald Denholm's expense and occupied by William Tennent, who was himself thirled to the Mill of Cleuch on the lands of George Lockhart of Carnwath. Lockhart sued to have it demolished as contrary to the astriction. The problem was said to be that the lint mill, fitted for *sheeling lint bows*, that is, crushing flax seed to extract the oil, was also capable of grinding oats. Carnwath feared that it would attract custom away from his Mill of Cleuch. The case went on for some years but its outcome was sealed by the fact that the lint mill had been built 'upon the encouragement of the trustees for the encouragement of manufactures'.[21] Kames decided in 1757 in favour of Tennent and refused to allow demolition.

Another case in the same year allowed a pot barley mill to be built within the thirl of a meal mill.[22] But the issue was not yet settled, and in 1760 the destruction of a barley mill was at first ordered, then countermanded in favour of a compromise which allowed the barley mill to operate as long as it should be 'put into such a shape as it should not be fit for grinding peas and corn into meal'. This was again objected to on the grounds that many rulings 'clearly establish the doctrine that the servitude of thirlage does virtually imply a restraint upon the proprietor of the subservient tenement from building a mill thereon which can interfere with, or be prejudicial to, the dominant mill . . . and it is vain to imagine that the caution proposed can give any effectual security against abstractions.'[23]

Clearly the Lords of Session themselves were in several minds on the question, but such cases as these seemed to the more enlightened of them to prove that the system of thirlage was acting as a drag on industrial development and would have to be changed. When the new flax-spinning mills, insistent as they were in competition for the old water mill sites, and backed by new and abundant capital, began to appear in the last decades of the century, the case for retention was lost. The new industries spelt the death of the old system. The same lords who pushed the case for Scotland's emergence as an industrial nation at their boardroom tables could not in honesty give judgments in court which impeded that development. The system which forbade the building of new mills of any description within the thirl of the old corn mills had to go. 'The right of thirlage', to repeat Kames' words, 'seems to have created a monopoly in favour of the proprietor of a mill and it seems to have been thought that the only safe and sure protection of that right was to be found in the prohibition to erect mills of any kind within the bounds of the thirl.'[24] But, by the end of the century, Kames' view that 'it is full time that this monopoly were at an end', pioneering as it seemed in the 1750s, had become one generally held.

Among those fighting most effectively to break the system were the bakers and brewers, traditionally powerful crafts experiencing a new importance caused by the demand for their products from the growing town populations. Before the tightening of the licensing laws and the effective prohibition of the small, illicit country stills, the ordinary country mills had been accustomed to grind small quantities of malt as casually as they ground oats or peas or bere. Similarly, while home brewing was common, householders often brought their malt to be ground at the mill where they bought their meal. In these circumstances malt had become by use and wont subject to multures in the same way as other grains. During the eighteenth century several attempts were made to limit the effects of thirlage by suggesting that it applied only to oats, but this was certainly not commonly the case. At the Baron Court of Stitchill, for instance, in 1665, 'George ffrenche confest he abstracted his multures fra Stitchill Mylle to the prejudice of the possessor thereof contrair to former Acts of this Barroun Court wherfor he is unlawed and amerciat in fyve pounds and to pay to Andro Nizbet (the miller) Double Multure for a fulle of malt confest befor be him. The qlk day it is judicially statute and ordained that non within this Barony abstract ther Multures Meal nor Malt in tyme cumeing fra Stitchill Mylle but that they bring their haill grinding corne and malt therto to pay Myll Dewties used and wont therefor under the payne of 5 punds and Double Multure to the possessor of the Myll for the corne and malt so abstracted.'[25] Similar instances are to be found in the records of other baron courts.[26]

In the towns, where brewing was, of course, carried on on a larger scale than on the farms of the baronial tenants, similar restrictions applied. In Edinburgh, for instance, a charter of King Robert the Bruce granted to the magistrates a thirlage within the royalty to the town mills 'by which the Good Town is enabled to restrain and hinder the brewers to make use of hand mills and other engines'.[27] The brewers of Alloa were thirled to the baronial mill which was the property of John Francis of Erskine, feudal superior of the town of Alloa. Perth city's meal, malt and barley mill was still exacting multures from the brewers in the 1830s.[28] All over Scotland the brewers were thirled either to the magistrates or to the landowner on whose lands their town had grown. Abstractions had been common and perhaps often condoned but the income to the mills from the brewers was a considerable one. What both brewer and miller had connived at throughout the eighteenth century was the dodging of taxes due to the Government. By law a person or company bound by his thirlage to grind malt at a certain mill was entitled to deduct from the amount of multure due to the miller a proportion of the malt tax due by him. If miller and brewer co-operated in ignoring the tax, both gained by it. Between the imposition of the Malt Tax after the Union and 1809 'it was constant practice all over Scotland for proprietors and tacksmen of malt mills to exact the full multure upon all malt ground at their mills without making any abatement or deduction for the duties.'[29] Thus the miller gained, and, as long as the customs officers were lax, or kept in ignorance, the brewer did not lose.

The end of illicit distilling affected country mills, used to grinding malt for their neighbours' heather stills, quite lamentably. 'Very little corn comes to this mill,' wrote the miller of Ussie in 1821, 'and of malt scarcely any on account of the near neighbourhood of the revenue officers.'[30] Instead of the many hundreds of families having their malt ground at the local mill, there sprang up a small number of large, legally run distilleries, each eventually setting up its own malt-grinding machinery.

Similarly, when the brewers felt the customs officers breathing down their necks they pressed to be allowed to deduct, as they were legally entitled to do, the amount of the tax from the multures they paid. While the amounts involved were trifling, no one troubled much about them but, with the raising and stricter enforcement of the tax, the loss in income to both brewers and millers began to cause resentment. There had always been some resentment on the brewers' part against the conditions of thirlage. Very early in the eighteenth century it was claimed that the Edinburgh magistrates' insistence on the brewers' thirlage to the town mills had chased the brewers out of the burgh into the shires. 'There are,' it was reported, 'upwards of thirty breweries now standing waste who have retired to the country and erected breweries there.'[31] The brewers, forced by their astriction to send their malt to be ground in Edinburgh, complained that 'of 12 bags of malt sent to the Town mills (notwithstanding all the pretences of an easy multure) they get not back ten, what by multure, servants' fees, extortions, thefts, insufficient grinding etc.'[32] The problem was not a new one. But the growing efficiency of customs officers, coming at the same time as some proprietors were being more assiduous in asserting their thirlage rights, drove the brewers to the law courts. There, as had been the case with other problems associated with thirlage, they found the law lords in a state of indecision. In 1766, for instance, when the Duke of Buccleuch looked to the courts to defend his right to exact multures on malt, the courts decided that the defenders were at liberty to grind their malt where they chose,[33] in spite of their having been used to grind at the Duke's mill at Dalkeith. But in 1769 the opposite decision was made in the case of James Bruce of Alloa against Robert Stein and others, brewers in Alloa, whose subjection to thirlage was confirmed.[34] This inability on the part of the law lords to agree on the question of thirlage betrayed a slipping of the grasp of the feudal system on the Scottish people. Its hold was becoming weaker as the strength of those subjected to it grew.

Concurrently with the brewers' fight the bakers had been attempting to break away from their mediaeval subjection to the town's mills. There were two main complications to their argument. One was the question of whether wheat for white flour, in many mills a new addition to the range of products, ought to be subjected to thirlage and pay multures in the same way as oat and barley meal. The bakers, of course, wished to have the right to grind at whatever mill they chose and to avoid the payment of multures. Between the incorporations of bakers and the magistrates who stood as owners of the town mills there would have been even longer wrangles on this point, one, again, on which the courts were for some time unable to reach a clear decision, had not other considerations interposed. One of these was that in many towns the ancient burgh mills had been allowed to fall into such a state of disrepair that the councils were unable to find the money to uphold them, and the bakers, being their largest users, took over the tacks of the towns' mills. This resolved the question of multures as the bakers would then have been paying the dues to themselves. In some cases, however, the bakers built new flour mills for themselves outside the town and then had to fight the magistrates' attempts to extend the burgh's thirlage rights to the new mills.[35]

There was, however, an interesting case which illustrated clearly the fact that, in spite of all the high-flown declaiming against the 'ancient tyranny' of thirlage, it was common economic expediency rather than principle which motivated the campaign for abolition. In Dundee, the Baxter Incorporation, having been for some years tacksmen of the town mills, found themselves facing competition from imported wheat flour which was being landed at Dundee's harbour and transported to Perth for the use of the bakers there. Some of the bread thus baked found its way into Dundee retail shops. In a swift *volte face* the Dundee bakers abandoned all objections to thirlage and attempted in the courts to prove that a thirlage of *invecta et illata*, to which the town's inhabitants were subjected, could and should be applied to all grain passing through the town on its way to be ground, which should be forced to pay multures to the town's mills just as if it were to be ground there. The Baxter Incorporation, as multurer of the mills, were, of course, less interested in the income from the multures than in the competition from the Perth bakers, but they were not above attempting to use thirlage to suit their own ends while it suited them. They did not, however, gain their way, the courts deciding that 'a thirlage of invecta et illata does not apply to grain imported at a sea-port within the thirl, when carried beyond it to be ground into flour and baked into bread though the bread be brought into the thirl and retailed there to the inhabitants.'[36]

One way and another, by the end of the century the upper classes were convinced of the need for reform. First, the law lords had seen the difficulties caused by endless litigation on the subject. The law, as it applied to the new situation existing in a country whose agriculture had been revolutionised, was not sufficiently clear and precedents from another age did not apply.

Secondly, the landowning class, in whose interests the laws of thirlage had been framed, now saw advantage in their abolition. Anxious to increase their money income in every possible way, they wished most of all to tempt the new industries within their domains, and they knew that this could not be done while the old restrictive laws applied. In addition there were estates on which landowners, even before the Thirlage Act, chose to encourage tenants to purchase their way out of their thirlage obligations. It was one way in which, if his tenants co-operated, a landowner could raise the lump sum of money so many of them so badly needed. There are instances of landowners wishing to have their multures 'purchased wholly up' for a sum of money.[37] And landowners were themselves among the first to seek commutation of multures in those cases of long-standing irritation in which the lands of one estate had become thirled to the mills of another.

Thirdly, the new enthusiasm for the rights of man, the extolling of liberty for its own sake, so fashionable among the intelligentsia after the French Revolution, even if it wavered in its firmness later, had produced a climate of opinion in which all tyranny was odious. It was convenient for the ancient feudal traditions to be pigeonholed in the category of tyranny, and the more lettered gentry, along with their dedicated followers in the Presbyterian ministry, took up the cause with uncritical joy. Thirlage was claimed to have carried along with it 'consequences not only hostile to improvements but even to the best interests of morality and religion.'[38]

Fourthly, the people themselves, the farmers and small tenants, emerging gradually from their long acceptance of the established order, were making their opinions felt in more than one way. They were 'becoming cunning lawyers';[39] that is, they were not entirely unprepared to go to court, especially with the moral backing of their parish minister, to challenge a miller's or landlord's right to exact multures. More important, perhaps, they were voting with their feet. They were simply failing to attend those mills which did not serve them efficiently or whose charges were too high. Transport improved, road surfaces were made more passable, and farmers were more able to afford horses and carts, so they were better able to stay away from a mill in their immediate neighbourhood and to choose one, if necessary, at a little distance from them. If an entire sucken acted in this way it was difficult to prevent it, especially where there was uncertainty about the outcome if mill proprietors did sue for abstracted multure. Thus, in many districts, millers themselves gradually ceased to exact multures from their customers, chiefly in recognition of the fact that they could no longer enforce payment. Instead they substituted a money charge for the service of grinding.

In Panmure, in Angus, the tenants of the Honourable William Maule freed themselves of thirlage some years before the Act, simply by agreeing among themselves to pay the rents of the three mills on the estate. The factor, on being informed that the tenants were 'desirous of obtaining freedom from this thraldom', accepted their proposal.[40] Stair held that, at any time, thirlage could be taken off an estate simply by the ceasing to exact multures. It could be ended on any estate, he said, 'in the like manner as it was constituted, either by prescription, whereby liberty is recovered to the thirled lands, which needs no positive act to deny the multures, but simply forbearance to lift or seek them is enough; or otherwise by any discharge or renunciation without further solemnity'.[41] But this was not clearly or widely enough understood, and in most cases where landowners and tenants agreed on the desirability of breaking the thirl a charter was granted by the estate to tenants freeing them of their subjection. Freedom could also be granted to individual and presumably influential tenants rather than to the whole sucken, as it was to Alexander Gordon whose lands were all astricted to the mill of Enrick 'excepting always the Mains of Carletoune when I or my heirs shall happen to live thereon which during our living thereon are no way subjected to this personal thirlage but if the said Mains are set in tenantry then and in that case this thirlage shall wark the said Mains'. This exemption was granted 'at my earnest desyre and from a freindly regard to the accommodatione, standing and wool being of my family'.[42]

The Act of Parliament known as the Thirlage Act was passed in 1799.[43] It did not, in fact, abolish thirlage so much as lay down the procedures by which estates might be freed of it. Its proper title is 'An act for encouraging the improvement of lands in that part of Great Britain called Scotland', 39 Geo. *III* c.35 1799, which is perhaps some indication of its true motivation. Its preamble read, 'whereas there is a kind of thirlage known in the law and practice of Scotland, called a thirlage of the invecta et illata to which sundry towns, burghs, burghs of barony, villages and other places in that part of the kingdom and the inhabitants thereof are subject which thirlage it is expedient to allow to be purchased by the persons subject to the same . . .' It provided that an inhabitant subject to thirlage might apply to the Sheriff to have the thirlage commuted into an annual payment. The fact of his having so applied had to be made known to all having an interest in the question, including the lessee of the mill. This was usually done by an announcement in the local parish church.[44] The procedure was that evidence of the annual value of the thirlage had to be put before the Sheriff and a specially qualified jury and on that evidence an annual payment in grain to be paid at the mill was fixed. In most cases there was not too much difficulty in reaching agreement from the evidence given by tenants, landlords and millers on a fair sum to be paid as compensation for the now abolished multure. Everything was taken into consideration, all the separate dues once payable to the miller and his servants, and a sum fixed 'in lieu of all multures, knaveship, miller's dues, services and prestations of every kind exigible from the said lands . . . besides the value of the mill-ring'.[45] Where the mill was under lease the sum thus fixed had to be paid annually to the lessee during the term of his lease and he had to agree to accept it as full compensation for his lost thirlage rights. In some cases the proprietor of the mill sought to have the amount paid as one lump sum rather than as a yearly payment. This sometimes proved more complicated. Colonel Stirling began, in 1803, an action to buy himself out of his thirlage to Sir Patrick Murray of Ochtertyre's mill at Carsehead which was not settled until 1815, the Colonel dying in the meantime and leaving the pursuit of his case to his nephew and heir. In the event the Sheriff ruled, 'being now well and ripely advised with regard to the value of the said thirlage . . . and having God and a good conscience before my eyes' that £900 was 'a just, adequate and fair value for a renunciation of a right of thirlage'.[46]

The Act allowed commutation to be paid either in corn or its value in money at the option of the payer at the fiar prices of the county. Colonel Stirling's was a large holding of land and the sums involved therefore very considerable. Most tenants had much smaller amounts to pay to the miller in recompense for the multures they now ceased to pay. The Portsoy tenants, paying the conversion of mill multures in proportion to their rents, paid in 1814 small sums of which 15/6d, fixed on a rent of £15.10s, was the largest.[47]

During the next half-century many estates were freed of thirlage, keeping the Sheriff courts busy with hearings of evidence. It would appear that most lands were free by the 1840s, but there were many exceptions. In Morayshire at the time of the *New Statistical Account* the Duke of Gordon's tenants were still astricted to Mill of Garmouth where they paid as multure one thirteenth of all grain ground.[48] In Banffshire on the lands of Boyndie, where tenants had until then paid the very harsh multure of one eleventh, the astriction was at that time in course of being abolished.[49] In Aberdeenshire and the North East it was only then gradually falling into disuse. As late as 1935 a miller in Aberdeenshire sued a farmer who was thirled to his mill for abstraction of multures and the miller won his case. There were then several suckens in Aberdeenshire and Kincardineshire where dry multure was still being paid.[50] While it might be supposed that it was the greater dependence of the North East on oatmeal for its staple diet that made it possible for the old system to retain its ancient hold on the inhabitants there, it is more likely that the much smaller farms and the many crofts there were both ignorant of the law and less able to pursue their rights in the courts. It could also be a possibility that the astriction was not considered so much of a burden as to require change.

It is certainly a fact that, once the hysteria of the campaign for abolition had died down, there was very little real objection to thirlage. Multures became recognised for what they were: an alternative form of rent. Where multures were converted to a money payment, extra rent had to be paid. Acknowledgement of this fact prevented many tenants from seeking commutation. The period of strong feeling against thirlage at the end of the eighteenth century had been one in which rents were rising very fast while increased grain production, at least in some areas, was bringing about an accompanying rise in multures. The outcry against thirlage was in fact a form of rent rebellion and the enthusiasm of the clergy for the battle was not wholly dissociated from their own obligation to pay multures on the produce of their glebes.

One of the factors persuading parliament to bring in a change in the law may have been the fear of the landowning class of anything which might again arouse the anger of the 'meal mobs'. Extreme fluctuations in prices and supply during the last decades of the eighteenth century had caused outbreaks of rick-burning and granary-breaking. There was already an atmosphere of unrest ready to fire up at any suggestion that prices were being unfairly kept up. Resentment against rising multures could easily have fanned the flames and certainly there must have been government anxiety to damp down heated arguments about thirlage which could have resulted in similar explosions.[51]

The real popular objection to thirlage was based on the tenants' dislike of mill services. The requirement to leave the cultivation of their own fields at the behest of an exigent miller was very much and naturally disliked. But what had not been foreseen was that, on commutation, landlords lost all interest in the mills, from which they could now derive no more financial advantage than from any other smallholding. The once valuable property, the mill of mediaeval foundation, with its multures and sequels, representing a considerable investment to the landowner, became nothing more than a neglected farm building. The suckeners were no longer compelled to keep it in repair, the landlord was no longer willing to do so. If the miller himself did not find its situation sufficiently profitable to allow him to hire labour and pay for materials for repair, it might drop into neglect and ruin. While a mill was let, the commuted multures had to be paid to the miller. But at the expiry of his lease or if he left his mill, the amount had to be paid instead to the landowner. There was, therefore, little incentive to the landowner to keep the mill in repair and the miller in his mill. The estate actually gained, during the period of commutation, by the miller's departure.

Because the Act was so drawn up as not to apply to those estates then subject to dry multure, that is the payment of dues to the mill whether the corn was ground or sold as grain, some tenants found themselves forced to pay multures to a mill which had long since ceased to operate. Judgment of the case of Spottiswoode v. Pringle in 1849 allowed the exaction of commuted multures although the mill had been in ruins for years.[52] In another case, in 1884, the Lord President of the Court of Session decided that the proprietor was not bound to keep up the mill and that lands once thirled to Kinross Mill must continue to pay commuted thirlage and dry multures. As late as 1901 it was asked in court in the case of Porteous v. Haig 'whether the proprietor of lands who had a title to a thirl mill which had ceased to exist was entitled to exact sums commuted for thirlage?' and the affirmative decision was given.[53]

Kames believed that mills had only been built by landowners in the expectation of the income to be derived from the high mill rents made possible by the miller's entitlement to multures. Experience in the nineteenth century seemed to prove that just as thirlage was necessary to encourage mill building in the first place, it was also necessary to ensure that mills were maintained in good repair over their centuries of use. Certainly the reverse proved to be true. Mills dependent upon the interest of a landowner for their repair were allowed to disintegrate after commutation. Only those let to millers who were competent tradesmen and situated in districts where there was sufficient trade survived the ending of thirlage.

It remains to be considered whether Kames' other belief, that thirlage was holding back improvement, was also confirmed. There is no real evidence that technological innovation was held up by the thirlage system. Kames was, of course, giving his attention to the question in the period before the real upsurge of industrial activity. He was swayed by his firm and dear belief that the hope for Scotland lay in the encouragement of the linen industry and the imitation of the Dutch. His case for the abolition of thirlage was based chiefly on his own wish, and that of his fellows on the Board of Trustees, for the building of large numbers of lint mills well dispersed throughout Scotland. These, by improving the quality of the raw material supplied to the domestic hand spinners, were in themselves to raise the standard of Scottish linens so that they might successfully compete with Holland for overseas markets. It is true that thirlage, strictly applied, could discourage the building of lint mills within the thirl. But there were many other disincentives to lint-mill building, not least being the lack of any real spontaneous interest in the subject. Those that were built were built chiefly in order to obtain the generous financial 'encouragements' paid out of the Trustees' funds. In any case Scotland's industrial future did not, as the future showed, rest with home-reared flax and handspun linens.

In no other respect can a case be made out for the delaying of industrial progress by thirlage. Even before the Act it had been possible to do away with the system whenever there was any real need to do so. Where the capital for, say, the building of a spinning mill was available and the landowner was keen to attract such an industry to his estates, thirlage rights did not stand in the way. Landowners insisted on thirlage where the income from their lands was otherwise relatively small. Given the possibility of a much higher income from industrial development, they were unlikely to worry about the loss of multures from corn-milling. Difficulties and lawsuits did arise from the invasion of the old thirls by the new industries but these were occasioned by fights over water rights, not over astriction. Thirlage could not then be said to have delayed the industrialisation of those Scottish estates otherwise well based to benefit from their situation near the centres of population and innovation.

The question of whether thirlage proved a disincentive to technological innovation within the old meal-milling industry has also to be considered. The answer must be that it did not. Certainly the old baronies could not often be thought of as seedbeds of invention, although there were distinguished exceptions, and those millers whose suckeners were unable to leave them, however inefficient their procedures, might seem unlikely improvers. Yet the same 'spirit of improvement' which revolutionised agriculture did breathe on the old meal mills. And where a miller's mind fell to devising improvements he was not discouraged in any way by the system of thirlage. The Meikles' significant improvements in mill machinery and the application of water power, for instance, all fell within the period where thirlage supposedly enslaved the Scottish people.

In fact, where there was a will towards improvement and the capital to finance it, the system of thirlage did not in any way impede development. It could, after all, be done away with simply by ceasing to apply it, and this is what happened where a landowner's interest in improvement and a miller's ability to invent happened to coincide. Where thirlage seemed to be delaying progress, there were in every case other factors involved and the chief of these was always the economic backwardness of the region.

NOTES

1. Bell, G. J., *Principles of the Law of Scotland*, 9th ed., Edinburgh, 1899, 1017-18; Stair, Lord, *Institutions of the Law of Scotland*, 3rd ed., 1759, 23-4; Jamieson, *Dictionary*; Erskine, John, *Principles of the Law of Scotland*, 20th ed., Edinburgh, 1809; Gibb, Andrew Dewar, *Student's Glossary of Scottish Legal Terms*, Edinburgh, 1946
2. Bennett and Elton, *History of Corn Milling*, 2, 122
3. Chalmers, *Caledonia*, 1, 787
4. Bell, *op. cit.*, 1017-18
5. Morison, *Decisions of Court of Session*, 16046
6. E.g. *Charters of the Abbey of Crosraguel*, Edinburgh, 1886, Ayrshire and Galloway Archaeological Society, 1, ix; but see also Franklin, *A History of Scottish Farming*, 99ff.
7. S.R.O. GD 46/17/18
8. Morison, *Decisions of Court of Session*, 16069

9. Court of Session, Jardine v. Douglas, Feb. 26, 1793; Morison, *Decisions of the Court of Session*, 16056, 16063

10. Morison, *Decisions of the Court of Session*, 16040, 16045

11. *Ibid.*, 16037

12. *Ibid.*, 16049

13. *Ibid.*, 16063

14. Court of Session, Jardine v. Douglas, Feb. 26, 1793

15. Morison, *Decisions of the Court of Session*, 16056

16. *Ibid.*, 16033

17. Hamilton, *Monymusk*, 236

18. *Rules and Articles by the Commissioners of the Annexed Estates in Scotland for the Improvement of Lowland Farms and for the Encouragement of Tenants upon the said Estates*, Edinburgh, 1773, 5; *Rules and Articles . . . for Highland Farms*, Edinburgh, 1774, 3

19. Gunn, Clement B., ed., *Records of the Baron Court of Stitchill, 1655-1807*, 2 (henceforth Gunn, *Stitchill)*

20. Morison, *Decisions of the Court of Session*, 16029

21. *Ibid.*, 16038. The *bow* is the globule which contains the seed of flax

22. Morison, *Decisions of the Court of Session*, 16051

23. *Ibid.*, 16049

24. Court of Session, Glasgow Magistrates v. Ray Crawford, 1822

25. Gunn, *Stitchill*, 36

26. Barron, *Urie*, 82; Hamilton, *Monymusk*, 128

27. Morison, *Decisions of Court of Session*, 8899

28. *Ibid.*, 16061; Court of Session, Alloa Brewers v. Erskine, 1816; M'Dougall's Trustees, Multure Account, 1837 (NRA[S] 1510)

29. Court of Session, Alloa Brewers v. Erskine, 1816

30. S.R.O. GD 46/17/591

31. Morison, *Decisions of Court of Session*, 8902

32. *Ibid.*, 8903

33. *Ibid.*, 16053

34. Court of Session, Alloa Brewers v. Stein, 1769

35. Warden, *Burgh Laws of Dundee*, 360

36. Court of Session, Incorporation of Bakers of Dundee v. Just and Miller, Feb. 23, 1813

37. S.R.O. GD 24/1/94

38. *O.S.A.*, 4, 244

39. Morison, *Decisions of the Court of Session*, 16038

40. *O.S.A.*, 3, 473

41. Shaw, *Stair*, 242

42. S.R.O. GD 10/1219

43. 39 Geo. III c. 55

44. S.R.O. GD 105/576

45. *Ibid.* The mill ring is the enclosed area around the millstones into which a certain amount of meal escapes during grinding and from which a miller could, at the end of the day, extract for his own use what was rightfully his customer's meal

46. S.R.O. GD 24/1/94

47. S.R.O. GD 248/3109

48. *N.S.A.*, XIII, 59

49. *N.S.A.*, XIII, 238

50. Findlay, *Oats*, 183

51. Lythe, 'The Tayside meal mobs'

52. Rankine, Sir John, *A Treatise on the Rights and Burdens Incident to the Ownership of Land*, Edinburgh, 1884, 400

53. Court of Session, Porteous v. Haig, 1901

4
Landowners — Ownership of the Mill

Meal mills of ancient foundation, excepting those small horizontal mills built for family or clan use, were originally, as we have seen, the property of king or abbey and had passed, before our period begins, into the hands of the burghs or the landed gentry, by whom they were let out to tacksmen millers.

In addition some mills had been built on the baronial estates at periods later than the break-up of church lands. Stair believed that farming tenants were not originally thirled to these mills,[1] that landowners extended their power by imposing thirlage and that they did so as a new means of raising rents from their estates. Whether or not he is right about the thirlage of the lands not being co-existent with the appearance of the first mills on them, it is certainly the case that thirlage was being both extended and more strictly applied during the eighteenth century and that the landowner expected it to be applied to mills newly built in that period as well as to the ancient mills on his lands.

We know that, although the vast majority of mills existing in the eighteenth century were survivals from an earlier age, some new mills were built by landowners during the century for the use of their tenants. Alexander Murray of Broughton, for instance, was planning the building of a new mill on the Water of Tarf in 1743, to replace the old Miln of Enrick, and was providing for the astriction of tenants to it.[2] The Drummonds of Blair Drummond built a new mill at Cambusdrennie at the very end of the seventeenth century or the beginning of the eighteenth and undertook expensive water engineering to bring power to it.[3]

Mills built by landowners were not always built with the convenience of tenants uppermost in mind. The barony of Callander, for instance, built the Miln of Tombea about the year 1736 and thirled the baronial estates to it but, it was reported by the surveyor to the Forfeited Estates, who found it in a ruinous condition, 'This seems to have been a project calculated for private ends which has not succeeded. This place lyes quite away from that part of the barony thirled to it' which 'incommodes the tenants excessively'.[4]

What were the motives, then, of landowners who built mills during the eighteenth century, there being no real evidence that they were inspired to do so by the needs or wishes of their tenants who would, if let alone, have preferred the use of their own household mills? What were the 'private ends' of the proprietor of Callander which seem indeed to have been disappointed?

Mills were a valuable property. They had been considered to be so from their first building, and the gift of 'clap and happer of the mill' from king to subject, from husband to wife, from father to daughter, had been one of considerable worth and much to be coveted. The value of mills lay not in any intrinsic worth in the buildings or their machinery but in the income to be derived from them. Mill rents had been for the monasteries and remained for the eighteenth century landed proprietor an important source of revenue, one moreover not subject to fluctuation, as were the profits from land cultivation. Mill rents were set in accordance with the value of the multures supposedly to be extracted from the barony's tenants. In times of bad harvest the amount of grain coming into the mill decreased but it was the miller, not the proprietor, who bore the loss. Mills, therefore, represented for their proprietor some security in times of fluctuating returns from farming.

In one interesting case a landowner's widow, left penniless on his death, and evicted from her castle, was enterprising enough to go and live at the mill on the estate and to take over its management. Lady Mary Allardice of Allardice, née Graham, made the Mill of Allardice into a profitable business and educated her daughter, Elizabeth Keith, to be her multurer. She extended the mill's trade by attracting outsucken custom and charging a very modest 25th boll for her work. Lady Mary put her connections with the gentry to good use even if she was reduced to the ranks of the tradesmen. When Elizabeth was sent for trial at Aberdeen Sheriff court on a charge of over-exaction of multures, her mother used her influence with Lord Forglen, the judge, to have the Sheriff reprimanded. Far from putting the lady in jail, the poor Sheriff was ordered to put her on his own horse and deliver her safely to her mother's door.[5]

The value of a mill to an estate lay also in the opportunity it gave for the landowner to exert some control over his tenants. The Sutherland estate was more explicit than most about this. William Young, the factor, wrote to the Marchioness of Stafford in 1811 about his plans to end astriction to the mills but to continue to insist on services. 'Perhaps this would authorise the Heritor to say go where you please within the Estate and still enable him to keep a little reasonable authority.'[6]

Another incentive to mill-building by landowners was the hope that, by improving the means of production, tenants might be helped to get through to a new season without the estate having to supply them with imported meal. On some estates the tenants' near starvation in seasons of dearth would have forced them to eat seed corn if the landowner had not either imported meal for them or fed them from his own girnal. This form of subsidy was expensive and the building of an efficient mill to replace the tenants' hand mills could be justified as a means to avoid waste and perhaps avoid expenditure on imported corn.[7]

The miller, in the eighteenth century very much a boss's man, was well placed to know just how much each farm and cot was worth and which of them might be falling into arrears with rent or services. The mill acted as an additional or, in some cases, the only, factor's office for the administration of the estate.

More important, until Malthusian views on population control penetrated into the fastnesses of the keeps and castles of baronial Scotland, the generally held view was that an estate thrived in proportion to the number of tenants living upon it. The aim until the latter part of the eighteenth century was to attract settlers, particularly, of course, those of an industrious character who were likely to prove good rent payers. To do so it was advisable to provide the necessaries of existence, among which was certainly the mill, without which the staple foods of the people could not be efficiently processed.

So both financially and for reasons of expediency it was to the landowner's advantage to have mills on his land. Yet, although there were instances of new mill-building in the eighteenth century, they were few and far between, the number of mills having certainly declined very considerably in almost every parish by the end of the century.

The first reason for this was the very large number of mills existing from ancient times. Even ignoring the primitive horizontal mills, they have to be counted in thousands, every stream of any strength and some that were little more than trickles carrying a mill at almost every turn. The problem for the eighteenth century estate, then, was rather to keep the mills in repair than to build new ones.

In addition, the very unclear state of the law threw some doubt on the possibility of raising as much revenue from new-built mills as from the ancient ones. Because thirlage was introduced before the keeping of written records and mills were built long before the barons chose to let out their land with feu charters, it came to be accepted that only use and wont justified astriction to mills. Thus 'a very remarkable distinction arose between mills lately erected and those which have been of old standing. A man who acquires a land estate made up of separate parcels, which were originally parts of other baronies, and builds a mill upon it for the first time, cannot subject his feuers nor even his tenants that have outstanding tacks. An old barony, which has had a mill upon it, not only time out of mind but as far back as the title deeds go, is in a very different situation. There the presumption will readily be admitted, that the people of the barony have been astricted to the mill; and the use and wont of going to the mill is legal evidence of astriction.'[8]

Now the eighteenth century did see just this breaking up of the old baronial estates into smaller holdings of land and the issuing of feu charters, very often for the first time. Dr Sanderson describes how the feuing of Strathisla, begun in the sixteenth century, resulted in the buying up of small feus in the late seventeenth and eighteenth centuries in a move towards consolidation of land holdings.[9] In some regions lands were divided, in others amalgamated. Land throughout the country was changing hands as interest in agricultural improvement directed a rationalisation of landholdings. But if the new proprietors found themselves in law on quite a different footing from the older landed gentry, unable to astrict their tenants, they were unlikely to show interest in the erection of new mills.

It would, however, be unwise to apply this finding too generally because the law courts seem to have been themselves uncertain of the law and its proper application. For instance, the lands of Kinvaid, in Perthshire, had belonged in the seventeenth century to a number of different owners. In 1726 Smyth of Methven became proprietor of the whole area. In 1765 he sold the lands of Kinvaid and the Mill of Drumsay, to which the tenants were thirled, to Dr Thomas Young. Young continued to exert thirlage to his mill as the preceding owner had done, but in 1789 David Smyth of Methven, grandson of the man who had sold Kinvaid and now proprietor of neighbouring lands thirled to Drumsay

Mill, challenged Young's right to exact multures. In this case the Court of Session upheld Young's claim and rejected Smythe's. [10] But doubt about a new landowner's rights of thirlage did exist and must have proved a disincentive to mill-building by the landed gentry during the eighteenth century.

Other considerations contributed. The widespread enthusiasm for land improvement which spurred proprietors towards change and expenditure during the eighteenth century was motivated almost as much by love of novelty as by the wish for financial reward. Scientific ingenuity delighted. The letters of the landed gentry to each other and to their protégés are full of an almost childlike delight in new mechanical contrivances or in the science of chemistry as it emerged from its state of mediaeval mystery. But meal mills were no novelty and the extreme ingenuity of their machinery was so familiar as to inspire little interest. Exactly the same thing applied to a later period of landlord investment in agriculture. The *Transactions of the Highland and Agricultural Society of Scotland* between 1799 and 1865 contain evidence of very widespread interest in scientific improvements. There are eleven articles on threshing machines, but there is not one mention in all those years of mills, milling, meal or flour. The old mills, built on the old principles, still worked so surprisingly well as to be taken for granted. They did not catch the imagination. As a result they did not attract large investment.

This is not to say that no money was spent on mills by estate owners. In the first half of the eighteenth century landowners undertook some new mill-building and some lade and dam construction to improve water supplies, and they accepted the responsibility for the constant repairs necessary to keep the mills in working order. For the most part, however, these were not money transactions. In the first place, money was not freely available to the landowning class either as cash or as credit.[11] In the second it was barely necessary, most of the materials being available on the estates and the labour provided by the feudal right to command mill services.

Towards the end of the century the increased prosperity of the land allowing higher rents brought more ready cash into estate offices, and extended banking facilities made credit more freely available. Together these made new mill-building on the estates possible. It remained, however, uncommon for the following reasons.

While an earlier age had seen mill rents as a source of income to be coveted, this was only so because of the relative lack of opportunity for other investment. As new inventions and new markets made other industries viable, landowners began to see mills as small profit makers. Prompted very often by the Board of Trustees for Manufactures, who had chosen the linen industry as the one most worthy of encouragement, they turned their attention to textiles so that spinning schools, waulk mills and lint mills began to appear even on estates so remote from markets as to make their success extremely unlikely. Where capital was available it rarely went to meal-milling but was diverted into areas where there seemed a prospect of much larger profits. Near the cities these hopes were fulfilled. Those landed gentlemen who found towns growing and reaching out towards their boundaries were glad to see the old meal mills converted into spinning mills and bleachfields. Men like Sir John Richardson of Pitfour, near Perth, were active in the financing of the textile industries which were to be powered by the same streams which turned the meal mills. The Smythes of Methven, whose family we have already encountered as proprietors of meal mills, were part-owners, with Richardson, of Huntingtower bleachfield.[12] His estates situated usefully near Greenock, Sir John Shaw Stewart, in 1796, let to James Bogle and Company, merchants in Greenock, 'all and haill that mill called the Easter Mill of Greenock, with the mill-houses and land, astricted multures . . . and that for the haill time and space of 99 years, to be peacable bruiked and possessed by the aforesaid company, with liberty also to the tacksmen to erect dams for collecting water'. That Sir John's interest in meal-milling was slight is shown by the power he gave to the new tenants to take down the mill and houses and 'convert them into any use they pleased on condition always of having buildings of equal value on the land'.[13] This was a common pattern and an understandable one. Where the town's proximity allowed an estate proprietor to benefit from merchants' anxiety to acquire land and water power for industrial use, he could hardly be blamed for doing so.

Even proprietors of land on a much smaller scale attempted to turn meal mills into spinning mills. The *Dundee Advertiser* during the 1820s carried a rash of advertisements claiming that this or that old meal mill 'would answer remarkably well either for a bleachfield or a spinning mill'.[14] Sometimes the mills were temporarily adapted for flax-spinning and the newspapers would then carry advertisements announcing that hands were needed, but very often these ventures were short-lived and unsuccessful and the mills back in the 'For Sale' columns within a short time. The tendency to put the water wheels to spinning instead of grinding machinery was increased of course where the labour force employed at the new mills began to use bakers' bread instead of porridge, tea instead of ale and milk. Food began to be supplied by the retail grocer trade instead of reaching the table straight from the processor. The need for the meal mills receded at the same time as the opportunities for other investment increased.

Away from the cities, however, the landowners' hopeful investment in textiles proved very often unwise and in many cases the mills which had been converted to textile use reverted to grinding cereals. Near Dundee, on the river Dighty, site after site was ceded to textiles as the town grew in size and prosperity, and the meal mills disappeared steadily.[15] But in the next county of Fife many of the mills on the river Eden, which had been converted to textiles at the height of the hopes for cotton, slipped back to cereals as cotton's fortunes waned.[16] The landowners' interest in spinning-mills faded as the possibility of large returns became more remote.

The end of thirlage very often took the responsibility for the mills off the estates' hands. As we have seen, one of the ways in which thirlage could be commuted was for the tenants astricted by it to combine to pay the mill rents to the estate for the duration of the miller's lease. At the end of that period the mill would be let only if it was either profitable in itself, because, perhaps, it was well situated and served a large community of willing customers, in which case a miller willing to pay the rent would easily be found; or because the farmer on whose lands it was situated wished to keep it going for his own use, to grind meal for boll wages and crush corn for the horses, in which case he might employ a miller to perform the work for wages. In either case it was the need of the farming community rather than the estate owner's hope of financial gain which kept the mill alive. Where the farmers had no real need for a mill, as was the case in the dairy and pasture regions or in the hinterland of large towns, the mills were gradually allowed to fall into disuse so that by the time of the *New Statistical Account* at the middle of the nineteenth century the number of meal mills had been very drastically reduced in almost every parish.

This is, however, by no means the whole story. Although neither interest nor financial investment in meal mills was large-scale or even common among landowners, it did appear where there was some unusual spur to motivate it. Sir Archibald Grant of Monymusk, for instance, who, earlier, had been chided by his factor into taking an interest in the old mills on his estate,[17] became eventually something of a pioneer in mill improvement. In Aberdeen town the taste for white bread was already making itself felt in the 1760s. But, although the farmers of the hinterland were keen enough to plant wheat for sale in the town's markets, the bakers continued to import English flour. They preferred it for the very simple and understandable reason that they could make a greater weight of bread from the same volume of English flour than could be made from flour ground from Aberdeenshire wheat. Bread was sold by weight. Bakers were swayed by economic fact, not by local patriotism. The coarseness and high moisture content of locally ground flour made it unpopular with the bakers, who were interested in making as large an amount of bread as possible from each purchase of flour, and unpopular with the customers who preferred the light, airy, white bread made from English flour to the dark and leaden loaves made from Aberdeen ground wheat. The comparative nutritional value of the two was then of interest to no one.

The Gordon's Mill Farming Club met to discuss the problem in 1764, members complaining that 'they could find no consumpt *(sic)* for the coarse flour which would stick upon their hands if they made wheat into flour for themselves.' They agreed that 'their best endeavours ought to be used to promote the manufacture of our own wheat, otherwise an entire stop will be put to the raising of that grain in this country'.[18] They felt that the magistrates of Aberdeen should be persuaded to improve the facilities and the management of the 'Flower mill' at Aberdeen. Neither the town's mill nor the other local mills, although well suited to the production of oatmeal and bere meal, could achieve a really fine, white, wheat flour. Bakers found it coarse and the farmers felt that the yield of flour from a given quantity of grain was disappointing.

Sir Archibald had already faced this problem by installing millstones suitable for wheat at his Mill of Monymusk and by employing an English miller. His flour was fine enough to please the Aberdeen bakers and so his investment at the mill proved worthwile. By improving the equipment and the management of his mill he captured a share of the market which ensured that the growing of wheat on the Monymusk farms would be profitable. Monymusk mill produced nearly a firlot more flour and a peck more bran from each boll of wheat than the Aberdeen town mill could achieve.[19]

Grant's interest in his mill was spurred by a change of demand from nearby markets. Where the market for oatmeal remained constant, or even grew, as it did in the rural areas of the North East, the same incentive did not exist and landowner investment was less likely.

Estates which were neither near growing industrial towns nor on old arable land nevertheless sometimes built new mills more out of irritation at the inefficiency of the old ones than from any real hope of profits. On the Sutherland estate the old mill of Golspie was 'sent to Anderson the Blacksmith's' — an interesting illustration of how portable a mill was and of how specifically the term 'mill' applies to the machine rather than to the building — and the foundation of a new mill and kiln laid at Skelbo.[20] This, the factor claimed, 'without exaggeration will do more business than any six I have seen in Sutherland'. There seems to have been some family rivalry, perhaps cleverly played upon by the factor, which spurred Sutherland interest in mill-building. Young wrote to the Countess, 'If we do not get on with something usefull and convenient Lord Gower will carry off all the meal trade.'[21] An illustration of how very badly some improvement to the mills was needed is that meal to feed labourers could be imported to Sutherland from Morayshire at a price 3/6d per boll cheaper than the local mill could supply it.[22]

It was, however, only in areas which had been left backward and unimproved for longer than most that such interest was common or even necessary by this time. For the most part the landowning gentry of Scotland ceased to take an interest in meal-milling when they ceased to derive advantage from it on the commutation of multures after the Thirlage Act.

Nevertheless, during the nineteenth century some new mills were built. They fall into two groups, their building occasioned by different circumstances and financed by different kinds of people.

Field studies show a large number of mills in the eastern counties of Scotland which have the physical characteristics of early nineteenth century building. Some of these, although listed as nineteenth century, are in fact of much earlier origin. Their architectural style results from the extensive alterations undergone in the first quarter of the nineteenth century but their foundations are older. Rebuilding and alteration took place during that period for a number of reasons. The blockading of foreign ports and the destruction of shipping during the Napoleonic Wars raised the price of corn. The increased demand for milling capacity put pressure on the old mills in a way that revealed their deficiencies, and the higher profits from wheat-growing made possible the provision of capital for mill-building. Where increased prices for wheat had encouraged the switch from other grains to wheat production it was necessary for local mills to be equipped with marble stones to grind the harder grain. Some mills still carry a plaque giving the date of their building and referring to the very high prices then being fetched for wheat.[23] Even in areas where wheat could not thrive, cereal farmers benefited because the switch from oat products to white flour was delayed by the blockades and traditional dependence on oatmeal extended for a little longer.

Between the end of the eighteenth century and the abolition of the Corn Laws two technical improvements were added to any mill with a reasonably large clientèle. Kilns were built on to the original rectangular-shaped mill often, but not always, at right angles, giving the meal mill what is now thought of as its traditional L shape. The kilns were often of brick which was later harled, but perhaps more often of dressed stone. The line between the old random rubble of the first mill and the squared and dressed blocks of the kiln is often clearly visible in mills standing today. To accommodate the kiln and its furnace the additional building had to be of two storeys. Where the earlier mill had been of only one or one-and-a-half storeys its roof was often raised to meet the ridge of the kiln addition, and the whole was tiled or stone-slated to replace the original and probably rotted thatch. Abandoning thatch made it possible for the miller to do without the mill services to which he had been accustomed in the eighteenth century because a large part of the tenants' service to the mill had involved the cutting and carrying of thatching material. A slated roof required an initial financial outlay but had a much longer life.

This addition of an extra storey made possible the installation of the other improvement to mills very common during this period when expenditure on mills was relatively prodigal. Elevators, introduced from the 1790s, transformed the business of the mill, allowing the streamlining of processes and cutting out much of the hard labour of carrying sacks.

These two changes, both of which required some changes to the building which housed the mill, gave a new lease of life to many mills which were already very old at the beginning of the nineteenth century. There may have been other mills built at the same time completely from new, but the fact that almost every water course already bore a mill suggests that at least the sites and foundations of older mills were very commonly used for the new.

The second category of mill built during the nineteenth century was larger, serving town rather than countryside, owned by a company rather than an estate, very often three-storeyed, invariably slated, built to employ numbers of workers and dating from a period later than that in which, as we have seen, the country mills were being renewed. The old town mills were, almost without exception, found to be ruinous and inefficiently tenanted at the end of the eighteenth century. Built as meal and barley mills, they no longer satisfied the needs of the towns' populations. Factories and textile mills began to employ large numbers of women who, having less time for the traditional slow cooking of porridge and bannocks, turned to the baker for wheaten bread. The bakers demanded white flour and if the local mill could not supply the quality they wanted they imported English flour. To answer this, large flour mills were built in some towns while in others the older mills adapted their machinery to deal with wheat.

The first of the Leith flour mills was built in 1824 on a scale then almost unheard of in Scotland, having 29 stones, employing 160 people and having the capacity for 40,000 quarters of wheat weekly. Other mills were built in Leith in 1855 and 1863.[24] In Glasgow the old Bishops Mills in Old Dumbarton Road were rebuilt in 1839 and renovated in 1853 and the Port Dundas Grain Mills built in 1843.[25] In Dundee the Town Council recommended that the old Baldovan mills should be enlarged and improved at a cost of £1,000 in 1825, having succeeded in 1823 in letting them for nineteen years at a rent increased from £200 to £502.[26] The Town's mills were situated on the river Dighty at a small distance from the town itself, which had always been ill supplied with water. Within the town a mill for grinding wheat by steam power was erected by private enterprise and supplied with a Boulton and Watt engine of 32 h.p. but it was not a successful commercial enterprise.[27] In 1843 a large new flour mill was built in Strathmartine to be turned by a water wheel but with a steam engine to supply additional power.[28] In Dunfermline, the Heugh Mill, erected in 1784 to grind wheat, there being then four meal mills in the town, was adapted for steam in 1819 so that it could deal with 7194 bolls annually.[29] St Andrews, unlike many towns, had possessed a wheat flour mill since early in the sixteenth century. At the beginning of the nineteenth century the old Abbey Flour Mill was sold. The new owners found themselves faced with rebuilding 'as the Floor *(sic)* Mill has now become so ruinous as to render it absolutely necessary to be taken down and rebuilt'. In the 1840s the question of reselling the mill was discussed but it was decided instead to install a steam engine. Gourlay, Mudie and Company of Dundee performed the work, installing an engine of 10 h.p. at a cost of £361. 10s.[30] By the middle of the century it was not possible for a town flour mill to compete in the market without steam power and a greatly increased capacity, and larger amounts of capital were required than were commonly available within the small burghs.

The essential requirement for the new large kind of mill built after the middle of the century was closeness to a port, because it was built in response to a demand for milling capacity for wheat imported from America. America at first exported her wheat as flour ground in the great milling town of Minneapolis, the popularity of this fine white flour putting many British flour mills out of business and very much reducing the profitability of others until an important change in American exports gave them an opportunity for expansion. When the railway system was developed between America's corn-growing plains and her eastern seaboard the railway companies, finding grain easier to handle than flour, offered much lower freight charges for grain than for flour. Similarly the shipping companies, anxious to avoid flour because of its notorious tendency to deteriorate, charged less for grain. Thus American grain began to arrive in British ports in bulk, ready to be ground by millers with the capacity to deal with it.[31]

In discussing the two kinds of mill built during the nineteenth century we are necessarily discussing two quite different levels of expenditure and therefore two quite different kinds of investor. In the towns the money to build or renovate mills came, at the beginning of the century, very often from the baking trade acting as an incorporation. The trade was experiencing considerable profitability as a result of the change in social habits brought about by the industrial revolution. Bakers were the main customers of the old town mills, the most critical of their shortcomings and the most likely providers of capital for their replacement. In many cases they were already tenants of the towns' mills and impatient of the magistrates' unwillingness to spend money on their repair and their contrasting readiness to raise the rents. The logical step was to build new mills for the bakers' own use or to buy the towns' mills. As magistrates found it more and more difficult to get tenants for the mills, they were willing and ready to sell. The income from mill multures had once been an important part of the towns' revenues. In the nineteenth century it was no longer a consideration and councils were anxious to be freed from their ancient responsibility for the mills. As the mills came on the market it was a simple step for ownership to be transferred to the Baker Incorporations who were so often already the lessees.

This was not invariably the case, however. In Glasgow, capital for investment in mill-building seems to have come chiefly from corn-dealing and from millers who had successfully turned their attention to the buying and selling of cereals, hay and seed corn as well as flour.[32] In the smaller burghs, where the population still retained rural characteristics and the towns' mills still dealt in oats and barley with only small quantities of wheat, milling provided something more than a decent living but did not make the kind of profits which attracted the larger capitalists. The leases of Cupar and Perth mills were both advertised for sale at intervals throughout the nineteenth century without being able to find a taker and both were forced considerably to reduce the upset price for selling. Cupar exposed the Town's mills at public roup in 1792. One was sold to John Inglis, a baker: 'earth and stone of the ground of the said mills and clapp and happer of said mills' at £1,015 sterling of grassum and £105 yearly feu duty. When Inglis gave it up it reverted to the town as feudal superior and was advertised for sale in 1843 at an upset price of £1800, the feu duty being unchanged at £105. It was claimed that 'The security is most ample, the property, which is in the hands of an enterprising and improving capitalist, being worth nearly £10,000 and a more eligible investment is seldom in the market.' There were, however, no offers until the upset price was reduced to £1650 when, of several offers, James Russell's was accepted. In 1916 Russell's heir, Mrs Bertha Welch or Russell, made a disposition in favour of the magistrates and the mills were again advertised for sale in 1918. They were described as 'presently on lease to Messrs J. and T. Rodger, millers' and their business was described as 'that of a country miller, supplying farmers, grocers and others in Fife with meal, flour and feeding stuffs'. In 1919 two offers for the mills were made, one from John Rodger, the tenant, and another from John Forrest, miller of St Martin's Mill near Perth, who offered the sums of £605 and £610.[33] One mill was destroyed in a disastrous fire in 1978 but has since been rebuilt and modernised and is still in the hands of the Rodger family. The other town mill has been acquired by the Hamlyn Milling Co. and is now used only for grain drying.

The fact that the feu duties of the town's mills were directed by mediaeval charters to be committed to the common good of the town made it very often impossible for magistrates, however much they would have liked to do so, to sell the mills outright. All they could do was to sell the lease to a tacksman who might either manage the mills himself or sub-let them in such a way as to make them a profitable investment. The finding of a purchaser for the lease was simple enough during the period of high prices for corn. Mills belonging to Perth city let in 1792 to Ramsay, Whittel and Co., flour millers, at £800 per annum; they also rented Balhousie Mill from Lord Kinnoull.[34] In 1828 Alex M'Dougall, a Perth merchant, became tacksman of the same city's meal and barley mills. He sub-let the mill to John Elrick at £301 per annum. M'Dougall died in about 1833 and his Trustees then found that Elrick had been falling into arrears and that the mill was not being profitably run. One of the difficulties seems to have been that they were charging a higher multure than the other local mills. They reduced the multures, spent a large sum on repairs and modernisation and for some years ran the mills without a sub-tenant but with a manager answerable to the Trustees. The encroachment of the new spinning mills on the water supply and the reduced profitability of meal-milling towards the end of the 1830s forced the Trustees to ask the Town to allow them to surrender their tenancy before their lease was up. The mills were advertised in the *Perthshire Courier* on the 9th, 10th and 24th of May 1840 and in the *Chronicle* on the 17th as 'well worth the attention of an industrious and enterprising tenant'. In December 1840, after a long and disappointing period in which no offerer able to provide sufficient security was forthcoming, Mr William Wallace, the miller at Ruthven, put in an offer of £205 per annum for the lease.[35] The amount of income to be derived from the ownership of town mills had obviously been considerably reduced in the preceding decades, although the rents were still higher than those obtained from rural mills even while the business of those small burgh mills was now very much that of a 'country miller'.

What is interesting is that, during the period when the mills were possible sources of profit, that is, from the 1780s until perhaps the 1830s, it was not difficult to find merchant companies willing to take them over as an investment. Only when their profitability had been very much reduced, when, that is, they represented not so much a financial investment as a comfortable living for one family, only then did working millers begin to offer themselves for the town mills as principal tenants, or, where the town was able to free itself wholly of the encumbrance, as outright purchasers. In 1861, for instance, James Hay, miller at Crail, offered £675 as purchase price for the St Andrews flour mill.

In the country mills it was, in most cases, not until after the First World War that millers found themselves in a position to become owners of the mills of which they were already tenants or to put in a bid for another. There were three reasons for this. The first was that, until the breaking up of the larger estates, the land on which the mill stood did not become available for sale at all. The second was the difficulty experienced by tenant millers in accumulating any substantial amount of capital. The third was that, in a sense, millers were, as tenants, already capitalists, with considerable investment in the contents of the mill although they did not own the building or the land on which it stood.

There had, of course, already been several upheavals in land ownership. The rebellions of 1715 and 1745 had removed from their estates gentry 'disaffected to His Majesty's person', not all of whose families found their lands returned to them afterwards. The management of some of these estates by bodies like the Commissioners of the Estates Annexed to the Crown, or the York Buildings Company, gave an opportunity to such millers as John Robertson of Brunty to expand their business, acquire some capital and to plough it back into ventures such as lint-milling, saw-milling or the improvement of their corn mills.

The next redistribution of land was made possible by changes in the Law of Entail. Entail or, in Scots, *tailzie*, involved the settlement of land on a prescribed succession of heirs, guarded by strict prohibitions and breakable only with great difficulty. In particular it very often made impossible the lengthening of leases and it also made the selling off of pieces of land virtually impossible for many estates. As millers would have aimed only at the purchase of the few acres on which their own mills stood, this provision made their hope quite vain. It was not until 1914 that the strict entailing of estates in Scotland was broken. The result was that the very great majority of all mills remained under estate ownership, rented by miller/tacksmen until modern times.

The agricultural depression of the late nineteenth century, the death of many young lairds in the First World War, and the succeeding depression of the years between the wars all resulted in the breaking up of ancient landed estates.

The large mills at Port Elphinstone in Aberdeenshire were run by Mr Tait of Crichie in 1845 and, after the Limited Liability Act, by the company of T. Tait and Sons Ltd. The early success of these mills was made possible by their very advantageous situation on the Inverurie Canal which gave them cheap transport to Aberdeen docks and access to markets throughout the kingdom. Foresight caused the owners to build large granaries so that grain could be bought during low markets and processed for selling at advantageous prices. The coming of the railways, with a junction at Inverurie and a private siding to the Port Elphinstone mills, ensured their continuing success at a time when most Aberdeenshire mills were small affairs serving only their own immediate neighbourhoods.[36]

After the sale of the Keithall estate, the North of Scotland Milling Company Ltd., successors to T. Tait and Sons, purchased the ground around the mills from Lord Kintore. When the opportunity arose they bought extra ground, on part of which stood the granaries, outright from Lord Falconer, and, eventually, in 1914, the Port Elphinstone mill itself from Lord Elphinstone's estates.[37] By such complicated transactions some millers were able to buy not only their own mill building and the land on which it stood but also the surrounding land, which allowed for expansion but, more importantly, gave water rights over that land.

The North of Scotland Milling Company followed a policy of buying up country mills in their region wherever they came on the market. By 1908 they owned the Royal Mills, Aberdeen, and the oatmeal mills at Turriff, Lethenty, Port Elphinstone, Insch and Ardtames. Some of these were large commercial mills, some, like Ardtames, very small farm mills. By this means they were able to afford the water engineering necessary to ensure a sufficient water supply, the investment in machinery and building, the covering insurance and the advertising which made continuing profitability possible. Their letterhead proclaimed the quality of their product, Grampian Scotch Oatmeal 'all cuts for home and export trade, groats, barley, etc.' The twentieth century saw the appearance of several trade names in oatmeal: 'Peter Pan' oats from Kirriemuir, 'Grant's Oat Flour' from Dundee. These helped to sell the product, particularly in England, where the taste for natural food products was being encouraged by the intellectual élite of the arts and crafts movement.

Like the North of Scotland Milling Company, the Angus Milling Company emerged from the activities of one country miller, tenant of the Meikle Mill in Kirriemuir. The mill belonged to the Kinnordy estate of the Lyall family but a piece of ground adjacent to the mill, bearing two thatched cottages, a corn barn and a yard, came into the hands of the tacksman miller. The cottages, which were bought in 1838 for only £50, were later demolished and a row of three two-storey tenement houses built to replace them by Isabella Whamond of the Meikle Mill, with a loan of £350 from the Kirriemuir Freehold Building and Investment Society. Isabella made a disposition of this property to J. A.

Whamond and Sons Ltd., grain merchants and millers, in 1920, which put them in the position of being able to buy the Meikle Mill from Charles Anthony Lyall, Baron Lyall of Kinnordy, when it came on the market in 1937. In 1938 Whamond changed the company's name to the Angus Milling Company. Thereafter they followed a policy of buying up meal mills throughout the eastern counties, including small glen mills like Glencoul, and up to the borders of the North of Scotland's territory in Aberdeenshire.[38] This expansion led eventually to the acquisition of both the North of Scotland Milling Company's Aberdeenshire mills and the Hamlyn Milling Company's Cupar, Fife property, the whole being combined under the original Angus Milling Company's management from the old Kirriemuir mill with the new name of Hamlyn/Angus Milling Company Ltd.

Thus the breaking up of some of the large estates and the selling of some of their old mills resulted in the formation of milling companies whose empires grew larger and larger, but for most millers the finding of large enough sums of capital for property purchases was very difficult. The exceptionally advantageous situation of Port Elphinstone, the minor but astute property dealings of the Whamonds, the anxiety of Cupar Town to sell even at a loss, these were the circumstances which made possible the entrepreneurship of the three large companies which were eventually to amalgamate to control almost the whole of the East of Scotland. The influence of different markets produced a slightly different pattern in the south and the eventual formation of two different trade associations, the North of Scotland Oatmeal Millers' Association and the South of Scotland Oatmeal Millers' Association. Both of these have recently amalgamated with BOBMA, the British Oat and Barley Millers' Association.[39]

In the West the pattern was different again, with different farming patterns, lower oats acreage, greater degree of industrialisation, access to and demand for imported wheat and earlier conversion to steam power. Thus a different kind of entrepreneur took over milling in the western regions with capital based on merchant corn-dealing during the period of high grain prices. Small oatmeal mills virtually disappeared from the central western districts of Scotland. In the eastern counties, however, and in the south, in spite of the activities of the large milling companies, some small country millers did survive, chiefly because the estates on which they stood remained unbroken and letting to tacksmen continued uninterrupted.

Nineteenth century millers did not, then, commonly become proprietors of the mill in which they worked. They acknowledged the owner of the estate as their feudal superior and landlord and continued to pay him rent. But it was necessary for them to acquire and expend some capital because of the way in which the *miln,* and the building containing it, were distinguished in Scots law. It was for the building and the ground on which it stood that the miller paid rent. The *miln* or the machinery of grinding was his own property, at least in so far as he had installed it. The ancient mills surviving until the end of the eighteenth century and containing ancient machinery were often, but not invariably, considered as a whole the property of the estate because the estate had in the first place installed the works. Even then, where a miller made improvements on his own account, he either removed them when he left the mill or was allowed a consideration for them at the termination of his lease. At the end of the eighteenth century, the landowners very often ceasing to take an interest in the repair and upkeep of the mills and the simultaneous technological improvements forcing expenditure if mills were to be competitive, millers had to find from their own pockets money to install new machinery or improved water wheels and to build kilns. Some doubt about the miller's subsequent ownership of such property delayed expenditure in cases where the relationship between tacksman and estate was not good.[40]

Hunter held that it was 'the general understanding of the country that the lessee supplies and takes away with him the machinery of a thrashing mill if voluntarily supplied by him'; that in cotton mills only an empty building was leased and the lessee brought with him anything he required in the way of mules and jennies, which were, in fact, often hired rather than bought. But cotton spinning mills and threshing mills, because they were new, had been given some legal attention and the law pertaining to them carefully thought out. Because the corn mills were so old and so accepted a part of the historical scene, the law regarding them had not often been questioned. Hunter considered that 'while cotton, woollen, iron and other manufactories which are the growth of commercial industry, would be held to be classed under the principle which denies that machinery put up by lessees becomes a fixture, some doubts might be roused with regard to an ordinary corn mill, as by the law of Scotland it is deemed a separate feudal subject.'[41]

Lord Stair thought that because the water wheel of a corn mill could not be removed without damaging the building it ought to be considered the property of the landlord and not removable by the tenant. In English law, which Hunter held should be authoritative on commercial questions, the courts there having had a longer experience of commercial dealings, grinding stones boxed to the floor by a frame and screwed to it were considered fixed and therefore not movable by the tenant, although the general principle was that machinery installed by a lessee during his lease could be removed by him at the end of it.[42]

There was obviously some confusion, but in practice very few cases came to the Scots courts simply because contracts between landlord and tenant were commonly more carefully drawn. In those cases involving machinery which did reach the courts there was usually an extra factor, such as the hardship experienced by Robert Wilson, subtenant of a mill on the property of Campbell of Shawfield. Wilson was evicted because the principal tenant, the farmer to whom Wilson paid rent, had fallen into arrears of rent and was himself evicted. Wilson had spent money on improvements for which he was not compensated and felt justified in suing the estate.[43]

Eventually the law became firm. It was agreed that, in cases of doubt, the law was always to be interpreted in favour of the tenant: 'The presumption is that improvements made by the tenant were for his own benefit and are removable, at least where made for the purposes of his trade or business . . . the erection forms part of the capital of the lessee, expended in order to ensure the realisation of profits by means of his capital.'[44]

This having been straightened out, millers were encouraged to spend money on improvements to the mills of which they were tenants, knowing that, on removal to another mill, they would either be free to take the new machinery with them or would be compensated for the expenditure by the incoming tenant. In most cases, of course, there was no need for the courts to complete their deliberations. Most millers felt sufficiently secure in the custom and tradition of the country and in their own personal relationship with the estate factor to go ahead with such additions as they required.

In some cases the capital expenditure for the improvements was provided by the estate and the tenant then paid interest on the amount thus lent. William Baird of Galdenoch Mill paid £1. 10s interest on his kiln along with his £30 annual rent in the 1780s but William Gaudy of Lunan Mill paid for his own kiln and entered in 1837 in his account book '2 shillings and sixpence for wire for the kiln, £2. 19. 6d for plate iron for the kiln, 6 shillings and 6d for a furnace for the kiln.'[45] Between these two, of course, had fallen a period of great profitability for the miller, when during the period of high corn prices he had been able to deal in grain and meal to considerable advantage. Thus, and from the sale of his pigs and poultry and the proceeds of his carrier trade, he had been able, if he were sufficiently acute and industrious, to acquire some small capital to be laid out on machinery.

Another source of income for the country miller was the sawmill which could be installed with only small expenditure in a lean-to against the main building and turned by the same water wheel. The need for sawn timber for fencing and enclosure was very pressing during the period of agricultural improvements and continued into the twentieth century because of the well-known tendency of fences to need repair. Thus the employment of hands to feed the saw at intervals from tending the corn mill could bring in a useful extra income.

In addition to money saved from income, some millers were fortunate in being awarded a lump sum rather than a yearly reduction in rent as compensation for giving up their multures. This would put a sum of some hundreds of pounds at a miller's disposal, certainly enough for him to re-equip his mill. For the most part, however, an annual sum fixed by a jury as fair compensation for loss of multures was paid to the miller at Candlemas by each tenant. This, of course, he needed to pay his own rent. The occasions on which the Sheriff was asked to fix a lump sum in commutation of thirlage instead of an annual one seem to have been usually to the benefit of the landowner rather than the miller. Where the mill was under lease, the Act provided that commutation be paid to the miller. But if the mill was not let at the time when the estate resorted to the courts to end thirlage, the proprietor himself benefited by the award. It was, therefore, in a proprietor's personal interest to engineer commutation during a time when the mill was empty. It is, of course, those cases which gave trouble of which evidence survives, and we can know little of the many estates where thirlage was ended by amicable and unsensational three-sided arrangements between tenants, miller and estate proprietor. In some of these, lump sums may have been paid which gave the miller a useful nest egg.

Costs of mill equipment varied very much, even within the same period and certainly from region to region. Kilns built at Old Deer, Aberdeenshire in the 1790s, nine feet in diameter, cost £3 sterling and were capable of drying eight or ten bolls a day.[46] This was perhaps a little smaller than the usual nineteenth century kiln which had a square floor of perforated iron twelve feet by twelve feet. In the 1840s the *New Statistical Account* reported that several new kilns had been built on a fairly large scale, presumably replacing those built in the 1790s.[47] A kiln built at Skebo in Sutherland cost £50. The variation in cost could be accounted for by the availability of materials and the extent to which the miller performed the work himself. If he were prepared, as apparently Gaudy was, to buy in the parts at a fairly low cost and to construct the kiln himself, his expenditure would be small. If all had to be purchased from suppliers and professionally installed, it must necessarily have cost more. The large mills, able to employ millwrights and buy the latest equipment, began, after the middle of the nineteenth century, to install patent kilns, of which the most popular was the 'Eclipse' built by Messrs Wandsworth and commonly known in mills as a Wandsworth. This was a self-acting, thermostatically controlled kiln, capable of drying up to 30 cwts of oats per hour. But in the country mills the simple kilns installed in the first quarter of the century, capable of holding 4 to 6 quarters, 6 to 8 cwts, lasted, with, of course, running repairs, for the next hundred years.

To install all the improvements at once would have required a considerable outlay of capital, one beyond the reach of most country millers, but by gradual expenditure of small amounts over a fairly long period, by working himself at repairs and improvements and making and installing machinery with only occasional help from the millwright, it was possible for a miller greatly to enhance the value of the contents of a mill during the period of his lease. If he then moved on to another mill he could either remove the installations for use in his new situation or, more likely, accept, from the estate or from the incoming tenant, a sum in compensation for the change in value of the mill effected by him since his entrance. This sum, representing more in one lump than he had perhaps previously owned, could be used as grassum to buy entrance to another mill, one whose larger clientèle or better situation would allow him to better himself. Sometimes millers who had built up the trade of one mill to a limit beyond which expansion was impossible would take on the tenancy of a second mill, managing both at one time, often without employing more than casual labour to help them.

The introduction of efficient kilns probably made a greater difference to the profitability of corn mills than any other single factor within the miller's control. Returns on their work of drying and grinding allowed millers to speculate a little in the price of grain, converting it into meal at their convenience. Those mills in possession of enough ground on which to build granaries were, of course, in a better position to speculate because they were enabled to store quantities of grain in anticipation of a price rise. Most millers, however, were limited to small-scale speculation by restrictions of space for storage. Significantly, those mills which were the foundations for the big milling companies were those already provided with granaries or barns before the period of their major expansion. The typical two-storey country mill could store only a small quantity of grain at a time.

If very many of the improvements to the mill which added to the value of the miller's property could be achieved by the gradual expenditure of small amounts rather than by the outlay of a large sum at one time, there were two exceptions. The water wheel and the millstones were very expensive items upon whose good repair the mill depended. Water wheels of iron, two feet wide and twenty feet in diameter, are quoted in the *Millers', Merchants' and Farmers' Ready Reckoner* for 1861 at £340. Most country mills had wheels smaller than that and, fortunately, the life of a wheel was very long and could be almost indefinitely expanded by careful management so that such an outlay for most millers was probably avoidable.[48] In many cases, the wheels already *in situ* at the end of the eighteenth century and almost certainly installed at estate expense were made to last throughout the next century, albeit with constant repairs. Similarly, although new millstones might cost £60 a pair,[49] only the large wheat-grinding mills bought new stones with any frequency. The country meal mills, by care and attention, made the old stones last for scores of years and, in some cases, bought secondhand when they were forced to replace. The stones discarded as having lost the edge to grind fine wheat flour were still suitable for a long life grinding oatmeal. Leith millstones were shipped to Orkney for secondhand use in the meal mills there.[50]

Thus, although a miller by judicious dealing and hard work might acquire some little capital and although if he chose to spend it there was considerable scope for its investment in mill improvements, it was also possible for him to get along and to expand a little without any large outlay of capital, and for most nineteenth century millers this was undoubtedly the pattern. Circumstances were changed by the effect of two world wars. Dietary changes, a falling agricultural population, competition from the retail trade, all made their mark on profits, but, during each of the wars, the nation's difficulty in importing foreign grain and animal feedstuffs made an opportunity for mills to be kept busy and financially successful.

The savings from this period meant that, when estates, anxious for one reason or another to raise ready money, became ready to sell, there were millers as sitting tenants ready to buy. Thus Mill of Benholm, tenanted since the sixteenth century, was bought by the Watson family in 1929. The Coutts family, who had been tenant millers at Kildrummy for generations, became owners of the mill. William Gavin of Peterculter, whose father and grandfather had been tenant millers, took over Upper Kennerty Mill as tenant in 1923, purchased Murtle Mill in 1938, Lower Kennerty in 1940, making it one of the best equipped in the county, and bought Wardmill from the laird of Drum in 1947.

NOTES

1. Shaw, *Stair*, 242
2. S.R.O. GD 10/1227
3. *N.S.A.*, X, 1276-7
4. Wills, *Reports on the Annexed Estates*, 6
5. MacPhail, *Papers from the collection of Sir William Fraser*, 57
6. Adam, *Sutherland Estate Management*, 2, 138-9
7. Horn, *Letters of John Ramsay of Ochtertyre*, 11; Cregeen, *Argyll Estate Instructions*, xx
8. Morison, *Decisions of Court of Session*, 16032
9. Sanderson, 'The feuing of Strathisla', 3
10. Court of Session, Smyth v. Young, June 14 1789; Morison, *Decisions of Court of Session*, 16073
11. Cf. Holderness, 'Credit in English rural society before the 19th century', 99
12. *N.S.A.*, X, 72-3; 188-90; 190-91
13. Court of Session, Henderson & Thomson v. Sir Michael Shaw Stewart, June 23 1818
14. *Dundee Advertiser*, 25 September 1823
15. Title deeds of textile firms show origins as meal mills
16. Jespersen, 'Watermills on the River Eden', 238
17. See p. 33
18. Smith, *The Gordon's Mill Farming Club*, 62
19. *Ibid.*, 63
20. Mrs Gunn, of Barry Mill, states that her grandfather was miller of the Sutherland estate's mill at Golspie in the early nineteenth century
21. Adam, *Sutherland Estate Management*, 2, 139
22. *Ibid.*, 111
23. One of these is Blythe Bridge Mill in Peebleshire, built in 1817, not now in use, Dept. of Environment, Historic Buildings Survey

24. *Ordnance Gazetteer of Scotland*, Edinburgh, 1885
25. Hume, *Industrial Archaeology of Glasgow*, 1-7
26. Dundee Libraries, Lamb Collection 279(10), 279(33)
27. *Dundee Advertiser*, 26 January 1821
28. *N.S.A.*, XI, 890-1
29. *Ibid.*, IX, 890-1
30. Macadam, *The Baxter Books of St Andrews*, 241, 260
31. Knowles, *Industrial and Commercial Revolutions*, 207 has a useful passage on this subject
32. Hume, *Industrial Archaeology of Glasgow*, 168, 182, 222, 234, 238-9, 243, 273
33. Hamlyn/Angus Milling Co. records. I am also indebted to Mr H. Andersen for information regarding the Cupar mills
34. *O.S.A.*, 18, 518
35. M'Dougall's Trustees, Minutes, 1828-40 (NRA[S]1510)
36. *N.S.A.*, XII, 664
37. North of Scotland Milling Company records, including plan of Lord Elphinstone's estate
38. Disposition of subjects, Westownend, Kirriemuir, 1826-1938, Hamlyn/Angus Milling Co. records
39. It has been suggested to me, by Mr Graham of R. F. Bell and Company, that the existence of the different associations helped to bring about the development of different milling systems in north and south Scotland. It is perhaps more likely, however, that this was the result of the influence of different firms of milling engineers
40. Hunter, *Treatise on the Law of Landlord and Tenant*, 2, 314, 383; *Juridical Styles*, 539; Court of Session, Peter Dallas v. James Baillie Fraser, May 26 1849
41. Hunter, *op. cit.*, 2, 317
42. *Ibid.*, 2, 314-9
43. Court of Session, Robert Wilson v. Walter F. Campbell of Shawfield, December 12 1839
44. Hunter, *op. cit.*, 2, 312
45. Gaudy's ms. meal account book
46. *O.S.A.*, 16, 472; Findlay, *Oats*, 168-75; see also Slade, Harry Gordon, 'Rothiemay: an 18th century kiln barn', Scottish Vernacular Buildings Working Group Newsletter, 4, 1978, 21
47. *N.S.A.*, XII, 157
48. See pp. 94-5
49. See p. 93
50. Mr Hugh Linklater of Orkney, in a BBC Scotland broadcast, 1979

5
Millstones — The Heart of the Mill

At the heart of the mill lie the millstones, their essential operation the same in the prehistoric quern and the nineteenth century mill. No material better than stone has ever been found for the production of good, nourishing flour from grain.[1]

Since the most primitive times human beings have found it desirable to grind the cereals they eat. Grains and pulses are not all of the same degree of hardness; but they all share the quality that, when stored, they become too dry and hard to be palatable without processing. When people first ceased to eat their food as soon as they found it, when they first settled in one place and showed the foresight to store some of their food, they then found it necessary to grind their corn into meal and to cook it before eating it. Simple hand-operated mills have been found all over the world from very early human settlements, of so basic a pattern that it varies only slightly whatever the period and region.[2] The principle, in hand and powered mill, is that the grain is fed through the eye of the *runner* or upper stone to be ground between the runner and the *nether* stone and falls from them on to a sheet or tray beneath.

Hand querns must have varied a lot both in their efficiency and in the length of time they might be used without replacement according to the quality of the stone used. Similarly the stones of the early water wheels had to be replaced more or less often according to the hardness of the local stone.[3] 'Constant grinding wears away stone' — the proverbs are full of the experience of millers.

Baronial tenants, although they complained about the time wasted in mill service, in fact made something of an occasion of bringing home the millstones from the local quarry. It was, at least, a change from the daily round and involved the co-operation of a large part of the community. It was a day out, an excursion, crowned with a dinner provided by the miller,[4] and the element of danger in it added excitement to the occasion. A millstone may weigh 35 cwt. To get it home without damage either to it or to its carriers was not a simple feat. At Urie, 'ilk plugh within the barronie', that is each tenant of as much ground as could be ploughed in a day, 'is to send sufficient men and two horse for home draweing off the milne stone off the milne of Cowie at what so ever time they ar to be brought home for the use of the said milne'.[5] At Threave tenants were bound to bring 'four men and four horses to help home the milnstone'.[6] In Stitchill tenants could buy out of the labour if they were wealthy enough, paying 'mill-stone silver' as wages for a substitute to assist in bringing home the stone.[7] Millers were advised not to wait until they were in desperate need of a new stone, which might happen at an inconvenient season of the year when the astricted tenants were occupied with their own harvests and unwilling to help. Good millers anticipated the need. 'Having always millstons lying besyd them a year or they be needed.'[8]

Although tenants of the baronies were bound to provide horses for bringing home the millstones the stones were, of course, very often quarried in places difficult or impossible of access to horse and cart. What is more, in very many districts of Scotland until the end of the eighteenth century carts were not of a sturdy enough construction to support so heavy a load, nor were the horses strong enough. The method of carrying the stone was to thread a long straight pole through the eye, thus making it possible to roll the stone along the ground to the mill. The rounded piece of wood was called a 'mill-wand' and it took the labour of several men to hold it. The length of the wand had to be proportionate to the weight of the stone but was also, of course, dictated by the width of the track along which the stone must travel. In some cases, on the other hand, the width of road tenants were bound by their leases to keep in repair was dictated by the length of pole required to bring home the proprietor's millstones. At Fishtown of Usan, for instance, on the Angus coast, whence fish for the royal table was conveyed to the court when in residence at Forfar, grants of land from the King always reserved a right of road for the royal cadger, or fish-merchant, all the way from the seashore of Usan to Forfar, a distance of some twenty miles, 'in breadth the length of a mill-wand'.[9]

Rolling the stone on its wand could be a perilous procedure, the quarries being frequently situated high on a hillside and the way home being both steep and bumpy. One account tells of 'a very terrible march of a millstone near Tillicoultry. A millstone being loosened and pushed off by a number of herds . . . came rolling and bounding from the side of one of the Aichill Hills to the bottom where above 5,000 people were hearing a tent preacher on a sacrament Sunday. The stone had acquired such velocity and force . . . that, as it came toward them, it would have killed some hundreds of them had it not, as it were by the interposition of providence, broke into pieces, which did no harm.'[10] The irreverent farm boys can seldom have had the pleasure of seeing the righteous so thoroughly put to flight. But there were other occasions for excitement. An earlier report describes a fight which took place between the tenants of the Earl Marischal and those of Sir Alexander Falconer of Halkerton in the Mearns, when both were engaged in fetching new stones for their Barons' mills. 'The Earl Mariscal, Andro Barclay, James Chope in Mylnedeall of Bervie and Alexander Conlie, quarrier, tenants of the Earl, complained that on the 7th July [1617/18] a large number of persons . . . went by command of Falconer and Halkerton to the number of three score, and all armed, to the Earl's quarry or "quarrel" at Knox of Benholm, where there was ane mylne stone standing won and dressed for the proper use of the Earl's own mylns. A battle ensued and Conlie's correll (collar) bone was broken.' In return the Earl's men waited until Falconer's men were trying to bring home stones for their mill of Halkerton and 'committed a fierce assault upon them and put Andro Barclay in the Place of Benholm'.[11] A group of men burdened with so cumbersome and run-away a load as a millstone is peculiarly defenceless and liable to attack.

The difficulty in transporting millstones meant, first, that mills were always locally supplied where possible and also that those miln-stone quarries which were to develop commercially were likely to be situated on the coast whence the stones could be shipped by sea. At Kinneff in Kincardineshire, 'where the rocks were in great repute',[12] at Pennan in Aberdeenshire and at Aberdour in Fife, millstones were quarried from the rock face on the seashore. There is a spot on the shore below Kinneff where millstones formed but not yet detached from the rock can still be seen at low tide. At Aberdour, where the quarry belonged to the Earl of Aberdeen, the millstones, when cut, were 'Pushed over the remaining precipice and fall at the foot of the rock on a small sand beach, dry at low water but covered by the tide when it flows. From this the millstones are conveyed by sea and landed at the mouth of the burn of Troup.' Twelve quarriers were employed there.[13] The stones of Pennan were reckoned to be one of the most useful for milling. At one time twelve men were employed there in cutting millstones from the rock and the stones were used all over Scotland. But by the 1840s only five men were employed and the demand had fallen so far that even these were finding it difficult to make a living. Quarries were let out to tacksmen in exactly the same way as other land and it would appear that the men employed in cutting millstones at Pennan were working on a piecework basis for the tacksman of the quarry. The rent of the quarry was £50 annually in 1845. The stone suitable for millstones was said to be inexhaustible but demand had fallen off because of the doubling of the selling price of the millstones.[14] This rise in price may indeed have played some part in the falling off in demand but it seems more likely that improved transport to other parts of the country, and a wider knowledge of improved practice, had caused millers to demand superior stone from further afield. The large millstone quarry at Blackford in Perthshire, which had furnished stones for all the mills for many miles around, was already experiencing a drop in demand by the end of the eighteenth century.[15]

The drop in popularity may have been because the stone itself proved inferior for milling purposes to imported stone, or it may have been that stones from outwith Scotland were more skilfully prepared or dressed. Associated with the change must have been the more frequent employment of trained millwrights who were aware of better products commercially available. The larger firms of town millwrights may have been subject to the pressures of salesmanship from the larger quarry owners which persuaded them to specify non-local stones.

During the seventeenth century Scotland had been an exporter of millstones. Scottish quarries exported millstones to Holland, Ireland and America. Smout noted mixed cargoes in the port books of Glasgow and Bo'ness which included 'Lusty Susans, political prisoners, grindstones, coal, linen cloth, knives, Bibles and bed-feathers'.[16] And an eighteenth century report said 'the mill-stones with which Angus is plentifully supplied are daily transported by sea to Fife and the Lothians where they are gladly received for grinding stones to their mills . . . Hewn stones are likewise carried hence . . . to Holland; and even to the distant regions of North America for upper and nether millstones.'[17]

During the eighteenth century, however, the qualities of French burr stones, a very hard chalcedonic hornstone quartz from La Ferte-sous-Jouarre, 70 km. east of Paris, came to be increasingly recognised. This was partly in response to the new demand for wheat flour. Wheat grain, being harder than oats and barley, wears down millstones more quickly. The grinding edge of French burr stones dulls less easily than other stones. Because pieces of quartz large enough for millstones occur only seldom, French burr stones were quarried in small pieces which were then trimmed to fit together in segments like those of the arch in building. They were stuck together with a mortar of plaster of Paris and an iron hoop was applied by coopers to the edge of the stone. This occasioned a need for the new trade of millstone builder.[18] The blocks of French burr were imported loose and built up into millstones by the importer. French burr grew to be of such value to the millers of Britain that in 1809 the embargo on trade with France had to be lifted for three months to allow their importation.[19] It is surely an indication of their extreme importance to the food supply of the nation that a war should be interrupted to allow them passage.

How widespread was the use of French stones in Scotland before the end of the eighteenth century is harder to ascertain. 'Burr stones' are reported as being in use at Little Gilmour in 1748.[20] The 'marble' stones used at Pitreavie in 1760 were probably of French quartz although they are not specifically so described. The fact that the mill was described as 'by no means fit for grinding wheat' because it had no marble stones would seem to imply that marble stones were already accepted as being necessary for the production of wheat flour by that date. The tenants, who wished to take their wheat elsewhere, complained that Pitreavie was 'a common corn mill which, though it may bruise the grain to pieces, is absolutely unfit for making sufficient flour'.[21] But Coulston, the miller, replied, 'Though the mill has not a marble millstone and is not particularly intended for a flour-mill, yet it is fit enough for the purpose of grinding wheat. Much wheat in Scotland is grinded by mills of the same kind.'[22] No doubt both spoke the truth. The grinding of wheat with the old equipment must often have been attempted but the better capitalised mills had apparently begun to use French burrs by the middle of the eighteenth century.

During the French wars the shortage of French burrs was felt in Scotland, as in England, and substitutes for them were found where possible, both from the old quarries, the traditional suppliers, and from new sources. James Brownhill, miller at Alloa in the second quarter of the nineteenth century, is credited with first using stone quarried from the Abbey Craig, a rock face near Stirling, to make millstones for grinding wheat. After his discovery Clackmannanshire stones were exported by the hundred all over England and Scotland

and were reckoned 'a useful substitute for French burr stones, which could not be obtained in Britain during the late war'.[23] Brownhill was awarded a prize of £105 for his discovery by the Society for the Encouragement of the Arts.

For the grinding of oats and barley French stones were not considered so essential, and so the mills of the oat-growing districts continued to use Scottish stone from Pennan or from Glamis, where a good quality stone was also to be had. The specification for the repair and renovation of the Perth city mills in 1837 at first required French burr stones but this was amended on the advice of the miller to allow for the use of Glamis stone.[24] By the end of the nineteenth century, however, it was usual for the runner to be a *peak*, that is of sandstone from the Derbyshire Peak district, where the geological formation is known as Millstone Grits, while the nether stone was nearly always, according to Findlay,[25] of French burr. Syson, however, says that both bedstone and runner are commonly of Peak stone in the oat-growing districts of northern England. Costs may have had more influence on choice in the North of England where the local Derbyshire stones cost, in 1861, £30 per pair, while the imported French stones cost more than double that at £70.[26] In Scotland, where both had to be imported over a distance, the cost may have narrowed so that the choice lay between the French burr and Scottish stone. Pennan stones cost £6 for one stone fourteen inches thick in the 1840s.[27]

In a court case involving the Bakers of Canongate against Mrs McDowal of Little Gilmour in 1811, a witness remarked on the vast increase in the expense of milling between then and 1748. Burr stones which in 1748 had cost £20, in 1811 cost £60.[28] Clackmannanshire stones, however, cost only from £16.16s to £21 a pair when French burr were costing £63.[29] In 1799 the mills of Balwhirry, Craigoch and Dinduff had their meal stones replaced at the cost of £64, £64 and £32 respectively, which might suggest the the first two were of imported French stone and the last was a Scottish substitute, but it may equally imply that the first two mills needed both runner and nether stones replaced while Dinduff made do with one.[30]

In 1837 the Perth specification read 'Stones, to be the very best, should be french burrs built on edge — or what would answer very well is a pair of good Glamis Greys drest burr fashion. However that's a matter than can be settled being about 12 or 14 pounds difference in the expense, that is to say if either is not more than 3 feet in diameter (which is plenty) and from 7½ inches to 8 inches thick hem and 10½ or 11 at crown runner if Greys — But if Burrs are preferred they require to be 11 at hem and about 12½ or 13 at crown — all burrs without any free stone.'[31] This last warning seems to imply that millstone builders were not above incorporating some sections of cheaper stone along with the imported French stones, and specimens have been found in Ayrshire of millstones with centres of local sandstone, built round with sections of French burr.[32] It is also interesting to note that these were smaller stones than Syson reports for England where, he says, the diameter may vary from two to six feet but four feet is most common and where the stone is 15 inches thick at the skirt (or hem) and 17 inches thick at the eye (or crown).[33]

Most mills, of course, after the introduction of two-step gearing, kept more than one pair of stones in action and the stones specified for Perth were an additional pair of *bread meal* or *batch* stones.[34] The mill-wright whose tender was accepted made his offer 'provided the additional Millstones required is of Glamis Grey, but if it is of French Burr it will be twelve pounds more'.[35]

Millstones in constant use wear down very quickly. Each stone is grooved on its grinding side with deeply scored lines which are divided into ten *harps* each with four *furrows*, the flat surfaces in between being called *lands*. In Scotland the furrows were called *roads* or *channels*. The purpose of these grooves is to allow the meal, once ground, to sift away from the grinding surface to prevent the space between the stones becoming clogged. The edges of the stones must be kept sharp and deep enough to ensure that the meal is kept moving and distributed towards the periphery of the stones. If the dressing is delayed the meal can gather in lumps, sheltering the unground grain from the grinding surface of the stones and slowing the action like a brake. Stones had in some circumstances, where hard wheat was ground and the work was unremitting, to be dressed at intervals as close as fourteen days.[36] At Benholm the miller lifts his stones apart by means of an endless chain and finds once a year often enough for dressing them. Both Mr Watson and his father before him, who took over the mill in 1929, attended to the stone-dressing themselves. A separate trade of millstone dresser existed in some districts during the nineteenth century, the travelling dressers taking their own tools with them and making regular and expected visits at the various mills on their routes. In Scotland the job was more often done by the local mill-wright.

The skill of dressing a millstone lay in roughening again the surface of a stone which had worn smooth, by cutting delicate and precisely measured furrows between each of the radial grooves, and recutting these grooves to correspond with the thickness of the grinding edge which had been removed. Each stone wore differently, the grain of the stone and the differing degrees of hardness causing the surface even of one stone to show varying degrees of wear. No machine was found to perform the work because judgment was required as well as patience and calculation, but the 1840s saw the introduction of an instrument which guided the hand of the millstone dresser and so aided the work of producing perfectly parallel lines.

Stones which began at from 11 to 18 inches thick were used until they had worn down to about 3 inches thick before being replaced.[37] In Scotland, when French burrs had grown too thin for effective work they were covered with emery to prolong their grinding life a little longer.[38] And sometimes stones whose useful life in flour mills had passed were then sold secondhand to meal mills where they were used for many years more. Orkney meal mills were regularly supplied with stones discarded by the flour millers of Leith.

A miller's skill lay in keeping his stones properly dressed and in adjusting the stones so that they worked at exactly the right distance apart. The harder grains, such as wheat, required very closely set stones, the softer grains requiring less pressure to break them down. The stones had not only to be perfectly adjusted for the type of grain but also perfectly balanced so that they hung evenly, not allowing one part of the stone to wear unevenly. In the early horizontal mills the pressure was regulated in the simplest way possible, by driving, with hammer blows, a wooden wedge between the stones.[39] Nothing more perfectly illustrates the difference between the crudeness of these early mills and the precision of the nineteenth century mills than this: a modern oatmeal miller, performing the same task, uses the paper labels off his corn sacks, inserted round the side of the stones, to achieve the infinitesimal leverage necessary.[40] In Scots, a *mill-steep* was the name for the lever used to bring the stones closer together or further apart.[41]

Another means of making this adjustment, known in the North of England as *tentering,* was by *lighter staff*[42] which gave the small country miller, who did not run his mill long on one job, the advantage of being able to raise his stones quickly when one customer's work was finished, and another's, perhaps of a different grain, or a different quality, was waiting for the mill. But this advantage was outweighed in mills working on larger batches of grain by the usefulness of adjustment by screws which were able to maintain the setting of the stones more accurately and for longer periods without adjustment. Screws, of course, required some capital expenditure and were therefore more likely to be found in large town mills than in the small country meal mills. John Duncan, advising McDougall's Trustees in 1837, stressed the need to introduce screws to the Perth mills: 'Screws are required for raising and depressing the millstone pinions out and in of gear as they require either mill to go or be at rest.' Gray specified screws only for wheat flour mills and then only occasionally, saying 'sometimes a screw nut is used for this purpose'. His normal practice was to use the mill steep or what he calls the 'mill-band': 'a lever which raises or depresses the mill-stone at pleasure according as the meal is wanted ground coarser or finer . . . or what is commonly called greater or smaller'. The lever worked by moving the free end of the *bridge-tree*, the bearer which carried the mill spindle. The squared top end of the spindle entered the *rynd* on the lower side of the runner or upper stone.[43]

The square orifice in the centre of the upper millstone which receives the spindle to turn it is called, then, the *mill-rynd*. Balfour, in describing the machinery of a mill in his *Practicks*, describes the rynd as 'resembling the rowel of an old spur'[44] so that, presumably, in his day the rynd was round. The fixed rynd was replaced in flour or wheat mills by a *balance rynd* which avoided the tedious task of setting the runner square to the spindle, but in oatmeal mills this advantage was wiped out by the difficulty of using a balance rynd where a large clearance was required, as in shelling oats.

The balancing of the stones is attended with special difficulty because they must not only be set at exactly the right closeness to each other but must also be precisely adjusted to the mill shaft. Even a slight imbalance will cause not only irregular grinding but also damaging wear to the working parts. The maintenance of these parts in good condition is complicated by the fact that mineral oil cannot be used at any point which might come into contact with the surface of the stones and so with the corn or meal. While the stones were lifted for dressing, the miller used to take the opportunity to grease the shaft at the point where it is normally encased in the eye of the millstone and out of reach. Best quality fine beef suet, preferably kidney suet from which all traces of membrane have been removed, is still used in meal mills. The miller takes a lump of suet in his hand and rubs it hard into the iron-work where it remains caked until melted by the action of the turning stones.

Where only one pair of stones was available, as in the early mills, the oats were first *shelled,* that is their husks were rubbed off by grinding with the stones set well apart. The shelled oats and husks were then separated by fanning, and the husks saved. This was the operation which, before the application of water power to mills, was performed by hand, in the open air on the *shieling hill,* or in barns so built as to allow the wind to blow through. Some old title deeds of mills still mention the shieling hill as part of the property.[45] The husks are now used for animal feed but were once consumed as *sowans,* which was procured by steeping the husks in water for a week or two so that the fine, floury part of the meal from the inner husk, known as *sids,* remained as sediment to be strained off, boiled, and supped with a horn spoon.

After shelling, the oats — at this stage called *groats* — were returned to the stones which, now set closer, ground them into meal. Allowing the stones to run empty was very bad for them, resulting in unnecessary wear of the grinding surfaces. To prevent this required either constant watchfulness or the invention of ingenious devices to warn the miller when the hopper was nearly empty.

The introduction of more complicated systems of gearing allowed the use of two pairs of stones and the mechanisation of the fanning and sieving processes. One pair of stones without grooving was then maintained as a suitable set for shelling. A chute from there carried the mixture of husks and oats into the *shieling and fanning boxes* where the husks were removed to fall out of a small door in the fanner into waiting sacks. The oats were then carried by an *elevator* to the second pair of stones. Elevators consist of a series of tiny buckets, or cups, fixed to a continuous leather or webbing belt working inside a wooden casing, which carry the oats upwards and return for refilling in a circular motion.

The second pair of stones ground the oats into meal which was then fed by a chute into the *meal sieve.* This was, of course, another operation previously performed by hand, and old mills often have hand sieves of woven cane or wire hanging still on their walls. The mechanised meal sieve is a hanging box, containing, as a chest of drawers contains its drawers, a series of rectangular wire sieves of increasing fineness. The sieve is swung and shaken backwards and forwards by a crank from the shaft, thus shaking the meal backwards and forwards over the perforated wire. The first sieve drawer catches the whole oats, of which a few always escape the stones and must be returned for regrinding. Imperfectly set or worn stones will let through quantities of oats and large particles of grain to be caught at this stage.

The second sieve will catch the *groats* and send only meal through to the third. The third may be the last, holding the meal and rejecting only dust, or there may be a fourth so that two grades of oatmeal, fine or coarse, are provided for customers with different tastes.

Water power was applied to grinding in pre-historical times in the Middle East. In England the grinding of flour had ceased by Domesday to be a domestic hand task and had become the province of the water-powered mill. But in Scotland hand-powered querns were still commonly in use in the eighteenth century.

In the Baronial Court books there are very frequent allusions to the crofters' irritating habit of preferring their own querns to the landlord's mill and there are constant orders for their destruction. There was, as the 1905 editor of the Records of the Baron Court of Stitchill puts it, 'constant battle and striving between the hand-mill of the cottar and the water mill of the land-owner'.[46] Early leases of mills gave to the miller the legal right to break querns which were being used in defiance of thirlage agreements.[47] In the case of McDougal of Logan v. McCulloch it was ruled, 'by the custom of the baronies, house-mills and querns are always broke'.[48]

The *Old Statistical Account of Scotland*, written at the very end of the eighteenth century, has dozens of references to the use of querns: 'The lower orders of tenantry make shift to grind their corn by means of quairns.' In Tirie, because of the lack of water, hand querns were still usual and 'the work of 50 women is yearly lost at grinding'. In Applecross the miller could 'accommodate only a very inconsiderable district of the parish' and the rest had to be 'grinded by a hand mill called a quern'.[49]

But in these parish reports of the end of the eighteenth century it is clear that while hand querns were still in use and were commonly known, it was only in the Highlands and Islands that people were dependent upon them. Even then it was not lack of knowledge about the labour-saving possibilities of water power, nor the innate conservatism of a remote and backward people, not even the poverty of such districts which maintained the ancient querns in use. It was quite simply the absence of a steady supply of water.

Where water could be depended upon it was in use in the eighteenth century except where severe infliction of thirlage rights by a landlord encouraged tenants and cottars to evade the payment of multures by using their own domestic mills.

Poverty, of course, did play a part in the preservation of the old querns and the slowness in some districts of the adoption of water power. Although the most primitive of water-powered mills was so simple as to be hardly more expensive to build than a hand mill, the operations involved in procuring a steady water supply could be expensive. Where mountain streams flow steadily and without interruption they can be applied directly to a wheel without first damming and storing the water. In Portugal there are, to the present day, very many corn mills operating on this principle.[50] But in Scotland highland streams are notoriously fickle. Raging torrents when fed by thawing snows, they are often mere trickles in a dry stony bed by harvest time when they are most needed. Nor does the ground around such streams lend itself easily to the building of reservoirs. The expense and labour involved in producing a water supply would have been prohibitive in districts where corn production was on a scale only domestic and much of the meal consumed had in any case to be imported. Only the presence of a concerned landowner, willing and able to organise the labour and finance the undertaking could have achieved the transfer to water power in such districts. And in many Highland districts it was just such a presence which was most lacking as the commissioners of the forfeited estates found, when, after the '45, they were faced with the administering of long neglected lands which had fallen to the crown after forfeiture by their rebel proprietors. 'It is very remarkable that there are no corn mills on this barony, and all the corns are grinded on quirns,'[51] wrote Captain John Forbes, factor on the Lovat and Cromarty estates, in 1755. And another reporter to the estates wrote, in 1765, with a stunned incredulity which survives the two centuries since that lowland gentleman was faced with the primitive ways of Highlanders, who were his contemporaries in time but not in habits: 'They usually pull their corns by the roots, cut of(f) a part of the straw at the top, which is burnt to dry their grain. The method of doing it is this. Two women sit down, each having a small stick in their hands. They set the straw on fire and by turning it nimbly with their sticks and putting on more straw with corn, they take care not to burn the grain. Then they separate the grain from the ashes, put it into a tub, where they rub it well with their hands and feet, and then winnow, clean and grind it in their querns, which are a kind of hand mills. From shearing their corns they will make bread in a few hours.'[52]

Factors can be forgiven some sense of superior culture when it is considered that in Lowland Scotland the milling of corn was already a profitable, industrialised process, powered by intelligently engineered water supply and producing fine oatmeal and wheat flour on a scale large enough to supply both home and export markets. Nothing more clearly illustrates the impossibility and indeed uselessness of attempting a chronological account of technological development in milling. Where a favourable soil and climate had attracted the attention first of monastic agriculturists and later of improving landlords, milling had advanced to a point centuries ahead in technical achievement of those co-existing lands which neither nature nor enlightenment had favoured.

Abbey mills, in touch with the most enlightened European influences and having at their disposal the skills of the best craftsmen and the knowledge contained in scholarly scientific works, had applied water power to corn milling since mediaeval times. By the end of the sixteenth century the baronial mills and the towns' mills were water-powered, with very varying degrees of efficiency, while on the farms householders struggled to preserve their independence from their overlords by a self-sufficiency dependent upon the quern. Thus there were two strains of development. One, proceeding from the monasteries, had already reached a stage of moderate complication and powered efficiency before the Union of Parliaments. The other, a native technology as yet unchanged by outside influences, worked out from first principles the next steps after human motive power.

NOTES

1. It is interesting that the well-known firm of millers, Allinson's, recently asked newspapers to publicise their need for millstones and to ask country people to keep an eye open for old stones lying disused in barns and deserted mills which Allinson's hoped to restore and put back into service

2. Alexander Fenton's *Northern Isles* gives a very good account of early grinding techniques. See also Bennett and Elton, *History of Corn Milling*

3. Stones like those found at Falkirk in 1911, made of pudding stone, cannot have lasted long; see Buchanan, 'Notice of a pair of quern stones found at Highland Dykes near Falkirk', 367-9

4. Davidson, David P., *Tourists' Guide in and around Montrose*, Montrose (1882), 65

5. Barron, *Urie*, 90
6. S.R.O. GD 25(8) 1056
7. Gunn, *Stitchill*, 10, 21, 221
8. 'Adwise and Memorandum of Francis Masterton to those who succeeded him at Parke milne', Macadam, *Baxter Books of St Andrews*
9. Davidson, *op. cit.*, reporting Mr Huddlestone, schoolmaster at Lunan
10. Hall, *Travels in Scotland*, 2, 368
11. MacPhail, *Papers from the collection of Sir William Fraser*, 178
12. *O.S.A.*, 6, 199
13. *Ibid.*, 12, 585
14. *N.S.A.*, XII, 269
15. *O.S.A.*, 3, 206
16. Smout, *Scottish Trade on the Eve of the Union*, 177, 232
17. Edward, Robert, minister of Murroes, *A description of the County of Angus*, Dundee, 1793, reprinted Forfar, 1967, 9
18. Syson, *British Water Mills*, 109; Findlay, *Oats*, 179; cf. Edinburgh and Leith Post Office Directory, 1854-6: J. Smith and Sons, Scottish wire work and millstone manufactory, millstone builders and importers of French burr blocks
19. Syson, *op. cit.*, 109
20. Macadam, *The Baxter Books of St Andrews*, 207
21. *Sufficient* means *satisfactory* in eighteenth century Scotland. This quotation refers to quality, not quantity
22. Morison, *Decisions of Court of Session*, 16047, 16048
23. *N.S.A.*, VIII, 51
24. McDougall's Trustees, Copy Report by Mr John Duncan, Minutes, 12 June 1837 (NRA(s) 1510)
25. Findlay, *Oats*, 179
26. Syson, *British Water Mills*, 109
27. *N.S.A.*, XII, 269
28. Macadam, *The Baxter Books of St Andrews*, 206n.
29. *N.S.A.*, VIII, 51
30. S.R.O. GD 135/39
31. McDougall's Trustees, *loc. cit*; Stirton, Rev. John, *Glamis, a Parish History*, Forfar, 1913, 31
32. Hay, Geoffrey D., 'The work of the Royal Commission', *Scottish Archaeological Forum* 8, 1977, 14.
33. Syson, *British Water Mills*, 114
34. See p. 4
35. McDougall's Trustees, *loc. cit.*
36. Syson, *British Water Mills*, 117-9; see also Gray, *The Experienced Millwright*, 56. Gray mentions the grooving of millstones only when he is describing a flour mill, not when describing oatmeal mills, although he describes the stones in some detail

37. Syson, *British Water Mills*, 123

38. Findlay, *Oats*, 179

39. Cruden, 'The horizontal water mill at Dounby', 43

40. Mr Watson of Benholm described this to me in some detail

41. Jamieson, *Dictionary*

42. Jones, 'Water powered corn mills', 341; see also Scott, *Engineer and Machinists' Assistant*, 2, Plates C II fig. 11 and C IV, 17-1 for detailed drawings of screws and wedges for adjusting stones

43. McDougall's Trustees, *loc. cit*; Gray, *The Experienced Millwright*, 49

44. Balfour, *Practicks*, 493

45. E.g. Disponing of property of David Cargill: 'The midmost of these three corn mills . . . with the haill gear of the said mill as she is presently going with all and sundry dams, intacks, leads and water gangs . . . and with all and sundry houses, biggings, yards, lofts, crofts, kilns and shilling hills pertaining thereto . . .'

46. Gunn, *Stitchill*, xv

47. Hunter, *Treatise on the Law of Landlord and Tenant*, 383

48. Morison, *Decisions of Court of Session*, 8897

49. *O.S.A.*, 10, 356, 399; *Ibid.*, 3, 375

50. Jespersen, 'Portuguese Mills', *Transactions of 2nd Intl Symposium on Molinology*, 81

51. Wills, *Reports on the Annexed Estates*, 40

52. *Ibid.*, 99. Note the similarity to F. Marian McNeill's account quoted at p. 38

6
Water — The Power of the Mill

When water power was first applied to the turning of millstones it may have been used as nature provided it and as it still is used in Portugal, for example, the wheel placed in a running stream and functioning only when the stream was full. But before our period opens the advantage of storing water had been recognised. Dams are mentioned in Scottish legal cases as early as the sixteenth century[1] and even the most primitive mills, those 'trivial things' so sneered at by the Duchess's factor in Sutherland, made some attempt at it, in the process 'destroying many acres of good land'.[2]

That mills did sometimes operate without dams even in the middle of the eighteenth century can be seen from Sir Archibald Grant's 'Memorandum on Lint and Corn Milns' where he suggests the introduction of a dam as an advantage rather than a necessity: 'If milln is upn burn consider where some large dams may be easily made for a reservoir in case of need . . . A large dam may be made in Kirktown parks which will fill if bank is made strong to contain many 1000d tuns and sluice only opened by degrees in great dryness and scarcity.'[3]

Where natural rock formations provided steep falls and a copious and unceasing supply of water, of course, millers sited their wheels to benefit from it. At Mill of Melrose in Gamrie the fall was steep enough to allow two wheels to operate, one above the other.[4] Sometimes falls of water, suitable for turning mills, were advertised in the newspapers by landowners anxious to attract industry to their lands and unable to provide capital for it themselves. And always where a mill on a natural fall was advertised for sale the advantage of such a natural water supply was stressed. Transfers of property included not only mill and machinery but such phrases as 'such right of waterfall as belongs to me as proprietor of the mill, . . . such right as I may possess to take water from the Dam or Weir near the mill'.[5]

However, where nature was not so kind, man had to labour to provide water for his mills. The first step was the building up of embankments on either side of a stream so that it might carry the full volume of its floodwater down to the mill rather than spread it over the surrounding fields.

This brought more water to the mill but made it no easier to regulate the supply. It was necessary simply to use the water while it was there and cease work when it was insufficient. This was a pattern of work to which all rural workers were accustomed until the end of the eighteenth century, a burst of heavy labour, and a long quiescent phase in which only such work as was obviously necessary was performed. The Protestant work ethic, making labour a virtue in itself and idleness a sin, was very foreign to Scottish country workers before the nineteenth century. To bring corn to the mill and then be forced to wait about until there was water to grind it seemed natural. The mill was, in any case, a focal point for the community, a place for conversation as well as work, and attendance upon it was a welcome break from field work. Corn grinding was in many areas a part-time occupation rather than a trade, and other activities could be fitted around it in a flexible way convenient to eighteenth century habits. 'When persons are thirled to a mill which they know in the heat and drought of summer to have scarcity of water they are obliged to be so provident as, at times when the mill has sufficiency of water to make her go, to grind as much as may serve them the time she stands idle and cannot go; and if they do not, *sibi imputent*, blame not the mill.'[6]

The more efficiently run mills had, of course, provided themselves with a steady water supply before the end of the seventeenth century and some of the dams and lades, Perth's Low's Wark and the Brechin town dam, for instance, are of mediaeval origin. But it was the change in farming methods which forced on most mills a re-appraisal of ideas about the sources of power.

One of the first accomplishments of the improving landowner was the drainage of his land. New leases began to include the clause: 'Power is reserved to the proprietor to change the course of water runs, to construct flow dykes on river sides and to make such leading drains as shall be judged proper.'[7] Before improvement the farming land in Scotland suffered from Scotland's heavy rainfall. Many acres of land were waterlogged and boggy, streams from the hills running down on to heavy clay valley bottoms, as in the Carse of Gowrie, or beds of reed and peat even more defiant of cultivation. In magnificent feats like Lord Kames's clearing of Kincardine Moss[8] and in many small reclamations of land, drains were dug, peat moss cleared, and arable land reclaimed for planting. By the introduction of drainage schemes 'fields of moss which would not carry a sparrow have been so completely dried that the plough has been introduced.'[9]

There was, because of the increased acreage under grain crops, an increased need for the work of mills. But many millers found themselves with a very much decreased flow of water to their wheels. The mill streams which had hitherto collected their water from a very wide natural drainage area were now diminished by the diversion of field water into artificial ditches. Ponds and lochs were drained with results many miles away. For instance, before the Lake of Kinnordy was drained, in 1740, the Dean river was 'a considerable stream'. After the loch's draining it was 'scarcely sufficient to turn a mill'.[10] And this was a common experience.

Lord Rollo's factor achieved the draining of the White Bog on the Dunning estate by deepening the channel of the stream which issued from it but 'the brook had formerly given off a supply of water to turn machinery which was now cut off. Hence, one of two things became necessary, either to relinquish the use of water for driving the mills, or to carry it forward at the same level as formerly by means of an aqueduct.'[11] In Fife Lochore had provided a natural dam for two waulk mills, six corn mills, one flour mill, one coal engine and two lint mills until the estate proprietors drained it. The proprietors gained by its draining one hundred acres of good land but the millers 'have sustained much loss for the want of a dam'.[12]

The law on the subject seemed to support the millers. In the case of Thomas Thomson against the Gudeman of Humbie it had been ruled: 'Gif ony man has ane miln . . . and is in peciabill possession of the samen, with ane dam and clouse[13] thairin, throw the whilk ane water passage cumis, leidand and conduceand the water for the dam to the miln; it may not be stoppit, nor he be troublit be ony persoun, be altering of the said clouse, or drawing off the water fra the said water passage or dam, or be making of the water to be of greiter force or strength than of befoir, or zit to be of less force or virre than of before quhair throw the said miln is or may be mair haistie or mair slow in grinding of corns nor scho had wont to be in times bygane.'[14]

But legal sympathies in the late eighteenth century lay with the Improvers, not surprisingly considering the Law Lords' own interest in agricultural science. Millers had neither the social standing nor the financial strength to make known the damage they often sustained by being deprived of water on which their mills had depended for centuries. The usual course of events was lackadaisical. The mill, without its usual water supply, turned erratically and less often. Tenants, bringing their corn to the mill, which they were obliged by their tenancy agreements to do, however inefficient its working, found themselves more and more often obliged to wait for lengthy periods. The rule was that, if delay at the mill were the fault of the miller, those living on the estate to which the mill belonged were entitled, after a wait of 24 or sometimes 48 hours, to go to another mill. But if the mill was out of action, or slow, through some cause beyond the power of the miller to avoid, such as a lack of water, then they must wait patiently for it to work. 'If the mill be ruinous, or the water insufficient or through great throng they must still wait to be served.' No matter how slow the service they must wait their turn: 'as in barbers' shops, he who is first wet is first shaven.'[15]

Not only were customers delayed but, because a mill irregularly supplied with water performs the operation of grinding jerkily and unsatisfactorily, they had to accept imperfectly ground meal. Sometimes farmers began to grumble to the baron baillie about the bad service they got at the mill. More often they ceased bringing their corn to the mill and fell back on their old habit of grinding in querns. Then they were brought before the barony court for abstraction of multures and, not unnaturally, gave as their excuse the bad service they got at the mill. The next step was for the baron, or estate proprietor, to take to the sheriff court the neighbouring landlord whose drainage works had deprived the barony mill of its water supply. Barony courts dealt with all matters of conflict between tenants or between landowner and his own tenants. Where conflict arose between one estate and another the matter had to be heard in a higher court. By steps like these a great many cases involving water rights were brought into the Court of Session throughout the eighteenth century and into the nineteenth. The very common occurrence of such cases (and of the thirlage disputes which so very often had their origin in the reduced efficiency of old mills) has led some scholars to suppose that the number of working corn mills had greatly increased during the eighteenth century. This is, I think, a false deduction. Many new mills certainly were built, but in most cases one new mill supplanted two or three older mills, resulting in a reduction of numbers.[16] The increased frequency of mention of mills is due to the greatly increased number of battles over water rights. That in itself arose from the agricultural improvements which, all over the country, were reshaping the countryside of Scotland, redirecting and governing her streams and draining her lochs and ponds.

It was, of course, also partly due to the change in tenancy agreements. Throughout the eighteenth century it became gradually more common for tenants who had hitherto held their land by virtue of yearly verbal agreements, to be given written contracts. These did not necessarily give longer leases, although they sometimes did so, but they began to define holdings of land more satisfactorily. Tacks of mills, which seem to have been given in writing rather earlier than other land holdings except for the larger farms, described the possession with some precision. Mills must be described in conveyancing 'by the name, the particular kind of mill, and with the appurtenances thereof, viz, the miller's house, kiln and damhead, lead, with the astricted multures, sequels and services thereto belonging'.[17] This meant that where a miller had hitherto made use of a particular stream he became aware of his legal right to it, at exactly the same time as estate improvements were in process of diminishing it.

The problem increased towards the end of the eighteenth century with competition from other industries. On the farms the introduction of threshing machines increased the demand for water. 'The husbanding of water is now becoming a subject of peculiar interest to the agriculturist. This arises from its scarcity in many districts, in consequence of the improvement of the land, and from the many uses to which machinery may be applied in farming operations, by the agency of water power.'[18]

While the courts busied themselves with the rights and wrongs of water rights cases, the more efficient millers set about the improvement of their own water supplies. One of the mill services which millers were entitled to call upon fellow tenants to perform was the cleaning of the lades and the building of the mill dam. 'The said day it is statuit and ordeanit be the Laird and bailzie with the consent of the haill tenants in our barrouny, that everie tennent and sub-tennent, cottare and greasmen, sall answer and obey the miller at the milne of Montquheiche as they salbe requirit to cast the laids, fens the dams, and bring water to the milne in stormes and at other tymes as they salbe requirit.'[19]

It was very general for leases to include this 'casting of the laids and dams'. Each tenant was required to clear a piece of the lade of the debris which accumulated there, branches, leaves, rubbish of all kinds, which impeded the smooth flow of water to the mill. They were by no means always willing to do so. Natural unwillingness to perform unpaid work had always brought a large number of cases of recalcitrance before the baron courts and the extra field work required of tenants on improved estates left them less time to spend on the miller's work. Robert Dick of Threave was complained of in 1732 because 'he refused to . . . cast and clean his part of the mill dam' for Thomas Clacher, the miller at Ladyburn mill.[20]

The first dams were formed by running a dyke right across the bed of a stream so that the water built up behind it. The flat area behind the dam was then surrounded by embankments of turf divots to hold in the water. This was the kind of dam inherited by many eighteenth century millers and, in spite of constant labouring to keep the weir in repair and the turf walls from crumbling it was inefficient both as a reservoir of water for the mill and because it caused damage to surrounding fields.

At a mill built by James Drummond of Perth 'on a small farm belonging to the King . . . a dam was formed by a dyke run quite across the Water of Garbh Uisge and just at the mouth of Loch Ludnig which it swells considerably and destroys a vast deal of ground on the Arnprior estate.' At Loch Eye 'the tenants of the mill had been in use, for a long period, to dam up the water by means of turf and straw.'[21] The very insubstantial materials used in embanking and the lack of understanding of the force contained in pent up water caused an endless series of disasters. Mr Forrest of Gimmers Mill, in Haddington, cannot have been the only miller to find himself isolated by flood water when, in 1775, 'the miller and a friend were marooned on top of a pear tree where they were obliged to remain five or six hours under the most dreadful apprehension of being carried down the river, tree and all.'[22] In flood, embankments and weirs were carried away and whirled on the escaped torrent into the mill race. A stick caught in a water wheel can do serious damage in a very few minutes by battering and breaking the floats, damage which can take many hours' work to repair and cause long stoppages at the mill. The escaped flood water further up stream flowed over fields, destroyed crops and sometimes drowned animals, involving the miller in constant litigation with his neighbours. The Arnprior proprietors sued James Drummond for the damage done to the estate 'but the late Rebellion put an end to the process'.[23] Drummond had then more serious charges to face.

The answer was to construct dams, lades and weirs of more substantial materials. It was made easier of achievement on estates where mill services were commuted into money payments so that the miller could hire labour, thereby ensuring more willing and efficient carrying out of his instructions, and could pay for materials. This was happening on some estates quite early in the eighteenth century. The Leswalt survey of mills in 1730 contains an estimate of the money required for repairs to the mills, including 'ten shillings sterling to make up the pool'.[24] Andrew Paterson's tack of Arbirlot Mill in 1766 obliged him 'to furnish his proportion along with the other tenants for cleaning the said mill dam'.[25]

But in most cases money contributions towards the maintenance of the water supply did not come until after the Thirlage Act. Even then, although multures were converted into money payments the farmers' leases often required mill services which they were now even more unwilling to perform. Millers who wanted improvement were dependent either upon the goodwill and understanding of their landlord or upon their own hard labour. In Stirlingshire proprietors of mills formed a society to obtain a fuller water supply. Having raised £2,000, the bulk of which was 'borne by a few individuals', they created a 60-acre artificial lake to feed their mills.[26] Millers' co-operatives to protect their water supply were also known in Denmark.[27]

In spite of the difficulties, all over Scotland dams were deepened, widened and built up with stone embankments, their beds properly bottomed with clay. The lades, or 'water gangs', which led into and away from them were cut deeper and with straighter, stone-built sides, their courses cleared and sometimes bottomed with stone flags. Some notion of the labour involved is given in this instruction: 'The bottom being prepared by cross cutting with the spade and moistened with water (if necessary), the first layer is to be laid on to the depth of about 6″ and gone over with the spade, and if of a dry consistence it must have plenty of water poured over it and carefully and regularly tramped and wrought by the feet of men, till it be thoroughly mixed and incorporated. The proper working of this puddle is a most material part of this operation.'[28]

At the end of the seventeenth century James Drummond 'accomplished what was at that time a great undertaking, by forming a water lead along the whole length of the north side of the moss, to the extent of three miles, for conveying the water of the Mill of Muck to the Mill of Cambusdrennie'.[29] In Kirriemuir the Witch Pool was converted into a reservoir for the mills and the River Gairie diverted into a channel cut for it out of solid rock.[30]

One of the frequent causes of the bursting of dams was the inadequacy of the means of letting the water through. This was known variously as a coul, a goal or a gaull, and was nothing more than a hole in the embankment filled often with the most insubstantial of materials. The Brechin dam dyke goal was closed only by a whin bush pushed into the hole by the millers, a bush, presumably often renewed, which served its purpose until 1740 when the goal was shut up by the tacksmen of the fishings on the river below.[31] The millers of Fearn used to draw the water from their dam by removing a stuffing of straw and turf from the hole in it.[32]

A more efficient method was to insert a grating of wood or iron which could be lowered or raised to allow water out of the dam and into the mill lade. This was sometimes referred to as a *trowse,* but that word is also used to describe the wooden spout or 'trough' which directed the water on to the wheel, so it is not easy to be certain which piece of equipment is being described in particular documents. An item of £24 is included in the cost of repairs to Balmossie Mill in 1723 'for hanging trouis to the said milne', and the word 'hanging' suggests that this may have been for a sluice gate.[33] At the mill of Galvenoch in 1730 the list of items required included 'ten fir dales for closing the water-gate'.[34] On existing mills it is, of course, usually impossible to know at what period certain improvements have been made. The Benvie mill has an ingenious arrangement whereby the grating type sluice gate on the dam, which is in this case at some distance from the mill, can be lifted by turning a handle inside the mill. This is connected by wire under the road to a pulley wheel which guides the wire a hundred yards down the road to the stream and lifts or closes the sluice there as well as at the dam.

More often the grating has to be lifted by hand in and out of place as more or less water is required. An improvement on this arrangement inserted a screw sluice which gave much more precise control over the flow of water issuing from the dam. In 1822 Thomas Dudgeon, tacksman of the Mills of Fearn who had until then been satisfied with their turf and straw arrangement, inserted a screw sluice and raised the turf embankment behind it.[35]

The adoption of the screw sluice was in answer not only to its convenience, but to a greater understanding of water power. The money and labour expended on dam building a generation earlier had not always resulted in greater efficiency at the mills, partly because the pent up water could be released but not controlled, with the result that too great a volume of water sometimes reached the mill. James Bogle of Easter Mill of Greenock built a new reservoir in 1796 of three Scots acres in extent and 20 feet deep. But in 1816 a flood swept away his embankment and destroyed a tan-work several hundred feet below. Bryce, the tenant in 1816, was blamed for not having and keeping in repair a properly controlled sluice.[36] John Scott, proprietor of lands on the water of Gogo, built, in 1815, 'jetties, breastworks and other obstructions' in an attempt to strengthen the river bank. But the force of the water hitting this strengthened bank in flood was increased as it was flung against the other bank and, in 1831, it destroyed the mill lead of the Mill of Gogo, cutting off the mill's water supply.[37]

Because water power had, from the end of the eighteenth century, been directed to the turning of machinery more profitable than corn mills, means of increasing its proficiency began to be studied. At the same time the old-fashioned corn mills, for the same reason, began to experience competition for the water which they had hitherto been able to use as wastefully as they chose and farmers, becoming increasingly often the boastful owners of threshing machines, took a new interest in the water supply to their lands. The Highland and Agricultural Society encouraged consideration of the subject, publishing pamphlets and awarding prizes for studies of water power.

In the countryside mills had to compete with the ubiquitous threshing mills, bone mills, coming into favour as the value of bone meal was understood, and saw mills, set up to provide the vast quantities of fencing needed for the new enclosures of fields. 'I hope you are aware,' one miller wrote plaintively to his landlord, 'that the saw mill and sawing yard is erected on the best piece of ground attached to the mill and that you will deduct my rent in lieu of the value of the said croft.'[38] Lint mills had come and gone in popularity, surviving only as long as the Board of Trustees for Manufactures chose to favour them with subsidies. Corn mills had always had to compete with waulk mills for sites. The Waulkers, because they were an incorporated trade, had more power and better organisation than the millers. In Cupar, for instance, each waulker inherited from his father rights to the exclusive use of the town's waulk mill and its water supply for one specified day of each week.[39] The millers using the town's corn mill had simply to wait their turn or, as in Rutherglen, to pay each day for the privilege of using the town's water.[40] As waulking evolved into large-scale chemical-using bleachfields it became a much more dangerous threat to corn milling, not only withholding water from ancient mill sites but sending it back downstream in a polluted state. Near the towns the industries on the river banks multiplied until not an inch of stream was wasted. One miller found a spinning mill built so close to his mill that the stream had only 18 inches in which to gather water before entering his lade.[41]

The pressure to provide water for growing town populations was another danger to mill supplies. In Dundee meal millers joined with some water-powered industrial firms to prevent the diversion of the Dighty water into the drinking supply of Dundee.[42] In Paisley, Seedhill and Sacel mills successfully prevented the forming of a water company to supply the town with water from the River Cart and forced upon the town an expensive alternative water scheme. But in Greenock mills benefited from the supply engineered by Shaw's Water Works.[43]

The husbanding of water became more and more important. The quantity of water required to perform a day's grinding or to thresh a stack of oats was calculated. The size of dam required to hold this volume of water was worked out. The horse power generated by a fall of water was found by multiplying the weight of water in pounds by the number of feet in height between the outlet of the dam and the mill, and dividing that product by 33,000. If the fall was 11 feet, the water running at eight feet per second, it generated ten horse power, the weight of a cubic foot of water being 62.5 lb. A mill dam of one rood in extent and three feet depth was reckoned sufficient for one day's work. Where the resources were available it was considered wise to build a second, higher dam to act as a night reservoir, collecting sufficient water for operations to start at first light next day.[44]

This kind of calculation, needless to say, was not often within the powers of the country miller, but was executed by professional engineers for the benefit of town mills or for industries other than milling and only later came to the attention of the agricultural community through the work of such bodies as the Highland and Agricultural Society. Country millers made the best of what they had, which was often a dam and lead of extraordinary antiquity to be kept in repair as best they could. The ingenuity with which they adjusted the flow of water to suit the idiosyncracies of their own wheel and machinery can be seen in a number of interesting devices in surviving mills. A peg board at Glenbervie and a similar one at Benvie allowed the hook which raised or lowered the sluice to be set with some precision in a series of different holes, thus allowing just so much water through to the wheel as the job in hand required. At Benholm a long wire through a small window overlooking the wheel and attached to a board opens the sluice to the wheel as much or as little as the miller wants. These were the improvisations of men immediately involved with the task of milling, discovering by trial and error the capabilities of their own mills. No two mills are exactly alike, just as no two streams flow in exactly the same way. Handled by the same family over a long period of time, a mill develops characteristics and responses of her own to which the miller adapts his ways. Where some small adjustment can ease his labour or improve the quality of his meal, he makes it. Where the mill rejects change and insists on its own ancient ways of working, he accepts it. Trial and error, rather than mathematics and engineering, have made most water-powered country mills what they are today. They remain in essentials remarkably little changed from their eighteenth century predecessors. Very few processes have been added, very few improvements of any importance made. Materials remain the same. But the trade of meal milling, nevertheless, could not remain entirely unaffected by the advances in engineering and the changed attitudes to profit making which began to be felt in the second half of the eighteenth century.

NOTES

1. Balfour, *Practicks*, 493
2. Adam, *Sutherland Estate Management*, 139
3. Hamilton, *Life and Labour on an Aberdeenshire Estate*, 142. See also Grigor, 'Kilns, mills, millers, meal and bread', 126; and Stephen, *The Book of the Farm*, 1, 218: 'If the stream does not produce this quantity a dam must be formed.'
4. *N.S.A.*, XIII, 276
5. North of Scotland Milling Co., Disposition by William Leslie
6. Morison, *Decisions of Court of Session*, 941
7. Souter, *General View of the Agriculture of the County of Banff*, Appendix, 31
8. Tytler, *Memoirs of the Life and Writings of the Hon. Henry Home of Kames*, 28-9
9. *N.S.A.*, VI, 87
10. *O.S.A.*, 12, 198
11. *N.S.A.*, X, 721
12. Beatson, *General View of the Agriculture of the County of Fife*, 9

13. *Clouse* — a sluice: Jamieson, *Dictionary*
14. Balfour, *Practicks*, 493
15. Morison, *Decisions of Court of Session*, 9411
16. Findlater, *General View of the Agriculture of the County of Peebles*, 92; *N.S.A.*, XII, 970; *Ibid.*, X, 1215
17. Hunter, *Law of Landord and Tenant*, 383
18. Findlater, James R., civil engineer, Dundee, 'On the construction of reservoirs of water for agricultural purposes', *T.H.A.S.S.*, ser. 2, 6, 314
19. Barron, *Urie*, 38
20. S.R.O. GD 25/8/1056
21. Wills, *Reports on the Annexed Estates*, 71; Court of Session, Dudgeon v. M'Leod, 19 January 1830
22. Anon., 'Forrests of Gimmers Mills and their Charter Chest', *Transactions of the East Lothian Antiquarian Society*, 5, 49
23. Wills, *Reports on the Annexed Estates*, 71
24. S.R.O. GD 154/460
25. S.R.O. GD 45/18/1983
26. *N.S.A.*, VIII, 123
27. *Transactions of the 2nd Intl Symposium on Molinology*, 96
28. Adam, 'On the construction of reservoirs of water for agricultural purposes', 310
29. *N.S.A.*, X, 127
30. *O.S.A.*, 12, 197
31. S.R.O. GD 45/18/2254
32. Court of Session, Dudgeon v. M'Leod, 19 January 1830
33. S.R.O. GD 45/18/1271
34. S.R.O. GD 154/460
35. Court of Session, Dudgeon v. M'Leod, 19 January 1830
36. Court of Session, Henderson v. Thomson, 23 June 1818
37. Court of Session, Johnstone v. Scott, 7 November 1834
38. S.R.O. GD 40/17/59
39. Hamlyn/Fife Co., documents giving water rights
40. *N.S.A.*, VI, 397
41. Court of Session, Sir James Foulis v. George M'Whirter, 1841
42. *Report relative to the proceedings in Parliament for obtaining a water supply to the town of Dundee*, 1836
43. *N.S.A.*, VII, 280
44. Adam, 'Reservoirs', 309. A good example exists at Knapp Farm, Longforgan. See also Young, David, Perth, *National Improvements upon Agriculture*, Edinburgh, 1785, Essay X, 'What are the best and cheapest methods of banking in rivers . . .', 149

7
Early Technology—The Machinery of the Mill

The simplest water-powered mills in Scotland bear a striking resemblance to the water-mills of other pre-industrial communities.[1] Known variously as *Norse, Highland* or *Greek* mills according to the writer's favourite theory about their origin, they are most usefully described as *horizontal* mills because their wheels are turned horizontally by the water. They were used by families and farm communities in areas where no patron appeared to build a more sophisticated version or where the poverty of the people made them anxious to avoid the payments of dues at a public mill and they were replaced, wherever an improving landlord had control, by mills of superior construction at varying periods up to the end of the first decade of the nineteenth century.[2] They remained in use after that time on farms which, having freed themselves from the restrictions of thirlage, were able at last to abandon their easily hidden hand querns and house mills and apply their own water resources to the more efficient production of their own grain and in such areas as had never known landlords' mills.

The last of these old horizontal mills in use on the mainland of Scotland was noted in Kinlochbervie in 1864.[3] In the Western Isles and in Orkney and Shetland they survived into the twentieth century.[4] It was not, in fact, ignorance of a better way of doing things that made the islanders retain their ancient mills. They were efficient enough for what was required of them. The crofting population knew that other forms of water wheel could make a less wasteful use of a water supply but, as one of them said: 'If I get all the power I need from the burn as it flows past where is the foolishness in leaving the rest unused?'[5]

The water wheel to which we are now accustomed is a vertical wheel, taking the force of the water on buckets or paddles which, in turning, turn an axle which transfers the power by gearing to the millstones. In the early horizontal mill the wheel was only in the most rudimentary sense a wheel at all. It consisted of a rounded block of solid wood around which blades were set diagonally at intervals. An upright post or tree trunk fixed to its centre was attached at its other end directly to the millstone. Thus, when the flow of water hit the blades of the wheel as it lay flat in the stream the stones were turned and grinding could begin. The pressure of the stones could be regulated by driving a wooden wedge between them. The whole was sheltered by a roof of thatch or of heavy stone slates and sat directly over the stream which powered it. The horizontal mill was the sort of contraption which might be discovered by any one with some ingenuity but no mechanical knowledge who chose to tinker at a stream's edge until the result was achieved. It was, in fact, a mechanised hand quern. Where mills like these were in use until a late date, various adaptations and labour-saving devices worked towards a greater measure of efficiency. In the Dounby mill corn was fed from a pyramidal wooden hopper on to a tray which gradually projected the grain on to the stones in quantities suitable to the rate of the stones' turning. The grain was caused to fall on to the stones from the tray by the joggling motion of the tray. A small piece of stone resting on the upper millstone was attached to the tray by a piece of string. When water was applied to the paddles of the wheel the resultant rotation of the millstones tugged the string, which shook and joggled the tray, which fed the grain in just the right quantities into the eye of the millstone.[6] This device thus performed the task of the 'feeder' worked off the mill spindle in geared mills.

From the moment this simplest of mechanical contrivances was introduced, grinding, which had hitherto been the business of women, became a man's job. The earliest illustrations invariably show men at the mill, but the quern was a woman's tool. When grinding was removed from the home to the stream the woman, housebound by the needs of children and food preparation, could not move with it; nor could she as easily as a man carry the sacks which now had to be taken to and from the mill, because there was no provision for storage in the early horizontal mills.

By the end of the eighteenth century and into the nineteenth 'these trifling things', in spite of the irritation of all the more enlightened souls who came in view of them, were still in use wherever the water supply was chancy and the people poor. William Young, factor to the Sutherland estate, trying to drag the people of Sutherland with him into the nineteenth century, wrote to the Marchioness of Stafford in 1811 of the numbers of little mills which 'waste the people's time and destroy many a good acre containing water for them. If I did not fear that your Ladyship might think I wanted grist to my own Mill I would almost say that the one at Golspie should be rooted out.'[7]

Sir Walter Scott described one he saw in Shetland in 1824. 'The wheel is horizontal with the cogs turning diagonally to the water; the beam stands upright and is inserted in a stone quern of the old fashioned construction. This simple machine is enclosed in a hovel about the size of a pig-stye — and there is the mill! There are about 500 such mills in Shetland, each incapable of grinding more than a sack at a time.'[8] Scott's use of the word *quern* illustrates one of the difficulties in dating the disappearance of hand mills because these very simple water mills are often referred to by the same word. For instance the minister of North Yell wrote in 1792, 'We pay no multures here, having no water mills but such as are called quirns, driven by water, on the same construction as the mills used formerly in the Highlands of Scotland.'[9] The number of mills mentioned by Scott is less surprising when one compares it with the large numbers existing elsewhere. The quantity of grain which could be processed at one time was so small that a cereal-producing district would require many small mills to cope with its harvest. Berwickshire, for instance, had no fewer than a hundred mills, twenty on the water of Leider alone.[10]

Those districts which had abandoned such mills within living memory described the old mills with contempt: 'In nothing has this part of the country received greater improvement than in mills and kilns. Formerly the latter were miserable machines, at which much time was consumed and the grain horribly abused.'[11] All the writers speak of the time-wasting occasioned by the horizontal mills. Their direct dependence upon the flow of water without intermediate gearing meant that the use of power was as inefficient as could be.[12]

Because the mill had to be built directly over the lade, the water to turn it coming 'through the house', these primitive mills were as often broken or carried away in spate as they were left dry in summer. In some districts they were known as 'winter' mills because they could operate only when the streams filled, in others as 'black' mills, presumably by analogy with the 'black houses' of the Highlands.[13]

The construction of the horizontal mills was commonly, as might be expected, entirely of wood rough-hewn in the vicinity of the mill, the millstones similarly, quarried and only roughly shaped, of such stone as was locally available. But they did survive the introduction of iron parts to more advanced districts and sometimes made use of iron for the shaft. 'Like the ploughs, they are of a singular construction. They are without wheels. A round piece of wood about 4 feet in length and fitted with 12 small boards in the same manner as the extremity of the exterior wheel of an ordinary mill, with a strong iron spindle fixing to its upper end, supplies the place of a wheel in these mills. The iron spindle, passing through the under millstone, is fixed in the upper. A pivot in the under end of the tirl (the piece of wood above mentioned) runs in a hollowed iron plate. The water falls upon the awes or feathers of the tirl at an inclination of between 40 and 45 degrees . . . The tirl occupies the same situation under this mill as the trundle in the inner part of an ordinary mill and performs the same office. The diameter of the tirl is always equal to that of the millstones.'[14]

In most districts of mainland Scotland these horizontal mills did not survive the end of the eighteenth century. The spread of knowledge and interest in land improvement, encouraged by the high prices for corn experienced until the end of the Napoleonic Wars, spurred on the improvement of mill machinery. Tenants were almost certainly less grateful than their parish ministers supposed when the 'wretched mills' were destroyed and new ones 'on the most approved principle of construction' introduced.[15] Slow and inefficient the old mills may have been, but they made their users self-sufficient and independent of the money economy their landlords were so anxious to introduce. It is unlikely that all were destroyed or that their use was always willingly abandoned. The *New Statistical Account*, written in the 1840s, not infrequently reports the substitution of new mills for the old within only a short period of the writing.

To sum up, it is difficult to assess how important to a community was the change from hand mill to the first primitive water mill. Certainly the fact that to find water it had to be removed from house and barn and from the control of women necessitated some extra degree of organisation. Carrying back and forth of sacks had to be arranged. The fact that the mill, to be worthwhile, most often served more than one household meant that each man's turn at the mills had to be justly provided for. The original building and equipping of the mill required co-operation between neighbours to lift the axle-tree and carry the millstones. All these steps were regulated in the baronies by the imposition of mill services and the fining of any man who took another's 'rowm' at the mill.[16] In Stitchill Mill, in 1663, for instance, Alexander

Barry Mill. The wheel house can be seen in the foreground. (*Peter Drahoney*)

The interior of Barry Mill. (*Peter Drahoney*)

The fire insurance plaque at Barry Mill. (*Peter Drahoney*)

The water wheel at Barry Mill. (*Peter Drahoney*)

The miller at Barry standing beside the hoppers. (*Peter Drahoney*)

For when the dam runs dry! Barry Mill. (*Peter Drahoney*)

Baledgarno Mill, Kinnaird Estate, Perthshire. The water wheel is located in the angle between the house and mill. (*Peter Drahoney*)

The estate houses adjoining Baledgarno Mill. (*Peter Drahoney*)

The remains of the over-shot wheel at Baledgarno Mill. (*Peter Drahoney*)

The miller's wife, Mill of Glendenstone. (*Enid Gauldie*)

Auchreadie Mill. (*Enid Gauldie*)

Harvest at Auchreadie Mill. Note the over-shot wheel in the background. (*Enid Gauldie*)

Kildrummy Mill, Aberdeenshire. Note the cock vane. (*Enid Gauldie*)

Benvie Mill, showing the kiln and the miller's house. The lade is underground. (*Enid Gauldie*)

The Benvie miller's house. (*Enid Gauldie*)

Lowry was so impatient as to push out of his way one Andrew who had preceded him: 'the said Alexander offered to stopt him and dispossess him and his rowme at his own hand brevi manu wherefor the said Barroun umlawed and amerciat the said Alexander for the said Bloodwyte in the sowme of £25.'[17]

In more remote and less regulated communities the providing of the mill and the fair use of it was the result of neighbourly co-operation. In most cases, at this stage, no one person served the trade of miller. The mill was fed and put to work by those in need of it as and when they required it. It was a tool of the community rather than a money-making device. The door stood always open, without locks and without attendants, ready for the first crofter to reach it with his sack of corn.[18]

Coarse as its product and slow as its speed were, it was still noticeably more efficient than the tedious hand mill. The larger and heavier stones it was able to turn could, if properly managed, produce finer meal within a shorter time. The rate was slow, the capacity small, but still it was faster and could grind more at a time than the old querns. However, the very frequent breakages in water mills gave the almost unbreakable querns one advantage at least over the horizontal water mills. Reversion to the use of hand mills when the local water mill broke down was so common an occurrence as to be recognised and regularised by law.[19]

Thus changes made by the first application of water power to the corn mill were not so very significant. They brought some increased capacity, some speed, but, allowing for the time wasted in breakdowns, not so very much. They had, perhaps, some slight influence on the organisation of society, but, again, in communities where co-operation between neighbours had always been necessary for survival, not so very much. In this early sunrise of technology large areas of Scotland still slumbered throughout the eighteenth century. In the Islands the form was not replaced but perfected so that the old horizontal mills continued to give service to farms even into the twentieth century.

The next step, the addition of gearing to the water-powered mill, was of a quite different degree of importance. It was perhaps the single most significant step taken towards a modern technology. It made possible the extension of generalised power to tasks other than the turning of millstones and it was this that allowed the development of industrial machinery. The impossibility of drawing up a chronology for technological development in corn milling cannot be too much emphasised. While in some parts of Scotland the quern was only slowly being replaced by the horizontal water mill, the Scots engineer John Rennie had already been called from his Lothian workshop to build the Albion Mills in London, steam-powered, with double-acting engines developing 150 h.p. and driving 20 pairs of millstones. Compare that 150 h.p. with the two or three h.p. developed by contemporary country water mills.[20]

The date at which gearing was introduced into mills in Scotland is unlikely, then, to be established with much certainty. The vertical-wheeled, single-geared water mill had been known since Roman times and the description of such a mill by Vitruvius was in English translation with illustrations in fifteenth century England. Sir Anthony Fitzherbert described mills existing in England in 1539 which clearly conform to the Vitruvian model, single-geared, with one pair of stones, and turned by a vertical wheel.[21] With the information available in written form it was inevitable that the monks in Scotland would avail themselves of it and apply it to their own corn mills. Equally it seems likely that it was the increased value of corn mills with geared machinery which caused mills to begin to be commonly mentioned in charters of lands from the end of the fifteenth century. For instance, a charter by John Lundy of that ilk, Knight, and Isabel his spouse, granted Robert, their son, 'the lands and barony of Benhame, viz the Manis, Casteltoune and Tulloch, *with the mill,* to be held of the King', in 1491.[22] The re-apportioning of monastery lands in the sixteenth century, of course, put vertical-wheeled mills into baronial hands, very often for the first time. They valued the new property accordingly and passed it on to those they wished to honour as a gift of some importance. At any rate, for the purposes of our present study, it is enough to say that water mills with some form of gearing were known well before the beginning of the eighteenth century.

In 1730 some tradesmen charged by their landlord 'to view the miln and appreciate her to see what money would make her sufficient' recommended the spending of eight pounds, fifteen shillings and ten pence sterling on, among other items, 'seventy shillings sterling for water wheel and axel rods and twenty one shillings to make up and cog wheel'.[23] The survey of the same mill in 1719 is not so specific but it does describe it as being 'a sufficient milne new built in timber, irone and new stones' and it seems reasonable to suppose that it was already at this time a mill with gearing. It was still in good shape without major alteration in 1741, or would be, it was reported, 'after the small runner is removed and ane old mill stane within the miln put on in its room'.

The interest of a landlord dictated that he should keep his mill in good repair, for if the mill was inefficient his tenants would either revert to the use of their own hand mills or else exercise their legal right to go to mills other than his own in times of its not working. Either way he was deprived of the valuable income from the thirlage.[24]

It was customary for the mill, whose gender, like a ship's, is always feminine, to be surveyed at the end of each miller's lease and the amount of expenditure required to bring it back into the condition in which he entered was estimated. The repairs and renewals had to be constant. Neglect over quite a short period of years could bring a mill into complete disrepair, as the Forfeited Estate Commissioners found on reviewing those consigned to their care after the neglectful years of rebellion. The fact that all going parts were wooden meant that the constant thundering of the water on the large wheel, the relentless rubbing against each other of all the bearings, the battering to which the teeth of cogged wheels were subject, caused wearing away and the need for constant replacement.

It was the introduction of the cogged wheel which necessitated the growth of the trade of millwright. The early horizontal mill had required nothing for its maintenance beyond the skill of any reasonably intelligent farmhand. But the replacement of cogs needed a supply of the proper hardwoods, good tools, an ability to judge and measure accurately and some skill and experience, although decisions about the number of teeth required for particular wheels were arrived at in haphazard fashion.

Gearing is by definition the interposition of mechanical parts between the prime mover, in our case the water wheel, and the working parts of the machinery, in our case the 'miln'. In practice it refers to the method by which motion is conducted from one revolving axis to another by the engagement of one toothed wheel with another. The first geared wheel, known as the 'trundle' or 'lantern pinion' in Scotland and as the 'wallower' in England, was not a wheel in any modern sense. It was formed by inserting a number of cylindrical wooden spokes (known as rondles or rungs) into equidistant holes in two parallel wooden discs which were set on a square shaft. The cogs of the pit wheel engaged with the trundle to turn the shaft. Wooden trundles, although replaced for sophisticated work by iron geared wheels, remained in common use in some parts of the country 'where cast iron is less common and in consequence less appreciated than in our manufacturing districts'.[25]

Gear wheels in use until at least the end of the eighteenth century were commonly of wood, the teeth formed of separate pegs of wood morticed into the rim of the wheel. (The whole wheel is a *cog wheel* and the teeth are cogs.) Wheels of this type were in common use all over Europe at the middle of the nineteenth century wherever the mill was at a distance from iron foundries and its capacity did not justify the extra expense of iron gearing. The wood had to be well-seasoned hardwood, beech, plane, hornbeam or hickory. However, the use of iron was not unknown in the mid-eighteenth century: 'Arbroath miln hath iron teeth' although 'it is only a clay thatched low house about 15f. broad'.[26]

After the beginning of the nineteenth century the kind of gear wheel which came to be commonly employed in mills was the mortice wheel, in which the body of the wheel was iron but the teeth were still of wood. There were significant advantages in the use of wooden cogging. In particular it made repairs both easier and cheaper, the replacement of one tooth being a relatively simple business. Old millwrights also claimed that the work of the mill was smoother, with less vibration, and they liked wooden teeth because they wore and rubbed each other until they achieved a more perfect adaptation to each other than their makers could have designed.

At its simplest a geared water mill consists of a large paddled wheel outside the building, connected by an axle through the wall to a smaller *pit* wheel. In turn the pit wheel, which is cogged, connects with the teeth or rungs of a much smaller *pinion* or *trundle* from which an upright shaft rises up through the bed stone to connect with the runner stone and perform the grinding operation. The shaft from the trundle to the stone is called the *mill spindle.* Its lower end turned in a metal, preferably brass, cup or pot fixed on the *bridge tree.* The top part of the mill spindle was squared to enter the square hole in the *mill-rynd.* The rynd was the iron cross in the underside of the upper millstone fixed there for the purpose of receiving the mill spindle. The squared end of the mill spindle rose a little above the rynd and had fixed on to it a *feeder.* This consisted of three or four protruding branches which revolved with the stone and struck the *shoe* of the corn *hopper,* shaking it just sufficiently to make the grain fall out of the hopper into the eye of the stone.

The next development was to take the mill spindle not straight from the trundle into the single pair of millstones but, instead, into a larger *spur wheel.* This larger wheel can then turn on its toothed perimeter two more small cogged wheels from each of which a shaft rises to turn a pair of millstones. (The new wheels thus added were known in England as *stone nuts* but Gray calls them pinions and I have found no Scottish description of millwork which uses the term 'stone nuts'.) This double gearing has already allowed the doubling of the capacity of the mill by the addition of another pair of stones. But once the possibility had been absorbed into the minds of the ingenious country millwrights it was soon realised how easily the number of gear wheels could be multiplied. As John Watt wrote to Matthew Boulton in 1782: 'There is no end of millwrights once you give them leave to set about what they call machinery; here they have multiplied wheels upon wheels until it has now almost as many as an Orrery.'[27]

While millwrights' enthusiasm for the possibilities of gearing was thus being fired, the experiments of the agricultural improvers were, at the same time, introducing different grain crops to neighbourhoods accustomed very often to the processing of only one kind. The different requirements of different grains in milling made very desirable the operating of more than one pair of stones in a mill. It is certainly true that the setting of stones can fairly easily be adjusted for the milling of different kinds of grains, but the desirability of being able to mill different grains on different pairs of stones, at the same time and without that prior adjustment, is obvious. We know that millers were experimenting with the different techniques required for different cereals throughout the second half of the eighteenth century.

In 1750, for instance, Alexander Corse had erected a mill in Blantyre 'chiefly for the purpose of sheeling barley, but which, with very little variation in its machinery, was fitted for grinding all sorts of grain and was frequently used to grind oats and pease into meal'.[28] In wheat flour mills shieling stones and dressing machines were introduced as well as the main millstones.

Until 1757 the law of thirlage as applied in the courts had done something to discourage the grinding of more than one kind of cereal in any one mill. But that the law was on this point ineffective is clear from the number of cases brought to the Court of Session involving millers who, in setting up to grind barley or wheat, were said to be infringing the landowners' thirlage rights over all growing grain *(grana crescentia).* A ruling of 1757 induced judges sitting after that date to be satisfied with cautioning millers equipped for the grinding of cereals other than those covered by thirlage rights to desist from grinding the thirled corns.

Hitherto they had been empowered to order demolition of the offending mill and frequently did so. In 1760 the Lords of Session recognised the ineffectiveness of their cautioning since 1757 and required the Lords Ordinary to take evidence 'how far the (barley) mill can be rendered incapable of grinding corn into meal without being totally demolished'. They heard that 'the general structure of all these mills is the same. Raising or lowering the upper stone, or perhaps shifting one stone for another which is the work of 2 or 3 minutes, is all the difference required in grinding one grain or another, or in making the mill fit for grinding oats or sheeling barley. Every barley mill must be so constructed as to be fit for the purposes of grinding; for besides the sheeling there is a second operation precisely the same with that of grinding oats into meal; viz, the grinding of the refuse of the barley, with such particles of the grain itself as are broken or crushed in the sheeling, into meal which, though of a coarser kind, makes a considerable article in barley mills.'[29]

Clearly, even before the introduction of more complicated gearing, the desirability of housing more than one process in the mill building had been recognised. Another ruling of 1760 noted that 'Improvements may be made upon mills of every kind.'[30]

It was not only barley and peas but wheat and malt which the millers came to deal with in one mill. Barley was dealt with by vertical millstones enclosed in a plate iron case 'pierced pretty thick of small holes to allow the dust and small refuse to escape through as it is rubbed off the grain'.[31] Malt was bruised between cast iron hollow rollers. Wheat had to be sieved through bolting cloths or a wire dressing machine as well as being ground.[32]

In 1768 the law lords heard that 'even although the mill is not properly constructed for grinding wheat the suckeners had for some time manufactured at that mill their wheat along with their other grain.'[33] It is clear that, while special stones were desirable for special grains, the old meal stones could be used to provide flour from any kind of grain, and they often were put to whatever use was then profitable. But where it was possible, that is, where the money and the skill were available, two or more sets of stones and machinery were installed.

In 1748 a lint mill was erected upon the lands of Sir Archibald Denholm 'and under the same roof was erected another mill, fitted for sheeling lint bows and also capable of grinding oats and, with some alteration, barley.'[34] Now this description does not make it certain that both mills were being turned by the same water wheel. It is not impossible that two separate water wheels with two separate shafts were situated under the same roof. But the expense entailed in such an operation suggests that both mills might have been turned from one wheel and points, therefore, to the use of two-step gearing. At any rate this instance illustrates the use of one mill for oats and barley. Gray's book of instructions for the millwright, published in 1804, which professes to crystallise his experience of the preceding forty years, gives plans for turning malt and barley mills off one wheel. He also illustrates flour mills with separate bolting and dressing machines turned off the same wheel which powered the stones.

Sir Archibald Grant of Monymusk, in his 'Memorandum on Lint and Corn Milns' of 1748, described 'a barley milln which works when lint millns dont and produces a penny barley, 14 st from one boll indifferent bear'. And he specified for his new mill, which was to have a lint mill at one end of the building and a meal mill at the other, that it was 'to have an other scutching milln by makeing the spur wheel of scutching axeltree long and rungs and same on water axel tree and coggs in spur wheel of communication and same spur wheel to move stampers'. He had some doubt about the efficacy of the arrangement, however, because he added: 'If too much strain for all at once: corn to goe in night and lint in day . . .'[35]

The generous encouragement given by the Board of Trustees for Manufactures in Scotland to landowners erecting lint mills on their estates spurred the attention of millers towards the possibility of turning more than one set of machinery from the same wheel. The Trustees spent £100 'for erecting lint-mills in different parts of the country for breaking and dressing of flax' in 1832 and awarded £60 to the inventor of the lint mill.[36] Alexander Robertson, at Mill of Brunty, was one of the few tenants of the annexed estates who gave their surveyors something to praise: 'It gives me great pleasure to see the spirit and industry of Alexander Robertson of this place, who, without a lease, . . . has, upon his own charges, built a very good lint miln of stone and lime with a slate roof and has added a barley-miln upon the same machinery; the same wheel serves both.'[37] This was in 1756.

In 1794 Robert Beatson described at Kilrie, near Kinghorn in Fife, 'a water powered threshing mill, with corn mill, barley mill and hoisting tackle, all moved by the same water wheel'.[38] Like the earlier introduction of lint mills, the late eighteenth and early nineteenth century craze among farmers for introducing threshing mills led to experiments which put the old corn mills to new uses. This particular one suggests the use of a crown wheel to make possible the addition of ancillary machinery for sack-hoisting. The crown wheel could be raised on a long shaft above the millstones, sometimes necessitating the raising of another storey, but allowing the application of another, separate set of gearing to be added.

By the end of the eighteenth and the beginning of the nineteenth centuries landlords and their tenant millers were beginning to benefit from the increased commercial advantages inherent in the possession of water power. Because there had been so many small corn mills the best sites on rivers were already in the hands of the corn mill proprietors who were thus well situated to take advantage of the new demand. The enclosing of arable lands had, for instance, brought a greatly increased demand for sawn timber for fences and saw mills appear as very frequent additions to the old corn mills. The improving of land by the addition of bone meal made the adaptation of mills for bone grinding a potentially profitable venture. Snuff milling, paper milling, bleaching, yarn milling and flax spinning were attempted with varying degrees of profitability on the old mill sites.[39] Most of them saw a brief but not a lasting period of profit making, which sometimes allowed quite extensive mechanical improvements. Others were thwarted in their attempts to extend. In 1808 the tenant of one of the 'common mills' attempted to turn his mill into a yarn mill but was prevented from doing so by the conditions of his lease.[40] In the 1840s Mr Yool, the tenant of Kemback Mill in Fife, had a water wheel of 16 h.p. which turned a meal mill, a saw mill and a bone mill.[41] James Gardner, miller and tenant of the Brownyside Mills near Airdrie, operated both grain and flax mills from the same water supply.[42] The Dunphail Mills at Edenkille near Elgin had 'an oatmill, barley mill, saw mill, thrashing mill and carding mill all under the same roof and wrought by the same stream of water'.[43]

These examples of multiple use cannot, unfortunately, all be taken as certain examples of multiple gearing. It was not entirely unusual for a row of water wheels to turn a row of differently functioning mills within the same wall. And, in one case at least, two water wheels were set one above the other on different storeys of the same mill house. The Mill of Melrose, at Gamrie in the County of Banff, took advantage of the steep waterfall on whose banks it was situated to bring power to two floors of the mill without an upright shaft between them.[44] But even this example proves the use of two-step gearing because each of the two water wheels drove differently functioning mills. On one storey the power turned a meal mill and a saw mill, on the other a flour and barley mill. Almost certainly most arrangements were the result of trial and error rather than previous calculation, and some attempts at complicated gearing may have ended in disaster. As with the first spinning mills, ambition sometimes overreached itself: 'when the frames were first started the breaking down of the machinery was so great that they had to fly out at the door and look in at the window to see how the pieces were thrown about. It was sometimes weeks before the damage was repaired and they got to spin. Their only consolation was that all the weak parts of the machinery had been found out.'[45]

In England, where single-geared mills had been known since the earliest times, double-geared mills are first clearly described in 1723 by Henry Beighton with an illustration of a water mill for grinding corn in Nuneaton.[46] From this time until the mid-eighteenth century double- or spur-wheel gearing was put into very general use. This two-step gear gave economy through a higher gear ratio and was therefore useful in an expanding trade with an increased demand for milling capacity. In England the earlier breakdown of the manorial system, forcing millers to respond much sooner to commercial pressures, resulted in a warmer and readier response to technical innovation. Development beyond the single-step gear, of ancient origin in English mills, was beginning south of the Border in the seventeenth century, at first by the use of two stages of angle gear. This helpful addition was quickly and widely adopted but was supplanted in the early eighteenth century by the introduction of the spur wheel.

The first originator of two-step gearing is not known, and its invention may well have been a happy accident. Where the need for repairs was as constant as it was in the old mills with wooden parts, adaptations dictated by economy, by temporary lack of some traditional material, by mechanical ingenuity or by sheer curiosity as to the result must have been common. Either in attempting a running repair or in making a cheap extension to an existing mill the idea was hit upon of attaching a new and shorter shaft at right angles to the old one simply by fitting a new trundle. This was so much simpler and cheaper to execute than had been the duplication of the entire plant that had hitherto been necessary when extra milling capacity was required that it was naturally taken up speedily and with enthusiasm.

At this stage the mills were made by local people from local materials. On the baronial estates tenants and sub-tenants were required by their leases to assist with bringing home the axle tree and millstones as well as keeping dams, lades and buildings in good repair. We know from surveys such as Leswalt's that materials were sometimes purchased, although even then it is unlikely that their origin was at any great distance. But where usable materials existed on the estate they were 'won home' by the tenants for the use of the mill. The Carron Iron Works opened in 1759 and Smeaton is credited with the first use of a cast iron axis for a water wheel in 1769. But the old axes were only slowly replaced with iron. The ancient wooden axle trees turned on for another century at least. It is certainly untrue to say of Scotland as Jones does of England that by the second quarter of the nineteenth century construction work in wood had all but ceased.[47] In Perth, for instance, the city meal and barley mill had its axle replaced in 1837, the millwright having reported that 'I cannot bring myself to believe that the water wheel, and axle of do. particularly, will even last the lease of 11 years.'[48] The specification required larch wood for the whole mill. The man chosen to carry out the work agreed that larch was suitable for the wheel. 'This I conceive will do quite well for the water wheel and seed house but would recommend foreign fir for the other parts as I think larch will not stand nearly so well as it cannot now be properly seasoned.' This concern over the seasoning of the wood sounds modern but, in fact, Britain was still suffering from the decimation of her woodlands to provide timber for shipbuilding during the Napoleonic Wars. Not enough time had elapsed for the renewal of the forests and so, as today, there was a temptation for timber merchants to supply under-seasoned wood because of the lack of time to weather it.

At any rate Perth mills were supplied with wood for their most important parts. This was not a backward country mill but an important town mill, serving a rich agricultural district, owned by a prosperous merchant, managed by an experienced miller and serviced by a skilful and important millwright. But the lack of seasoned timber and the improvements introduced by Smeaton, which were sometimes beyond the capabilities of wooden construction, eventually forced the use of iron for shafts, axle shrouding and gear teeth. Nevertheless wood served many mills well long after Smeaton, and millwrights continued to be found up to the present day to make and mend the wooden machinery surviving in the old mills. By 1847 wooden gearing had become rare, except that some millwrights liked to use one wooden cogged wheel working against one iron one for reasons of smoothness, but wooden water wheels were still common, even although new ones were usually then built of iron. Wood, it was said, 'once of almost universal use in constructive mechanics, is fast giving place to iron, and in a few years hence we may expect that a wooden water wheel will be as rare, and as much an object of antiquarian interest to those who take pleasure in reviewing the industrial arts, as wooden gearing had already become. Many of those wheels still continue to exhibit in their constructive details, a very superior style of workmanship; and an attention to durability which, in several instances within the knowledge of the writer, the lapse of a century has hardly conquered . . .'[49]

The period of technology based on wood and the succeeding technology of iron parts overlapped in corn mills, the new technology never completely replacing the old. Similarly there cannot be said to be a time at which the skilled millwright-tradesman entirely superseded the miller who did his own wright work. Until the third quarter of the eighteenth century millers did all their own mending and replacement. 'The miller's dues, or the wages for labour are a separate article consisting of a certain quantity of meal instantly paid out of every boll . . . for this payment the millers not only grind the corn but support the machinery.'[50] The local wright was called in not so much for the most complicated work, which was seldom beyond the miller's own skill, but for those tasks which required bought-in parts rather than those which could be constructed *in situ*. Even during the nineteenth century, when the larger mills were employing professional millwrights, the small country miller continued to do his own work. Today, in those water-powered mills that survive, he must do so, as his forefathers did, if he is to survive, because profits are too small to allow for the payment of a skilled tradesman. The period of the miller/millwright can be seen, then, never really to have ended, overlapping at both ends and co-existing with the trained and specialist millwright who came into prominence at the end of the eighteenth century and prospered until the Second World War. The country miller was a man whose technical skills varied, of course, from district to district, ranging from creative and ingenious engineering to sluggish making do. It was a variation caused by the variations in the educational resources of the community, the interest taken by the local landowners, the demands of the local farmers and the conditions and length of the miller's own lease.

Studies of the best means of harnessing water power naturally focused on the best means of constructing water wheels. Andrew Meikle studied the subject all his life. John Smeaton, John Rennie and Sir William Fairbairn each carried the experiments further towards real economy in practical use. Experiments on the power produced by water wheels had been made in France by Desagulier and Beridot and published in Britain by the middle of the eighteenth century but it was their widely differing results which drove Smeaton to begin his own more successful studies.[51] His tables of results remained the basis of water wheel construction for the next hundred years.[52] They were used by the engineers who followed him and in the instruction of apprentice millwrights. But even without them improvements were made by a host of individual millers and millwrights who tried a trick here and a trick there to improve the effectiveness of their wheels. There are three main types of vertical water wheel, named for the part of the wheel struck by the stream of water applied to it, the undershot, the overshot and the breast wheel.

The undershot wheel, which is turned by the action of water flowing under it, was that most often used in early times. It could be constructed without the expense and labour of extensive sluice building, simply by situating it on the bank of a lade. Where the lade was narrow the banks had only to be strengthened and sometimes, but not necessarily, heightened to support the bearings in which the axis turned. At the ancient site of Mill of Benholm, where the wheel is now turned by an overshot wheel from a mill dam, there is a point on the main stream above the issue of the present wheel's tail race, where masonry embanking suggests the very much earlier existence of an undershot wheel. It is to be expected that a mill of this age would originally have had the simplest form of wheel.

Undershot wheels were not, of course, always small in size. At Balbirnie Mill, near Brechin, which was originally an abbey mill, the wheel is undershot and turned by a very powerful water supply taken by a long lade from a weir on the River Southesk. It is 15 feet in diameter. The Mill of Cowie wheel is 14 feet.

The undershot wheel is the simplest and cheapest to build and it is possible to use it effectively where there is only a small head of water. Its efficiency depends on the force with which it is struck by the water rather than on the volume of water in the stream. Its power is very much reduced by loss of water at the sides of the wheel and by the resistance to the paddles leaving the stream of the water flowing below the wheel. It is, therefore, most suitable for use on narrow, fast-flowing streams not subject to seasonal diminution of supply.

The overshot wheel is calculated as being at least two and a half times as efficient as an undershot. It turns entirely by the weight of water falling upon it. Where the undershot wheel is turned clockwise by the water running underneath, the overshot wheel, because the water falls just beyond its top centre, is turned in the opposite direction. The great advantage of the overshot is that it needs only a quarter of the amount of water to turn it effectively. In the period when corn mills were finding their traditional water supply endangered both by land drainage and by competition from other industries, it was obviously desirable to install an overshot wheel were the capital could be found to do so. But because a fall of water must be provided to turn it, the installation of an overshot wheel most often required the construction of a mill dam so situated that the lead from it could be brought to fall over the top of the wheel.

The disadvantages of the overshot wheel, especially to engineers beginning to have some new appreciation of the possibilities of water power are, first, a waste of power because water falls out of the buckets before they reach the bottom of their turn and, secondly, a tendency to erratic bursts of speed where the load is decreased. These disadvantages could be overcome. The flow of water could be regulated by the miller to produce smooth working: careful adjustment of the gate to allow a greater or lesser flow from the lade on to the wheel. When the gate is fully opened all the water issuing from the dam falls upon the wheel. When it is partially closed by a variety of devices from within the mill where the miller is watching his machinery, the water rejected by it falls short of the wheel to join the tail race.

The enclosing of the wheel within a close-fitting arc could prevent the loss of water from the buckets and the resultant loss of power. This was particularly necessary with breast wheels. At Perth in 1837, when the water wheel was renewed, hoop iron was fixed to the outer surface of the buckets 'to prevent the timber chaffing away with ice sticks or dry hard substances thereby lessening the wheel in diameter and leaving too much space for the water to pass under the arc'; and the arc was to be made 'as true as men can make it by dressing of any high stones and raising up any that are too low to correspond with the wheel exactly'.[53] In other words, the wheel turned within a close stone-built shroud with only just enough space between the rim of the wheel and the stonework to allow the wheel's movement. Thus water attempting to escape from the buckets was cast back into them on hitting the wall of the arc.

Henry Stephen gives a specification for a mill wheel arc in his *Book of the Farm:* 'All the inside of the arc, where it comes in contact with the water to be of square dressed rubble stones and to be laid and neatly jointed and pointed with cement. Openings for entry and exit for water to be formed and to be built with scuntions and lintelled. Bottom of wheel pit to be laid with flagstones to prevent its breaking with water.[54]

The first water wheels had only flat boards attached to their axles to meet the force of water. Later the wheel was constructed with shafts to an outer rim and the boards were more effectively placed on the rim of the wheel. The flat boards or *paddles*, however, could not use the water to best advantage. They were, therefore, where economy of water was important, and increase of power desirable, replaced in overshot wheels by *buckets*. These were, at first, merely the same flat boards with the addition of raised sides, but they retained the water falling on to them instead of expelling it immediately, so using its weight to produce faster turning of the wheel. When the flat-bottomed buckets were deepened and curved they could retain the water almost to the bottom of its fall, thus ensuring even slighter wastage of power. A further improvement was the *ventilated bucket* described by Fairbairn in 1849,[55] and first used by him for James Brown of Linwood Mill near Paisley in 1827.[56] In this type there is a gap at the inner edge of the bucket which allows the air held in the empty bucket to escape readily and so allows the whole bucket to fill with water without air resistance. In Scotland the wooden paddle wheel was called a *start and awe* wheel, the *start* being the piece of wood which supports the *awe*. Where the flat board was replaced by a bucket it was described in Scotland as an awe with *sole plank*.

The type of wheel selected was governed, of course, by the geography of the region and the kind of stream running in it. In the South-West of Scotland the low breast paddle wheel is the most common. In the East of Scotland the overshot wheel is more often, but far from invariably, seen.

John Smeaton, as we have seen, studied the theory of efficiency in water wheels and he built many models, the first, in 1759, a wheel of two feet in diameter, to put his mathematical experiments to practical test. He showed how to increase the power generated by water wheels right up to the limits possible for wooden wheels. Before his time the possibilities of the breast-shot wheel were little understood, but after Smeaton's demonstration the breast wheel often replaced the old undershot wheels. Next General Poncelet, a French officer whose period of imprisonment by the Russians gave him time to develop his mathematical abilities, demonstrated an improved method of construction for small light iron undershot wheels, which ensured their extended popularity. By tilting the angle of the paddles and curving them he very much increased their efficiency without correspondingly increasing the expense of their installation, and he replaced the vertical sluice gate with an inclined one easily adjusted by means of a hand wheel. His simply expressed theory was that the water must enter the wheel without impact and leave it without energy to achieve the wheel's maximum efficiency.[57]

The various improvements which had been made in design began to place greater strain on some of the old wooden constructions than they could easily withstand. The Carron Iron Works had been opened at Falkirk in 1759 and Smeaton tried a cast iron axis for a water wheel there ten years later. He next replaced the wooden float boards with cast iron plates.[58] Murdoch, James Watt's assistant, used cast iron work at a mill in Ayrshire soon afterwards.[59] But iron for mill work was still in the experimental stage and neither of these attempts proved wholly satisfactory. Breakages remained common enough to prevent enthusiastic or immediate replacement of wood with iron. John Rennie, using wrought iron instead of cast iron, and sometimes cast iron of a superior manufacture, introduced iron into the construction of water wheels with more effect.

Wheels, whether under- or overshot, were most often situated against the gable end of a rectangular building and open to the elements. There are, however, many exceptions. Where power for more than one set of machinery was wanted and the intricacies of multiple gearing perhaps beyond the imagination of the local millwright, two or more wheels might be lined up along the long wall of the mill. Where a mill, usually a town mill, had extended its operations to both sides of a water course there might be two wheels side by side. This arrangement was suggested for Perth City Mills so that one wheel might power the oats and barley mills on one side of the lade, the other at the same time driving the flour and malt mills on the other bank, the whole thing, both wheels together, being encased in a stone wheelhouse, the top arched to allow the wheel to turn close to the stonework. The back wall of the wheelhouse had openings to allow water to enter the wheel, the front was open to allow its issue after use. At Craig Mill water was taken from the Dighty in a short lade through the mill to the wheel which, again, turned under a stone arc. At Midmill, which later became a bleachfield, a very large wooden undershot wheel turned in a lade flowing on the surface floor of the mill. In some few cases, such as the very interesting and well-preserved meal mill at Benvie, the wheel was installed under the floor of the mill and the lade brought underground to it. At Biggar in Lanarkshire a wheel constructed by James Watt, 'an ingenious millwright in Biggar', operated 50 feet below ground level.[60] This was a useful arrangement where later building had left a mill situated on the wrong side of a road from its original dam and lade.

Sometimes wooden wheelhouses were built to shelter the wheel, as at Balbirnie, which may have served to prevent icing up, but it is the action of the water on the wheel rather than the weather which wears out a mill wheel.

The choice of water wheel type continued to depend more upon the topography of the site than on the needs of the mill. The improvements in the design of wheels made by Smeaton, Rennie, Poncelet and, later, Fairbairn, were not made because their greater power was required by much innovation in the machinery of corn mills. Although the first applications of the new wheels were, in the case of the Scottish engineers, to corn mills, the spur to their adoption and development came with the application of water power to other industries and the experiments, not surprisingly, ceased with the substitution of steam for water power in manufacturing industry. The internal arrangements of the corn mill were left almost untouched by the half-century of studies of the efficiency of water wheels.

Two other methods of powering corn mills remain to be considered. Tide mills which, by damming water at high tide and letting it out gradually to turn a water wheel, took advantage of the power of the sea, were built at Aberdeen, Kirkwall, Burntisland, Musselburgh, Port Allen on the estuary of the Tay, and at Petty near Inverness.[61] Elton and Bennett quote a description of the Kirkwall mill on the Peerie Sea where 'the ebb or flow causes a current of great rapidity to run and an ingenious Orcadian has taken advantage of this to use it as the motive power of a great mill which he has planted on the causeway'.[62] At Burntisland the corn mill driven by the sea was said to work an average fourteen hours a day.[63] The sluice gate can still be seen which pent up the tidal water at Port Allen. Obviously this could never have been a common type of mill, the possible situations being so limited and the period of working not easily extended as long as that claimed for Burntisland.

For less obvious reasons windmills were also never common in Scotland. Donnachie has made a most interesting study of the windmill in Scotland[64] and Butt lists survivals in his *Industrial Archaeology of Scotland.*[65] Findlay says there were at least three for oatmeal in Aberdeenshire in the sixteenth and seventeenth centuries.[66] There was also one at Ceres in Fife, built for Captain Ker of Greenside, which threshed and ground corn and sawed wood 'and serves admirably the three purposes'.[67] The remains of a windmill used for threshing can still be seen at Bolshan farm in Angus. Andrew Meikle, we know, made experiments to improve the working of windmills.

Windmills are both expensive to construct and less reliable in action than water mills, there being no means of damming the wind as water can be dammed. The strength and gusts of winds in Scotland made windmills an even more dangerous prospect than in most parts of England, and the usually abundant water supply made the cheaper alternative almost always available. There was another disincentive to the expenditure by landowners in Scotland of the extra capital required for windmill building. In England tenants were bound to attend their landlord's windmill and pay *soke* rights there,[68] but in Scotland the law lords ruled that 'a tenant is not obliged by the nature of his thirlage to go to the pursuer's windmill, but only to his water mill to which he is thirled'.[69] This was not universally recognised. and the Dunbarney tenants in Perthshire were still thirled to the windmill there as late as the mid-nineteenth century.[70] But where there was doubt about the certainty of thirling tenants to the new mill, there was a powerful disincentive to windmill building in Scotland.

NOTES

1. Fenton, *The Northern Isles,* 388-90; Bennett and Elton, *History of Corn Milling,* 2, 26-8; Jespersen, *Mill Preservation in Denmark,* 225; Hay, 'Watermills in Japan', 321
2. See p. 35
3. Sage, *Memorabilia Domestica,* 1st ed. 1889; reprinted Edinburgh, 1975, introduction by D. Withrington, xi n.
4. Cruden, 'The horizontal water mill at Dounby', 81; Fenton, *Northern Isles,* 396-410
5. Bennett and Elton, *History of Corn Milling,* 20
6. Cruden, 'The horizontal water mill at Dounby', 43-5
7. Adam, *Sutherland Estate Management,* 2, 139
8. Quoted Sage, 1975, 65n.
9. *O.S.A.,* 13, 286

10. Macfarlane, Walter, *Geographical Collections*, Scottish History Society, Edinburgh, 1908, 184

11. *O.S.A.*, 6, 106

12. Usher, *A History of Mechanical Inventions*, 335-6, tables amount of h.p. per user for different kinds of mill

13. *O.S.A.*, 14, 149; Bennett and Elton, *History of Corn Milling*, 113; Morison, *Decisions of Court of Session*, 15976. See also Jespersen, *Mill Preservation in Denmark*, 224 and 'Portuguese Mills', *Transactions of 2nd Intl Symposium on Molinology*, 81

14. *O.S.A.*, 5, 193

15. *N.S.A.*, X, 576

16. Gunn, *Stitchill*, 29. Jamieson, *Dictionary*, gives *space* or *official situation* for *rowme*

17. Gunn, *Stitchill*, 29

18. Bennett and Elton, *History of Corn Milling*, 2, 27

19. Shaw, *Stair*, 243; Hunter, *Law of Landlord and Tenant*, 319

20. Usher, *Mechanical Inventions*, 335; Smiles, *Lives of the Engineers*, 225; Boucher, *John Rennie*, 6

21. Fitzherbert, Sir Anthony, *The Boke of Surveying*, 1539; Jones, 'Water powered corn mills', 305

22. S.R.O. GD 4/10

23. S.R.O. GD 154/460

24. Morison, *Decisions of Court of Session*, 9411. See also p. 30

25. Scott, *Engineer and Machinist's Assistant*, I, 68, 141; Gray, *The Experienced Millwright*, 44; 'Water powered corn mills', 315

26. Hamilton, *Scotland in the 18th Century*, 142

27. Smiles, *Lives of the Engineers*, 216

28. Morison, *Decisions of Court of Session*, 16049

29. *Ibid.*, 16050

30. *Ibid.*, 16058

31. Gray, *The Experienced Millwright*, 46, 49

32. *Ibid.*, 50

33. Morison, *Decisions of Court of Session*, 16057

34. *Ibid.*, 16039

35. Hamilton, *Life and Labour on an Aberdeenshire Estate*, 142-3

36. Wills, *Annexed Estates*, 65

37. States of the Annual Progress of the Linen Manufacture, S.R.O. NG1/14/27

38. Beatson, *General View of the Agriculture of the County of Fife*, 13

39. Jespersen, 'Watermills on the River Eden', 238; Turner, 'The significance of water power in industrial location: some Perthshire examples', 102, 114; Gauldie, Enid, Scottish Bleachfields, B.Phil. Dundee University, 1967, Appendix

40. Hunter, *Law of Landlord and Tenant*, 1, 472-3; Morison, *Decisions of Court of Session*, Appendix, *Tack*, 17
41. *N.S.A.*, IX, 725
42. Court of Session, Alex. Donald v. Robert Walker, 1856
43. *N.S.A.*, XIII, 191
44. Butt, *Industrial Archaeology of Scotland*, 39; *N.S.A.*, XIII, 275-6
45. Gauldie, Enid, *The Dundee Textile Industry, through the Papers of Peter Carmichael of Arthurstone*, S.H.S. Edinburgh, 1969, 15
46. Jones, 'Water powered corn mills', 354
47. *Ibid.*, 317
48. Alexander Gow to the Trustees of Alex McDougall, Sept. 1837 (NRA(S)1510)
49. Scott, *Engineer and Machinist's Assistant*, 68
50. *O.S.A.*, 7, 258
51. Gray, *The Experienced Millwright*, 44
52. Scott, *Engineer and Machinist's Assistant*, 205, 228
53. McDougall's Trustees, Copy Specifications and Repairs, 25 July 1837
54. Stephen, *Book of the Farm*, 1, 238
55. 'On water wheels with ventilating buckets', paper given before Institute of Civil Engineers, January 1849
56. Scott, *Engineer and Machinist's Assistant*, 217; Donnachie, *Galloway*, 34
57. Singer, Charles *et al.*, *History of Technology*, 4, 202-5, Oxford, 1958; Syson, *British Water Mills*, 79; Scott, *Engineer and Machinist's Assistant*, 228
58. Syson, *British Water Mills*, 54; Smiles, *Lives of the Engineers*, 226; Jones, 'Water powered corn mills', 317
59. Smiles, *Lives of the Engineers*, 226
60. *N.S.A.*, VI, 365
61. Findlay, *Oats*, 178
62. Bennett and Elton, *History of Corn Milling*, 223. *Peerie* means 'little'
63. *N.S.A.*, IX, 416
64. Donnachie and Stewart, 'Scottish Windmills', 278-80; Donnachie, *Galloway*, 40-42
65. Butt, *Industrial Archaeology of Scotland*, 35-6
66. Findlay, *Oats*, 178
67. *N.S.A.*, IX, 526
68. Bennett and Elton, *History of Corn Milling*, 319
69. Morison, *Decisions of Court of Session*, 8898
70. *N.S.A.*, X, 818

8
Millwrights — The Genius of the Mill

To understand the emergence in eighteenth century Scotland of the great millwright-engineers one must first stretch the imagination to suppose children without toys except those made for them by their parents and friends. Millers, because of some manual dexterity, some mechanical ingenuity, a curious turn of mind and a life which included among long hours of hard labour other hours of enforced idleness, were great toymakers. Donald Sage described, with the same nostalgia a later generation preserved for its toy trains, the toy mills he had as a boy: 'The revolution of the water wheel occupied far more of my waking, and even of my sleeping, thoughts than the revolutions of kingdoms do now. The mill was distinctly visible from the manse windows, and its stillness and its activity were among the first unusual objects that attracted my attention . . . the rim, the spokes and the circular shower of drops which, by the rapidity of its motion, it threw up around it . . . John Ross, the miller of Kildonan, a stout young fellow who held the mill in lease from my father, presented me with a windmill. His present rivetted my affections and I followed him like his shadow.' Then, later: 'My brother and I were, as boys, of mechanical turn. We were always building houses and mills in imitation of those at Kildonan. We built a clay house at the back of the manse, and below the bank of the mill-lade we had mills as closely resembling their larger and far more useful prototypes as our limited capacities could produce.'[1]

Another little boy who played with mill toys was John Rennie: 'The millwright had taken a strong liking to the boy and he let him have the run of his workshop and allowed him to make his miniature water-mills with tools of his own.'[2] Not surprisingly, among the many little boys who played with such things, only to discard them when another activity attracted them, there were a few bright children whose attention was more permanently engaged by them who continued, when the others had gone fishing or birds' nesting, to wander back to the mill to watch the magical turning of its machinery. Of these, some, like Rennie, grew up to be world-famous engineers, progressing, through the knowledge gained in corn mills of the possibilities of machinery, to design steam-powered mills, bridges, docks and canals. Others, without the backing of an educated or moneyed family, remained in the station to which they had been born, to become the ingenious millers and millwrights who were to instigate and carry out the improvements in mills achieved between about 1780 and 1850.

Among the best known of Scottish millwrights was Andrew Meikle who died in 1811 at the very great age of 91, a remarkable man in every way. He was the son of the James Meikle who was taken with Mrs Henry Fletcher of Saltoun on her famous trip of industrial espionage to Holland, then greatly in advance of both England and Scotland in technology. They returned with not only 'the whole art and secret of bleaching', then more efficient in the Low Countries than in Scotland, but the plans of the pot barley mill which was to be so profitably imitated all over Scotland and with an idea for a winnowing machine. James Meikle's winnower in imitation of the Dutch[3] was a simple contrivance consisting of an enclosed fly wheel which blew the chaff out as it rotated, the cleaned corn falling clear.

Henry Fletcher was the brother of Andrew Fletcher of Saltoun,[4] known as 'the Patriot' for his vociferous opposition to the Union. He drew up an article of agreement with James Meikle in 1710, putting clearly in writing what he wanted him to do. Meikle, who is described as 'wright in Wester Keith', was to travel to the Low Countries 'to learn there the perfect art of sheeling barley' and 'how to accommodate, order and erect milns for that purpose'. He was then to arrange passage on the first man o' war returning to Scotland. Either Mrs Henry did not want his company on the way back or they feared his apprehension by the Dutch with valuable industrial secrets on his person.[5]

On his return he was settled by the Saltoun family at Houston Mill, East Lothian. There his son Andrew was born in 1719.[6] Andrew Meikle is best known for his invention of the threshing mill, patented in 1788, a device which was to revolutionise agriculture by reducing drastically the number of servants needed on farms and by allowing the speed-up and commercialisation of corn milling. Without the thresher the delivery of corn from the farms to the mill was so slow as to make any speed-up of grinding unnecessary and of little advantage. But although the threshing machine is Meikle's best-known invention it was by no means his only one. He seems to have had little commercial ambition and to have produced most of his improvements in mill work chiefly for his own delight in their ingenuity. He was certainly ahead of his times in applying multiple gearing to his own mill and in fact stretched the possibilities of gear wheels and extended drive to such an extent as to alarm his neighbours. Samuel Smiles passed on an amusing story illustrating Meikle's delight in providing motive power for anything that could be turned, moved or rocked: 'One day a woman came to the mill to get some barley ground and was desired to sit in the cottage hard by until it was ready. With the first sound of the mill wheels the cradle and churn at her side began to rock and to churn, as if influenced by some supernatural agency. No one was in the house but herself and she rushed from it frightened almost out of her wits. Such incidents as these brought an ill name on Andrew and the neighbours declared that he was "no canny".'[7]

The importance of the threshing mill has, unfortunately for this study, obscured the other inventive work of this long-lived man. The thresher was patented in 1788. Meikle was already 69.[8] During his life up to that date he was doing the work of a country miller, grinding small orders of oatmeal and barley flour such as Samuel Smiles' old lady brought to his mill, adapting his machinery to increase its efficiency and, incidentally, attracting the attention of neighbouring millers by his ingenious adaptations. He began to be sought after at greater and greater distances to make repairs and give advice. Meanwhile the estate on which Houston Mill stood had fallen into the hands of Mr George Rennie who had built for himself the house of Phantassie. Rennie's son John was the kind of little boy who today would be found at the local garage, taking motor cycles to pieces. In the eighteenth century he played near the mill stream, haunted the mill, and made for himself little wooden water wheels to turn in the lade. By the age of 12, in 1773, his family, who had well-based pretensions to a rather grander walk of life for their son, accepted the permanence of his obsession and allowed him to become apprenticed to Andrew Meikle at the mill. Andrew's son George was also learning the trade. There was obviously a useful cross-fertilisation of ideas between them. Although the period of Meikle's fame comes after Rennie's apprenticeship to him, and although the interest taken in him by a landed family like the Rennies obviously helped to publicise his ingenuity, it would be unwise to give too much importance to Rennie's influence on Meikle. Rennie was a child, almost a disciple, of a man already recognised. Meikle had taken out his first patent in 1768 for a corn-dressing machine, but although this was his first patented device it was by no means his first invention. Smiles calls the 1768 patent 'one of the very first taken out by any Scotch mechanic',[9] and the case is that few millers or wrights had then either the capital or the knowledge of the business world to spur them into patenting their mill improvements. This machine was patented with the help of a surveyor, Robert Mackell, who was one of the gentlemen who took an interest in Meikle in an age when mechanical innovations were a very fashionable interest for Scottish professional men. In 1772 Meikle patented the spring sail for windmills. Until then it had been necessary for the miller to turn the sails into the wind, a heavy and laborious task. Meikle's invention provided automatic adaptation to the wind's direction. His work on increasing the power of windmills and water wheels went on throughout his life.

A first attempt at a threshing machine had been made some years before Meikle produced his first improvement on it in 1776 and his successful machine took another twelve years to perfect. After its patenting he was called for by landowners all over the country to make improvements to their corn mills. This was a period during which the commercial pressures upon the ancient mills were just beginning to be widely felt. Proprietors of mills were beginning to recognise the advantage of having one modern and efficient mill to which their tenants would willingly bring their corn rather than a number of decrepit mills to which only constant harrying by the factor could drive them. Landowners grew interested in the efficiency of their mills, as well as the income from them, in many cases for the first time. Hearing of some one as clever as Meikle they sent for him to give advice as to what should be done to put the old mills in order. At first, naturally, the orders came from landowners neighbouring Phantassie and from the Lothians. But nothing so clearly illustrates the shortage of skilled millwrights in eighteenth century Scotland as the wide extent of country covered by Meikle in the last quarter of the century. It was at this stage that Meikle, already an old man, was glad to make use of the clever young Rennie to execute some of his orders from far afield.

In 1779 Rennie set up a millwright's business of his own. He was then only 18 and most of his work was the overflow from Meikle's shop. His first job was to build a threshing mill at Phantassie for his brother George who had inherited the estate, his second to design machinery for a corn mill at Invergowrie, near Dundee.[10] The river embankment of this mill and one corner of the wall are all that is left of a mill which was one of the earliest pieces of work of a world-famous engineer. Rennie next advised on and built the machinery for Bonnington Mill in Edinburgh. This was the mill where, in 1780, he first attempted the use of cast iron pinions instead of the old-fashioned wooden trundles, or lantern pinions, then in common use. The experiment was successful and he continued to extend the use of iron parts in millwork. He then designed machinery for the town mill of Kirkcaldy, Proctor's Mill at Glamis, and Carron Foundry Mills.[11] His next years were filled with work of this kind. But because he was interested not only in the practical application but also in the theory of mathematics he attended the classes of Professor Robison at the University of Edinburgh between 1780 and 1783, continuing to execute orders for millwright work all the time he was at college.

Meanwhile James Watt and Matthew Boulton had been planning the building of a flour mill in Blackfriars in London, to be driven by steam. They had been having trouble with the design and had been unable to find millwrights with sufficient skill to help them. Watt made contact with the reputedly brilliant young Rennie in Edinburgh and he agreed to travel to London to supervise the fitting up of Albion Mills. The work was so successful as to make Albion Mills and its young millwright internationally famous. Watt and Boulton had installed two double acting engines producing 150 h.p. Rennie harnessed this power to turn 20 pairs of millstones, each 4′ 6″ in diameter and producing 150 bushels of flour each hour. It was a phenomenal rate of production for the eighteenth century: flour mills turned by water seldom ground more than five bushels of flour in an hour.[12] It turned the milling of flour into a modern industry and it made John Rennie famous. 'Noble lords came and saw and in due course came back as customers with orders for mills.' Rennie was proud of the smooth working of his machinery and wrote to his brother George: 'so quietly did she go that many workmen in the building did not know it.'[13] This was in itself an astonishing achievement because the average corn mill of the time shook and clattered so that every one within and without the building knew when it started work.

Rennie was asked to fit out flour mills all over Britain and Europe. The Leith mills he superintended himself. For corn mills in Spain, Portugal and France he designed and made the machinery in his own workshop and sent it abroad with assistants to see to its installation.[14]

By the time Albion Mills burnt down and Rennie took over the site for an enlarged millwright's and engineering business of his own, he had become the foremost engineer of his day.

Even after he had branched out into large-scale engineering, designing docks, canals and bridges, he continued to be sought after for millwork. Glasgow Town Council, for instance, at the end of the eighteenth century found the leases of all their town mills running to a close and, in the hope of raising more money from them, decided to put them in good repair and advertise tacks with longer leases to attract millers of some repute. 'In anticipation of reletting all the mills at an advantage it was recommended that a report should be obtained from a competent millwright as to any suitable improvements and that the mills should be let on 19 years lease.'[15] In the usual way of town councils the affair had to run through the hands of a number of subcommittees before it occurred to someone that the reputable engineer then constructing Broomielaw Docks might give the mills some attention. In 1807 the Lord Provost produced before the Council a report which the committee had obtained 'from Mr Rennie, engineer, relative to the improvement of the mills and stated that it was the opinion of the committee that plans ought to be got from Mr Rennie of the alterations and improvements which he had suggested.'[16]

Meanwhile George Meikle, Rennie's fellow apprentice at Houston Mill, had been achieving a more modest fame of his own. It was George who had been engaged by Lord Kames to advise on the draining of Kincardine Moss. He invented there an enormous wheel with buckets to raise the water which was one of the wonders of its age.[17] Leaving his father, he set up business on his own account in Alloa.[18] It seems likely that he came to Alloa on the encouragement of Hugh Reoch, a farmer from East Lothian — where of course the Meikle family were well known — who had taken a 200-acre farm at Hilltown of Alloa. The barony of Alloa had been allowed to run down so that agriculture there was abysmally inefficient until, in the 1770s, the old tacks began to run out and the land was let on longer leases and firmer conditions to intelligent farmers such as Reoch who put the land in good heart and, by example, 'quickened the diligence of his neighbours'.[19]

In 1787 Meikle built a water-powered threshing mill at Kilbagie in Clackmannanshire. This was in the year before his father's thresher was patented and was by way of an experiment. Six were built very shortly afterwards in the neighbouring county. Meikle was, as a result, asked to fit up the old town mills of Alloa to modern competence. He installed two water wheels, each nineteen feet in diameter, that is, very much larger than the usual wheel, which drove wheat and oats mills in one end of the 93-foot long building, malt and barley mills in the other. 'The machinery alone cost £500 and is uncommonly well executed . . . the mills . . . can be wrought on a great exertion and are capable of grinding 400 bolls in a day.'[20]

In 1795 he was consulted by Lanark Town Council about the need for improvements to the town's mill, which had the attractive name of Mousemill. He advised adding a storey to the mill to accommodate new machinery for wheat and corn, and the installation of a new barley mill and an improved kiln. The newly equipped mill was insured by Glasgow Fire Office for £250 in 1808, a sensible precaution as it burned to the ground — the fate of so many mills — in 1810.[21]

George became, then, a relatively prosperous millwright. He was not, however, as long-lived as his father and died only two days after his father's death, on 30th November 1811. Andrew had failed to make a fortune with his threshing machine and mill improvements, having generously allowed them to be copied all over Europe without financial advantage to himself. When the nineteenth century opened he was feeble as well as old, poverty-stricken and in need of care. On 26th December 1809, a meeting of the important landowners whose estates had benefited so immeasurably from his inventions was held to discuss what could be done for him. The meeting was the result of letters sent to them by James Macnab, describing Meikle's pitiable condition. Those who attended agreed to subscribe ten guineas, but the response was poor and ungrateful.[22]

William Fairbairn was another of the famous engineers who devoted some of his early attention to the improvement of corn-milling machinery. In his *Treatise on Mills and Millwork* he devoted ten pages of his first chapter to the history of mills, and he had some interesting things to say. The first machinery for corn mills, he said, was brought to Scotland from the Low Countries. This is probably a reference to James Meikle's trip to Holland and his introduction of the pot barley mill and winnower. 'As however such contrivances became more used a class of native artificers sprang up who made it their business to attend them . . . They designed and erected windmills and watermills for grinding corn, pumping apparatus and all the various kinds of rough machinery in use in those days . . . The millwright of former days was to a great extent the sole representative of mechanical art and was looked upon as the authority on all applications of wind and water . . . he went about the country from mill to mill, an itinerant engineer and mechanic of high reputation.'[23] Fairbairn himself was extensively employed in building cornmills abroad and throughout Great Britain. One, designed for His Excellency the Seraskier Halil Pacha of Constantinople, was said, in 1847, to show the very best methods of modern construction.[24]

We have seen that the Meikle family, James, Andrew and George, spanning more than a century between them, along with John Rennie, were responsible for spreading information and practical skill in mill work throughout the whole of Lowland Scotland. Another family to have very considerable influence on the millwright trade was that of Umpherston of Loanhead. By the 1780s there had already been four generations of Umpherstons practising as country millwrights in the same place. A number of apprentices lived in the house with Umpherston and, after a day's work in the shop, he would discuss with them some of the new ideas in mechanical theory which were beginning to circulate. It was, for instance, a startlingly new idea to them that bevel wheels could be made at angles other than 45°. The few books then published on practical mechanics were prohibitively expensive and the libraries which might have lent them were out of reach of country workers, but Umpherston subscribed to *Hall's Encyclopedia*, which was then appearing in periodical numbers and was eagerly read by millwrights. One of Umpherston's apprentices was his nephew, James Carmichael. After serving his time, he went from Loanhead to Glasgow to work for Messrs Thomson and Buchanan and there he helped Robertson Buchanan to work out the tables for his *Treatise on Millwork*. Until the very end of the eighteenth century millwrights had no useful textbooks in which to find solutions to the problems which occurred when they attempted the multiplication of gearing. The problems were only then being approached theoretically. Buchanan's treatise went into edition after edition. It was revised first by Thomas Tredgold, who added notes and additional articles, and later by George Rennie, who published his *Practical examples of modern tools and machines, being supplementary to the edition of Buchanan on millwork* in 1842. Another useful book was William Templeton's *Millwright and engineer's pocket companion* of 1833. The need for instruction for the many hundreds of young apprentices employed in the new steam-powered spinning mills caused the publication of a number of similar volumes from the second quarter of the nineteenth century. The corn millers benefited from the increased interest taken in practical mechanics, even country millwrights whose trade was confined to the maintenance of old water-powered meal mills being inspired by the climate of intellectual activity in their subject. The best-known textbook for the meal miller, Andrew Gray's *Experienced Millwright*, published in Edinburgh in 1804, showed very little in the way of new inventions, but it demonstrated the best practice and the proven methods of construction in a trade which had hitherto been without such a guide.

James Carmichael and his brother Charles, who also served an apprenticeship with their maternal uncle Umpherston, moved in 1810 to Dundee where they established what was to become the famous and important firm of James and Charles Carmichael. They left the world of the country millwrights to become maritime and locomotive engineers, to construct steam engines and machinery for the spinning mills. The textile trade absorbed many of their generation who had been trained in the shops of those country wrights who served the old meal mills.[25]

But although these were among the most famous names, there were scores of others who stayed in the old trade, many of them of considerable skill and inventiveness. Some continued to work as millers while they adapted and improved their own machinery and that of their neighbours, some leaving the mill and concentrating on the founding of a millwright business. Dr Butt describes one John Innes who, being engaged to supervise the building of the meal mill at Dalmon, Stornoway, remained to become its first miller.[26] It would certainly have been more usual for him to be miller first, millwright second. Perhaps he reverted to the mill when he found one set up to his own liking and showing the possibility of a good living.

In the first half of the eighteenth century millwrights were seldom differentiated from wrights in general. The millwright of the early nineteenth century was a blend of joiner, wheelwright and miller. The Old Statistical Account mentions very few indeed in its lists of parish occupations, while by the time of the New Statistical Account they are beginning to be men of some local standing. Eighteenth century millers who needed parts for their mills which they could not make themselves would turn to the blacksmith for metal work, the joiner or 'wright' for the kind of woodwork which might require tools not on the miller's own workbench. It is worth considering how few would be the parts requiring this specialist attention. Spindles and shafts could snap and require a smith for their replacement, but it would be an infrequent occurrence. The mill rynd was a piece of iron fixed to the upper millstone, but once in position it would last the life of the stone. The trundle or lantern pinion into which the teeth of the spur wheel engaged was a wooden contrivance whose parts were easily enough replaced. Iron teeth on the cog wheels began to be substituted for the hardwoods of which they had formerly been made only after about 1780. Iron was used for the water wheel by John Smeaton in 1769 for the first time, and entirely wooden wheels remained in common use long afterwards. Some shrouding with iron became common in the early nineteenth century but was by no means always adopted. It was required by John Duncan, the millwright from Balbrogie, in his first report for the Perth City Mills, but was omitted on grounds of economy from the final specification.[27]

Certainly it was the introduction of iron parts to mill machinery which brought about the common employment of the distinct trade of millwright. This was especially so in the period, before the setting up of specialist parts manufacturers, when each millwright had to improvise the parts for individual mills. The individual adaptations to particular circumstances are the characteristics which give each remaining water-powered mill its own special quality, and perhaps it was the need for a sensitive response to the mills' problems which first gave them their feminine gender. At any rate, as Smiles wrote, 'millers were under the necessity of sending one portion to the blacksmith, another to the carpenter'[28] when they were attempting their own running repairs. As millwrights emerged they were at first forced to use the apparatus of the older trades. 'In the course of their trade they worked at the foot-lathe, the carpenter's bench, and the anvil, by turns,'[29] said Smiles, in almost exactly the same words as those used by Fairbairn in his *Treatise on Mills and Millwork.*[30] Both books were published in the same year. Could both have been quoting from an earlier work?

There were many jobs which the early millwrights were only very slightly better equipped than the miller to do. They were in some cases unaware of the importance of precise calculation, as, for instance, of the number of teeth engaging on cogged wheels. Even if they recognised the need they were unable without modern machine tools, and without tables or established methods of mathematical calculation they could only fall short of precision. The cutting out of spaces to hold the wooden teeth of a gear wheel, for instance, was a tedious business and open to mistakes.[31]

We know that many mills were being rebuilt and refurbished by the middle of the eighteenth century and that the necessary skills to carry out these improvements existed within the miller fraternity. The adaptation of oat-milling machinery to suit wheat, for instance, was carried out with the minimum of difficulty by the miller on the spot who was forced to make the change if he hoped to keep his trade.[32] Some repairs and changes were clumsily made, resulting in frequent changes and exasperating delays at the mill for the customers. One of the complaints of the Commissioners for the Annexed Estates was the difficulty experienced in finding craftsmen of any sort. As most of the commissioners came from the civilised environs of Edinburgh where Mr Meikle or someone else of his kind could easily be found, the lack of men skilled in the mechanical arts was frustrating to them in their attempts at estate improvement. 'Farming is the only respectable profession in these countries, but if artificers were put upon a more respectable footing than at present it would tend both to the promoting of industry among them and to the improvement of agriculture. They have few tradesmen just now and those are the dregs of the country. Wrights, masons, wheel-wrights, plough-wrights, millwrights etc. when wanted, the inhabitants are obliged to bring from other countries at a great expense. I should, therefore, humbly propose that a number of young lads, sons of the principal tenants, should be bred to these several occupations.'[33]

One miller/millwright who was obviously not typical of the region was Alexander Robertson of Miln of Brunty. Before 1755 he had, as well as enclosing and improving the mill farm land and rebuilding the houses, built a lint mill and a barley mill turned by the same stream as turned the older corn mill, and moved by the same wheel, which must mean that he had some notion how to extend the drive from his water wheel. He employed several men at the mill and made all the improvements himself. 'He is quite a common country man . . . and he is of that turn of temper as to be happy in communicating to his neighbours everything he thinks would turn out to their advantage.'[34]

The first quarter of the nineteenth century saw a fairly rapid multiplication of the numbers of millwrights in that part of the country. Mr Crichton of Dunblane, engaged in the erection of a number of different kinds of mill on his estate, brought in George Morgan, a young man of 22 from Kincardine on Forth. He superintended the building of meal mills at Machary and the Hosh in 1829. Orders flowed in from neighbouring farmers, and in 1832 he set up business as a millwright in

Crieff. His first contract was the outfitting of the meal mill at Dalvreck. His became a very large firm surviving into the twentieth century. Crichton, however, was not the only millwright in Crieff. William Robertson, who died in 1843, had a great deal of business in the surrounding countryside and was thought of as 'the principal millwright in Crieff'. It may have been because Robertson was over-extended and perhaps keeping his customers waiting that Mr Crichton found it worthwhile to bring in George Morgan. There was, apparently, business enough in Crieff for both of them, as well as for another who was also known for the excellence of his work called Thomas M'Duff.[35]

Another Perthshire millwright was James Frazer, described in the *New Statistical Account* as 'artist, inventor and millwright'.[36] He was miller at the mill of Dowally where he erected a wheel which drove a saw mill and a threshing mill, turning lathes and grindstones as well as bellows for a furnace. This was a man of much more than usual ingenuity. As well as his mill business he designed a ferry boat for the river crossing at Logierait which used the principle of the Archimedes screw as early as 1822, but too late to benefit from patenting the invention. The ingenuity of millers did not always reap a financial reward. William Nairne of Mill-hole near Logie Almond, 'a man who had the gift of speech and much mechanical ingenuity', invented a machine for reeling yarn and a power loom shuttle which were both put into very general use in factories without financial benefit to himself.[37] James Brownhill, however, miller at Alloa, was another ingenious miller and, perhaps because his substitution of local stone for French burr was a money saver easily adopted by other mills, he was rewarded by a grant from the Society for the Encouragement of the Arts.[38] Robertson of Brunty, on the other hand, had applied to the Board of Trustees many times for an 'encouragement' without receiving one.[39]

All the men practising the new trade of millwright were not, of course, equally brilliant. Even in the ancient business of corn milling, changes to the machinery were inclined to be hit and miss, so small a change of balance could affect the smooth running of the wheels and stones. Perhaps even more difficult to acquire than the mechanical skills was the business sense and organisational ability needed to run a millwright's shop. Without established parts manufacturers and uniform pricing the estimating of final costs was chancy even for an experienced man. Undoubtedly some young millwrights, anxious for business, offered competitive tenders so low as to be impossible of fulfilment without loss to themselves. Such a one was Alexander Gow, who, in offering for the repairs to Perth City Mills in 1837, put in a tender which amounted to less than half the price estimated by the more experienced man, John Duncan, who had drawn up the specifications for the job. By 27 August 1838 the managers were complaining of the 'extra ordinary delay in completing his contract' and 'as there appears to be no probability of Gow's finishing the work unless compelled by legal measures' they requested the miller 'to get out of Gow's hands any articles which he may now have completed for the mills and which may be lying in his own premises . . .' after which the Agents were directed to present a petition to the Sheriff against Gow. Gow was not inefficient at his craft. When the work was finally completed, in December of 1838, it was passed as done 'in a substantial and workmanlike manner and in excellent working condition and every way adapted to the purposes intended'. He had simply, like so many small tradesmen, found it difficult to handle the financial side of his business competently.[40]

However the fact that it was, by the 1830s, customary to invite competitive tendering for millwright work shows the extent to which the trade had grown in the previous fifty years. In the 1780s the few recognised millwrights practising in Scotland were sent for from great distances to advise and carry out mill work, there being no question of local competition. Now, even a country town had in its neighbourhood a largish number of millwrights to choose from so that each had to compete in efficiency and in pricing for the work available.[41]

There were several reasons for the increase in the numbers of millwrights. First, of course, was the general improvement in agriculture and the increased grain production which created a demand for more efficient milling. Especially during the period of the French Wars, the farmers' increased prosperity along with their new freedom from the restrictions and discouragements of thirlage, gave them an interest in the building and improving of the mills on their land. More particularly, the introduction of the threshing machine, taken up by farmers with enormous enthusiasm at the beginning of the nineteenth century, had three important effects. In the first place it removed a disincentive. Hand threshing had allowed so slow a delivery of grain to the mill that there would be no advantage in speeding the grinding process. The analogy is with hand weaving. As long as spinning was a domestic, hand process, there was no incentive to invent powered weaving. The hand looms were already delayed by the slow supply of yarn. Once spinning became water-powered the hand loom weavers enjoyed a short-lived heyday of prosperity while they were in great demand to make up the yarn now flowing so much faster from the mills; but commercial pressures soon ensured that their craft, too, was speeded up, powered and modernised. So with grain. The invention of the threshing machine meant that farmers could deliver larger quantities of grain to the mills at one time and that they expected it to be quickly processed.

The greater pressures thus put upon the mills required a greater measure of efficiency from the ancient mills. Parts which had survived a century of desultory use yielded to constant and more hurried action. Because threshing machines were a new invention, their working not yet understood by the average countryman without some demonstration, they were normally installed by wrights. It was natural that the millwright, called in about the thresher, should be consulted about the mill itself. Thus the attention of new and skilled men, knowledgeable about the best milling practice because they travelled the district while installing threshers, was given to the grinding process.

Threshing machines were very often horse powered and special round or octagonal horse mill houses were built for them, of which a great many remain.[42] But where an efficient water supply existed, which of course it did on those farms where corn mills were already sited, it was found much more economical to use water power. Water was 'the readiest, steadiest and, what is more important, the cheapest power . . . horses are, of course, held as the most expensive of the powers, next to them steam, and last of all wind.'[43] The threshing mills, then, were very often so arranged as to be driven by the same motive power as the corn mill.

With the introduction of steam power to grain milling, the millwright trade divided into two quite distinct varieties. Large firms of millwrights, supplied by machine parts factories, evolved to serve the town-based, steam-powered, white flour roller mills which processed imported wheat. In the countryside, where the grinding of locally grown oats continued to be performed in small water-powered mills by traditional methods, country millwrights continued their small-scale businesses. Much of their work entailed the renewing of small metal parts but occasionally a firm would get a contract to refit a whole mill. Duncan Thompson and Son, Craibstone, then the firm most experienced in meal mill work, were engaged in 1920 by Mr Robert Dunbar to renew the whole Mill of Cowie, near Stonehaven. Five millwrights were kept busy there for fifteen months. Mr George Davidson, now retired, was one of those young men and he has described the improvements then made: 'Everything was of the latest, a 12 quarter kiln, with built in hoppers under the colm of the kiln with shaking spouts all round to convey the dried grain to where it was wanted. We had thirteen sets of elevators which did away with a lot of manual work for the miller and his staff. We also installed a new water wheel, fourteen feet diameter, four feet wide. This was a start in aw wheel, under shot.'[44] This mill is now out of action after running for fifty years.

The variety of the problems presented by different mills produced a variety of solutions. Not every millwright solved the same problem the same way. Where the experience of one firm differed widely from that of another, expertise in one field could lead to a prejudice on the millwright's part in favour of one method of operation rather than another. In some spheres this could produce quite noticeable regional differences, first in the engineering of the mill and, as a result, in the mill's product. The adoption of different systems for the sifting of the different grades of oatmeal, for instance, may have affected the cut of meal most often produced, a coarser cut being popular in Midlothian than in the north. Even after the rationalisation of mill parts there remained scope for skill, ingenuity and invention in the work of the millwright.

NOTES

1. Sage, *Memorabilia Domestica*, 1975, 78, 94
2. Smiles, *Lives of the Engineers*, 195
3. But probably of Chinese origin. See Berg, Gosta, 'The introduction of the winnowing machine in Europe in the 18th century', 35
4. Later Lord Milton, one of the Board of Trustees for Manufactures, at whose meetings he had the opportunity to publicise the Saltoun mills
5. *Farmers Magazine*, 1800, 158-9; Fenton, *Scottish Country Life*, 91, 99, 104
6. Gray and Jamieson, *East Lothian Biographies*; see also Walker, 'Fixed farm machinery', 52-74
7. Smiles, *Lives of the Engineers*, 211
8. In his old age Meikle was reduced to poverty which was alleviated only very slightly by the efforts of a few landowners to raise subscriptions for him from among those who had benefited so much by his invention. S.R.O. GD 9 332/1; 332/2
9. Smiles, *Lives of the Engineers*, 203
10. Boucher, *John Rennie*, 78; Smiles, *Lives of the Engineers*, 213. This was

a flour mill. The *Dundee Advertiser* carried an advertisement on 26 October 1810 'for the flour mills of Invergowrie, a man who understands the whole business of a flour mill'

11. Smiles, *Lives of the Engineers*, 213; Boucher, *John Rennie*, 123
12. Usher, *A History of Mechanical Inventions*, 335
13. Boucher, *John Rennie*, 11
14. *Ibid.*, 13
15. Marwick and Renwick, *Extracts from the Records of the Burgh of Glasgow*, 26, 34-5
16. *Ibid.*, 621. Incidentally he had to sue Glasgow for payment of his fees
17. Gray and Jamieson, *East Lothian Biographies*; Tytler, *Kames*, 28-9
18. Smiles, *Lives of the Engineers*, 210
19. *O.S.A.*, 8, 597-9
20. *Ibid.*
21. Robertson, *Lanark*, 274
22. S.R.O. GD 332/1; 332/2
23. Pole, *Life of Sir William Fairbairn*, 26
24. Scott, *Engineer and Machinist's Assistant*, 85
25. Gauldie, Enid, *The Dundee Textile Industry, through the Papers of Peter Carmichael of Arthurstone*, S.H.S. Edinburgh, 1969, 87-8
26. Butt, *Industrial Archaeology of Scotland*, 40
27. M'Dougall's Trustees, Copy Report by Mr John Duncan, Minutes, 12 June 1837 (NRA[S] 1510)
28. Smiles, *Lives of the Engineers*, 216
29. *Ibid.*, 131
30. Fairbairn, *Treatise on Mills and Millwork*, 26
31. Scott, *Engineer and Machinist's Assistant*, 84
32. Morison, *Decisions of Court of Session*, 16074, 16049
33. Wills, *Annexed Estates*, 86
34. *Ibid.*, 19
35. Porteous, *History of Crieff*, 182
36. *N.S.A.*, X, 997
37. Gauldie, *op. cit.*, 100 and n.
38. See p. 93
39. Wills, *Annexed Estates*, 19
40. M'Dougall's Trustees, Minutes, 14 December 1838 (NRA[S] 1510)
41. See also Donnachie, *Galloway*, 37
42. Hutton, 'Distribution of wheel-houses'; Walker, 'Fixed farm machinery', 52-74
43. Smith, Robert, junior of Huntly, 'On the extended application of water power', *T.H.A.S.S.* 2, 7, 64
44. In Scotland a wooden paddle wheel is called a *start and awe* wheel, the *start* being the piece of wood which supports the *awe*. See p. 132

9

Later Technology — Improvements to the Mill

Partly as a result of the extra attention by millwrights — and partly occasioning such attention — some interesting additions were made to corn mills during the late eighteenth and early nineteenth centuries. The mills, which had remained essentially the same in design from Roman times until the eighteenth century, now saw some changes.[1] As the *Engineer and Machinist's Assistant* put it: 'The operation of reducing the fruits of the harvest into a state fit for becoming the food of man, is naturally the earliest in point of date as well as the first in point of importance, to which the aids of mechanical science have been applied and although the machinery required for effecting it is not, perhaps, of such a nature as to admit that indefinite improvement of which many of the processes in the mechanical arts are susceptible, it has, nevertheless, from time to time, undergone important ameliorations . . . Modern practice differs but little from that which has been in use for many centuries: the corn being caused to pass between two horizontal stones . . . the lower stone being immoveable, while the upper one revolves upon a spindle . . . Simple as we have announced it to be it has partaken so largely of the mechanical improvements of modern times as to have changed the character of the corn mill from a rude and unwieldy combination of timber, stone and iron into a highly elegant and efficient piece of machinery.'[2]

One of the additions made to those mills which processed wheat flour and which, therefore, made the distinction between a 'flour' mill and a 'meal' mill, was the *bolting* machine. Again, it would be easier to be certain of the date of the bolter's arrival in Scottish mills if the word were used only for the mechanical contrivance. But 'to bolt' means merely 'to sieve' and a 'boulter' in an inventory may mean nothing more than an ordinary hand sieve. An inventory in the Dunglass papers lists 'three Bouteing cloaths, two wide sieves, three punches, a door, a bush chisle, a white iron scap, a harp, an old spindle, a bout miln and Trouch'.[3] In general, it is fairly safe to say that bolters were most often introduced into flour mills at the point where the local baker trade, the Baxter Incorporation, or individual baking firms, took over the leases of town mills. Sieving the flour to produce as fine and white a grade as possible had hitherto been a tedious and wasteful hand operation carried out by apprentices in the bakers' shops. Given the power of the mill, it was natural that they should seek to extend it to the sieving process. In England bolting machines had been fitted into mills from the beginning of the eighteenth century and bolting by bakers had ceased by the end of the century.[4] In Scotland, because wheat flour was not so generally used, the introduction of the machine was probably later but its use in town mills was probably general by the end of the century.[5] That the bolting mill was introduced by the baker who took a tack of the mill and not by the mill proprietor is shown by an agreement between the town council of Cupar, Fife and John Inglis, baker in Cupar, in 1792. Inglis leased 'all and haill the flour, corn, malt and barley milns and kilns belonging to the burgh of Cupar, the whole machinery thereof *except the fence for boulting the flour* [my italics] which is the property of the tacksman but for which he is bound to leave a boulting miln in good order . . .'[6] Later in the same document the word 'tinie' is used instead of 'fence'. Both are probably descriptions of what the machine looked like. It consisted of a fine wire screen fitted on to a frame over which the flour was shaken or brushed. Later models were cylindrical and fitted inside with a revolving brush. The best-equipped mills had both cloth bolting and wire bolting machines. Gray describes a mill which contained both, and a good description of an 'improved' mill designed by Fairbairn gives illustrations of the later form.[7] The mill bolter gave the miller complete control over the quality of the flour because the processes were now all in his own hands, whereas shelling had once been the farmer's task and bolting the baker's.

In the long run it was probably the installation of grading, cleaning and sieving machinery of varying degree of sophistication which made the difference between the most efficient mills able, because of the known quality of their product, to capture a share of markets at some distance from them, and the unimproved country mills. A high quality white groat, which makes the best meal for some customers, can only be produced by cleaning and sifting between each stage of milling. Kennerty Mills in Peterculter still produce this white groat by water power, as do Chirnside Mills in the Border country. In early mills riddling and sieving were done by hand in round sieves with different grades of aperture made of whatever material lay commonly to hand, but often of split cane. During the eighteenth century mill fanners and sieves powered by water were introduced for the preliminary stage of removing chaff, thistles and other bodies from the oats and for the final stage of grading the meal as it fell from the stones. But some mills began in the nineteenth century, and continued during the twentieth, to introduce further refinements, to riddle before and after kilning, for example, before and after shelling and with a wider range of sieves after grinding. This had three effects. It produced a purer, higher quality meal, but a smaller volume of it, because a large part of the impurities otherwise incorporated in the finished product had been removed. This meant that the meal had either to sell at a higher price or the loss of the extra weight had to be compensated for in other ways. But secondly the extra processes produced a much greater volume not only of the inner husk from which sowans could be made, but of mill-dust, sacked at each stage as it was rejected from the machines. This dust, although not wanted in the meal for human consumption, was nevertheless a food product with nutritional value and it was this, with an admixture of husks, that was sold for animal food abroad and was known to Aberdeenshire millers and farmers, whose own beasts fed on the best crushed oats, as *cheatabeastie.* In England a similar substance was known as *Jonathan,* and in a court case 'it was contended for the defence that the article was not sawdust as stated in the summons but the husks of oats & not a foreign substance within the meaning of the Act of Parliament'.[8] Thirdly, the extra processes necessitated a greatly increased sack handling between one machine and another. It was partly for this reason that they were unlikely to be introduced before the adoption of elevators, those ingenious devices which carry the product of each machine up to the roof of the mill whence it descends by simple force of gravity along chutes to the next process.

The greatest change in the work of the mill was the introduction of automatic mechanical handling. A great part of the labour of the mill had consisted of carrying the grain and meal from department to department as it passed from one stage of processing to another. From the moment when the grain first arrived at the mill it had to be constantly moved about by the miller and his assistants.

The invention which was to change this came from America, where Oliver Evans, author of the *Young Millwright and Miller's Guide*, which ran into thirteen editions, had invented the 'elevator'. This was an endless belt, with cups or 'buckets' attached at intervals, which was boxed in and, powered by the same drive which turned the millstones, automatically fed the meal from the stone floor into the sieves below. Evans's elevators were introduced into Liverpool in 1791 and, because they saved so much time and labour, were, over a period of years, installed in all corn mills.[9] It was natural that millwrights, called in to repair water wheels or to advise on the general efficiency of a mill, should recommend the adoption of this very useful process. The spread of the use of elevators, however, was not rapid in Scotland. Gray does not show their use or even mention them in his book in 1804. Perth City Mills did not have them before they were recommended by John Duncan in 1837.[10] But as and when they were installed they made new work for the millwrights and ensured a steady increase in the numbers employed in the trade.

Another innovation at the end of the eighteenth century was the greatly improved kiln situated within the mill. Oats has always required careful drying to make it milleable. Jones uses the existence of a kiln as one of the features distinguishing the 'upland' mills, where oats were ground, from 'lowland' wheat grinding mills.[11]

The drying of the corn was, in the days of the baronies, usually considered the business of the farmer, not of the miller. The primitive process of 'graddan' prepared the corn for grinding by what can only be described as a quick burning over a field fire. 'Aigar meal' was prepared from grain dried very slowly in a pot over a fire before being ground in a quern.[12] Corn drying was later performed in a corner of the barn on a small hearth prepared for the purpose. Survivals of this type of kiln have been recorded by Fenton in Orkney and Shetland.[13]

The next stage was the building of a rounded, stone addition to the barn, of two storeys, the fire chamber on the ground, the drying floor above it. The drying floor on which the grain was spread was at first of wooden planks spread with straw mats: 'Kilns for drying grain are sometimes made with timber ribs which was the universal practice about a century ago; many are made with brick floors but the cast iron floors are daily gaining ground.'[14] It is not hard to imagine how often disaster must have occurred. The infrequent survival of these farm kilns on the mainland of Scotland, though of course partly due to the inexorable course of farm modernisation, must also be due to the frequency with which they burned to the ground. The fact that their warmth attracted vagrants must have added to the dangers. The farm kiln made a warm and comfortable haven in a damp Scottish winter. In 1700, in Moray, a band of thirty gypsies, who wandered the country stealing food and cattle and causing riots, made the kilns of farm houses their usual sleeping places.[15]

Towards the end of the eighteenth century the drying floors began to be built of perforated bricks or tiles. In parts of Aberdeenshire brick pavements in corn kilns were said to be 'the latest improvement' in 1795: 'Brick pavements for kilns deserves the attention of every farmer.'[16] Partly because of the later mechanisation of the brick trade and the extremely high cost of transporting such heavy articles as bricks and tiles, the fashion for tile floors was short-lived in Scotland. They were fairly quickly superseded by wire floors which were lighter, more efficient and cleaner to use. Thus while brick floors were still being introduced as a useful innovation in the Lothians in 1829,[17] in Argyll and in Caithness in 1811 and 1812,[18] in Stirlingshire cast iron floors were built at Gargunnock in 1793, and in Aberdeenshire at Wester Fintray in 1811.[19] This probably reflects distance from brick and tile works which made the cost of tiles for kilns prohibitive. It may also point to the effect of the abolition or survival of thirlage in the district.

Where thirlage was abolished the drying process usually moved from the farm steading to the corn mill. Having now to attract customers rather than await their inevitable attendance upon him, the miller found it advantageous to offer the extra service of drying. Thus in Angus at the beginning of the nineteenth century many corn mills were being built 'and each mill had a kiln contagious [*sic*] to it for drying corn. In some cases these were made of flatbricks perforated with holes; but they were generally made of strong wire cloth supported by bars of iron.'[20] But in Aberdeen at the same time 'drying is always performed by the farmer himself at home, for which purpose a drying kiln is one of the most indispensable houses on the farm.'[21] And in Banff there was 'no public kiln, the grain being usually dried on the owner's or a neighbour's kiln'.[22]

The miller of Ussie found it difficult to attract customers by 1821 partly because 'there is a very great disadvantage attending to this mill which is that there is not a kiln attached to it.'[23] Obviously practice varied very widely. But some of the older mills had provided drying facilities. The mill of the barony of Stitchill was one of these, as we know from the case of the Alexander Lowry found guilty in 1663 of 'Blood-wyte' because he impatiently pushed out of his way another man who, having come earlier to the mill with his corn, 'had first bedded the kylle', that is, spread his grain for drying in the kiln.[24] Tenants were never, however, bound by law to bring their grain to the mill's kiln, although some millers managed to extract extra dues for this separate process: 'a certain amount of meal is also paid for the use of the kiln in drying the grain though there is indeed no thirlage to kilns and it may be dried at home.'[25]

It should be noted that, prior to the abolition of thirlage, even when drying facilities were available at the mill, the miller did not himself provide that service. The farmer or his servant had to carry the grain to the kiln and attend to its drying. Only after the abolition of thirlage, that is at times varying from district to district between about 1790 and about 1850, did the miller take on the labour of attending the kiln. He did so then partly because, as we have seen, he now needed to attract custom by the provision of the extra service but partly also in the interest of quality. The flavour of meal is very much affected by the way in which it is dried. Over-fast drying, always a temptation, produces a harsh and fiery-tasted meal: the best flavoured is obtained by long slow drying.

The experienced miller could tell when grain was ready by cracking a sample between his teeth. One miller described how his father's teeth had been worn down into half-moons by a lifetime of cracking oats.[26] The new varieties of oats introduced in the late eighteenth and early nineteenth centuries all had different qualities requiring different drying times. Coarser oats needed longer drying to make them milleable. Modern oats could not endure the primitive burning treatment of the Highland crofters without disintegrating. As customers became more selective in their purchases of meal, so millers had to grow more cautious in accepting oats for grinding. Robert Shirra Gibb, a farmer in Lauderdale with fifty years' experience of oat growing, wrote, in 1927, of his difficulty in persuading the local miller to take the new variety 'Golden Rain' which from the farmer's point of view, was an excellent oat. The miller, handling a sample, thought it would make a yellow meal and perhaps therefore be less saleable. 'I pointed out that the kernel was as white as any oat he ever saw. I asked him to make them into meal and report to me. When they produced beautifully white meal, above his average quality, all he could find to say was that "the meal had not much taste". This, however, was simply because they were of such fine quality that they required only a short time in the kiln and were not as much roasted as the sample against which he tested them.'[27]

It is hard, perhaps, for us, our palates bombarded by such a battery of tastes, to understand how wide was the range of taste in oatmeal for those who depended on it for the chief part of their diet. After all, the same machinery produced it in each mill. It was kiln-dried, ground and sifted in the same manner in every mill. The ways in which a miller's skill and knowledge could affect the quality are not immediately obvious to modern senses.

Skill had, first, to be exercised in the selection of oats for milling. This was not, of course, possible for a miller whose clients were thirled to him and had to bring him everything they grew of whatever quality. The exercise of judgment in accepting oats only became possible after he entered the commercial market. Whatever the variety of oats brought to the mill, he used his eye to judge it, his teeth to crack a sample from the kiln, his thumb to test the meal for fineness, his experience to decide how closely set the stones should be, and how long the grain should lie in the kiln.

The drying process involves expenditure of both time and labour. When the kiln is 'bedded' the oats are spread over the pre-heated floor. The fire must have been lit some hours previously. In the eighteenth century millers were bound by their tacks to have the mill ready for service at first light, which meant — for those mills which already had kilns attached — rising to fire the kiln some hours before daylight. In the nineteenth century millers, no longer bound by the conditions of a feudal tack, but now subject to the demands of commercial competition, had still to rise early to fire the kiln to be ready for their earliest customers.

After spreading, the oats have to be constantly watched and turned. The miller has to enter the dry atmosphere of the kiln with a long-handled wooden shovel to turn over the hot piles of grain, which must not lie too long in one position or too thickly piled in one place. It is heavy, back-breaking work, constantly repeated over a period of hours varying from three to six.[28] No absolute recipe for perfection can be given. Not only the variety of oats, but their moisture content, the state of the weather when they were harvested and the conditions of their storing, affect the length of time they must lie in the kiln before becoming just brittle enough for grinding.

The fuel used in the kiln varied from district to district and from period to period, as might be expected. On the farm the fuel might be either peats, in districts where they were available, or the husks left over after threshing. In the mills, similarly, the local availability of fuels affected choice. The larger mills, which were increasingly to be found either near docks or near transport junctions such as Inverurie, and those in south-west Scotland, used anthracite. A particularly suitable variety for use in mills was produced at Rankieston in Ayrshire.[29] Where transport costs and smallness of scale would have made anthracite prohibitively expensive husks were used, as in Old Deer: 'the only fuel employed to dry the grain is the sids or husks or what has formerly gone through the process.'[30] And in Sutherland 'the only fuel required is the shelling seeds collected at the milling of the grain which is a considerable saving in the course of a season.'[31] Husks continued to be used for the firing of kilns all over Scotland until the Second World War, and it is considered by those who remember the custom that firing the kiln with husks gave the meal a very sweet taste. Then the difficulty attending the importing of animal feedstuffs forced the crushing of the husks and chaff for use as fodder. Until the war husks not consumed in the kilns had been used as litter for poultry and pigs. In some places they were ground along with an admixture of other lower-grade material as animal feed, and much of it was sold abroad. Since the war the demand for home-produced fodder has been instrumental in keeping some small water-powered mills at work when the acreage of oats grown has so sharply decreased.

It may have been partly the abolition of thirlage which caused the transfer of kiln from farm to mill. The improvement of machinery in mills was not similarly affected. It was done earlier and independently of whether or not the mill's customers were astricted because it made the miller's own work easier. Kilns, on the other hand, made his work heavier and harder. They would not have been introduced at the miller's own instigation had it not been for two new considerations brought about, perhaps, or at any rate to some extent, by the fear of losing no longer astricted customers. Farmers were only too naturally anxious to rid themselves of the time-consuming process of drying their own grain, especially after the threshing machine had made it otherwise possible to cut down the number of hands employed on the farm. Mills which offered drying as part of the service would naturally attract customers away from old-fashioned mills without kilns. Aberdeenshire was late in abolishing thirlage and the results in a parish like Old Deer were immediate: 'what used to be a great and general grievance, when almost every estate was thirled or astricted to a particular mill and obliged to pay a heavy assessment, usually from 1/11 to 1/16 of the whole grain crop . . . is now happily removed, the last of the multures having been converted last year [1844]. There are now eight meal mills, six of them with and two without drying kilns attached . . . the ordinary charge for drying and grinding oats is now 6d. per boll of meal'.[32]

Added to the farmer's demand for drying at the mill was the miller's own wish to have control over the quality of the meal he produced for sale. The flavour of the meal was so much affected by its correct kilning that a miller's reputation for good meal could be enhanced or ruined by injudicious drying. Where he had to sell his meal, as he began to do more often during the nineteenth century instead of merely returning it to the farmer from whose parcel of oats it had been made, he naturally wished to be his own judge of when it was ready for milling. An unscrupulous miller had the means of correcting mistakes made in the kiln. If the oats remained too long over the fire the meal made from them would have a darker appearance than usual but the colour could be restored by the sprinkling of a little sulphur on the kiln fire. It is a trick that might get a bushel of meal sold to the unwary but would be unlikely to go long unsuspected because, although the colour might have been restored, the taste could hardly have remained unaffected. Those bothy men who ate meal for breakfast, dinner and supper would not be fobbed off with such a damaged product but would demand from the farmer, and he from the miller, the best 'ploughman's meal' that could be produced.[33]

The miller, then, on two counts, was spurred into the building of a kiln to his mill. He was forced, if he wished their custom, to take on the drying of oats from farmers who had, at last, the upper hand over him and wished to be rid of the task; and even where farmers were still willing and able to fire their own kilns the miller would prefer to do it himself to give him control not only over the quality but also over the quantity of meal he produced. Correct drying affects the fineness of the resultant meal. The finer the meal, the greater the volume produced from a boll of oats. Where meal was sold or paid for by volume rather than weight, as it long continued to be,[34] it was obviously in the miller's interest to grind as fine as possible.

The new kilns built at mills during the nineteenth century were not cylindrical in shape like the old farm kilns. It was, if not by any means always, often the addition of the new rectangular two-storey kiln which gave the old Scottish meal mill its very typical L-shaped plan. In the larger, mostly West of Scotland, mills it also resulted in the addition of an extra storey to the mill. Drying of oats at the mill required, for the first time, storage of oats at the mill. Where the dried oats had been brought from the farm by a servant who not only carried them to the mill but carried them back after grinding, the miller had now to find room for oats bought by him from the farms and stored to await the firing of the kiln. It was obviously not worth his while to fire the kiln for one small parcel of oats, and so he would stack the sacks until he had accumulated a sufficient quantity. This meant both the need for more space and consequently more sack handling, from granary or sack loft to kiln and from kiln to stones. Those millers with the capital to do so added a third storey to the their mills where they installed a sack hoist driven off the water wheel by a crown wheel in the loft. Thus sacks could be mechanically handled for storage to the loft and the stones could be mechanically fed from large hoppers hung above them.

Smeaton illustrated the use of the sack hoist in his earliest designs for large mills, and Andrew Gray also described them. John Duncan described the sack tackle in Perth as 'very improperly placed and out of order' and advised that 'two peculiarly made bevel wheels be applied at top of upright shaft in order to carry the motion of said tackle further up in the roof where it will work easier and be out of the way.'[35] In the East of Scotland, at least, most meal mills remained two storey buildings with a kiln at one end and only a very small amount of storage space. This reflects the kind of customer attending the mill. In the oat-producing counties the customer was most often still the farmer requiring meal for his own household and for the wages of his farm servants. In the towns and in the pastoral and dairy areas customers might be buyers on a larger scale for bakeries and groceries, and the miller had to keep larger stocks of grain and of meal on hand.[36]

The most telling change in the outside appearance of the mill was made by the addition of a ventilator for the kiln. Until then it was differentiated from other farm buildings only by the presence of the water wheel. Now the roof line was altered and the mill's characteristic appearance formed by the protrusion of a cone-shaped vent. In the South-West unobtrusive slits in a louvred wooden structure only slightly higher than the roof ridge made this a less significant feature, but in the East the wooden 'granny' rose high enough to be seen from a distance and was often topped by an exuberant weather vane, sometimes bearing the usual cockerel or a flat fish, but more often a symbol particular to mills, a wrought iron pig. The pig on the vane was an advertisement of the miller's prosperity and of his availability to his customers. It is unfortunate that so few of them survive.

Meal mills in Scotland were almost invariably stone-built. There were, perhaps, some few exceptions. In one part of the North-East 'clay biggins' were common enough on farms and one writer stresses that a particular type of clay or mud construction had advantages for mill buildings. *Auchenhalrig work*, named after the village of its origin, was said to be 'better calculated [for mills] because the materials are so strongly united that when the machine is at work the whole fabric shakes together as one compact body and there is seldom a rent to be seen in it'.[37] In Angus, near Inverkeillor, there survives the shell of a brick-built mill, its construction plainly influenced by its proximity to Anniston brickworks.

Of the eighteenth century mills surviving until the end of the century and so often described as decrepit, insufficient or derelict in reports of that period, some were certainly of a very primitive form of construction. Like the black houses of the cottar people they served, they were constructed of unmortared and unlimed stone, roughly patched and thatched with divots of turf. Some of these still existed well into the nineteenth century, like Wandell Mill in Lanarkshire, whose buildings were 'wretched and little suited to a farm of its extent at the present day'.[38] Most of the cottages in the nearby village were still built without chimneys and with only a hole in the roof to let out the smoke from the central fireplace, so the miller could hardly expect to fare better.

Turf was the usual roof covering for eighteenth century mills, and one of the mill services required of tenants at very frequent intervals was the carrying of divots for the 'thacking' of the mill. Robert Dick of Threave was bound by his tack 'to thatch a bay on each side of the miln'.[39] And at Stitchill, 'in all tyme comeing the mylne, but not the houses belonging to it, be furnished with strae by the Tennants proportionate to the husband lands within the Barronie ordaining them to carry the said strae according to their proportions to the Mill and that the said mill be furnished with divots.'[40]

Thatch of this kind rots and it needed to be replaced yearly and was never wholly watertight, a matter of less moment when grain was not stored at the mill but merely brought there for grinding, and immediately afterwards removed. The Forfeited Estates Commissioners drew up rules for the proper maintenance of the mills in their care. They banned the use of turf and divot and insisted on a 'proper' roof covering of 'thatch, fern or heather, sewed with tar-rope yarn, or covered with some better materials'.[41] The commissioners forebore to specify slate because they were well aware that it was seldom available to their tenants. However, their surveyor in Strathpeffer, Captain John Forbes, wrote in 1755, 'There are two milns upon this barony, well enough supplyed with water and sufficient for the sucken. They are also in good repair, having been lately built by the present factor in consequence of orders from the Barons of the Exchequer, only it were desirable to have them slated.'[42]

As millers began to compete in the commercial market by purchasing grain and dealing in meal, they were forced to provide dry and safe storage at the mill. This was the period in which slate roofs first appeared on mills. Andrew Paterson had a slated roof at Arbirlot in 1766, but he was a man of better financial standing than most tenants of mills, having been, in fact, accepted as a tenant because of his commercial success and supposed ability to keep the mill in repair rather than the previous tenant who was preferred by the neighbouring farmers.[43] And Alexander Robertson at Brunty had built his mill with a slated roof as early as 1756. But these were exceptions. The continual application of tenants to the remaking of mill roofs and the constant estate reports that roofs have fallen in and require repair, together with the frequent remarks in the mid-nineteenth century New Statistical Account that a new mill with a slated roof has been built in the parish, suggest that slates became commonly used only from about 1840. The parish report of Aberdour where the meal mill had been 'lately new roofed and slated' is very typical.[44] At Benholm the part of the mill dated 1811 has a roof of old stone slates, probably locally quarried, whereas the later additions have the more usual grey slates. Although many ancient mill foundations survive, the buildings have most usually been altered, added to and repaired so often as to leave evidence of their early origin only for the unusually observant.

This is partly because the construction of eighteenth century mills was usually very inferior and unlikely to survive the weather of two centuries. But it is also because the structure of mills, to an extent much greater than in other buildings, was subjected to very great strain. Water wheels in use shake the whole building to which they are attached, and all the machinery within vibrates and rattles until windows and door frames quiver. Even sound buildings treated in this way are liable to develop cracks. The mill designed by George Meikle for the town of Alloa in the 1780s was one of the first of a superior construction and its description sheds interesting light on how the cracking of mill walls was expected: 'From the time the foundation stone was laid, it was not quite 12 months before the mills began to work and, not withstanding the great stress upon such new walls, they were so well built that there is not the smallest crack to be observed.'[45] A weaker structure will not so much crack as collapse. That is why, at the end of the eighteenth century, just when business was beginning to pick up and more likely to be demanded of the old mills, many towns found their mills, like Glasgow's, quite 'untenantable'.[46]

It was, of course, in the towns that expenditure on larger and better constructed mill buildings most often became possible because of the new demand from fast-growing populations for the products of the now flourishing bakeries. In most cases towns gave up the problem of rebuilding and keeping in repair, either to the Bakers' Incorporations or to the new brand of capitalist/grain merchant/millers. And the new large mills resulting from this arrangement, even if they were not built for steam, were very soon to give up water power and meal milling in exchange for steam boilers and imported wheat, so passing beyond the bounds of this study. The Bishop Mills in Old Dumbarton Road, Glasgow were rebuilt in 1839 for William Wilson, miller and grain merchant, and, although originally powered by a water wheel, later installed a turbine engine. Port Dundas Grain Mills were built in 1843 for Andrew Hamilton, another miller who found the capital to turn to steam.[47] In Dundee the town agreed to spend £1,000 on improvements at Baldovan flour mill in 1825, but this mill was soon absorbed into the textile industry.[48] Even in the small town of St Andrews the Bakers' Trade installed a steam engine at the town's flour mill in 1847. It was built and installed by Gourlay, Mudie and Co. of Dundee, and was a small engine of 10 h.p. intended as an auxiliary to the water power of the mill.[49]

In the countryside the water wheels remained, hundreds of them turning steadily until the Second World War. There the most common form of construction was random rubble for all walls except that entered by the axle of the water wheel. The 'water wall' was built of dressed stone blocks carefully mortared with lime to withstand the constant rushing past of the water and the vibrating of the wheel. It was understood even before the eighteenth century that a more solid form of building was required for the water wall of the mill. At

Camaghuaran in 1755 the Forfeited Estates Commissioners specified that the contractor for the new mill which 'appears to be forming on a very good plan' should be 'only obliged to build the gable end of the mill and three feet of the side walls with lime'.[50] Much earlier the Monymusk tenants had in 1715 refused to rebuild the water wall at the mill when asked by the miller and had to be ordered by the baron court to 'read the wall and carie the lime and the sub tenants and crofters to serve the masson and gather and bring fogg'.[51]

The arrangement whereby each new tacksman was bound to leave the mill as he found it seems not to have applied to the water wall, which, perhaps because of the greater expense involved in procuring dressed stone and mortar and the necessity of hiring a mason for such work, would seem to have remained the responsibility of the landowner and his factor rather than of the outgoing tenant. Andrew Paterson, tacksman of the mill at Arbirlot, obliged himself in 1766 'to maintain and uphold the mill, house, walls and roof wind and water tight while the walls stand . . . excepting allienarly the walls or roof of the said mill shall faill and come down during the currency of my tack not thro my fault or neglect. In that case the Earl of Panmure is obliged to rebuild the walls of the mill and give her a new roof and . . . as some defect is said to be in the water wall at present that is to be repaired on Lord Panmure's charges.' But because he was a preferred tenant Paterson may have been able to drive a better bargain than the ordinary run of millers.[52]

The rubble for the main structure of the mill was usually quarried locally and may sometimes have been harled. At Aberdour the two mills built in the mid-nineteenth century were 'built of granite and partly of a sort of red rock or sandstone which abounds in the parish which, when harled, is very durable'.[53] But the ashlar for the water wall and sometimes for the lower part of the other walls would have to be purchased from a quarry where there were masons employed to dress the stone. The quarry at Turriff supplied 'stones for mill-courses' at 6d each.[54] This habit of building the first few courses of a mill and the one gable of dressed stone and the rest of rubble might easily lead one to suppose that a mill had been built and rebuilt at different periods, but it was in fact common practice in mill building and was well adapted to the needs of mills. The leaflet handed out to visitors to Balbirnie Mill, now a tourist attraction as well as a working meal mill, supposes the superior masonry of the area near the wheel to be evidence of the early possession of the mill by the wealthy Bishops of Brechin. It is more likely to have been the usual strengthening of the part of the wall which was subjected to the most strain.

It was not only the wear and tear of daily working which occasioned a very frequent rebuilding of mills. Particularly after the introduction of kilns, mills were only too likely to catch fire. Millers who had crofts to keep, as many of them did, were often caught between the demands of livestock and the need for constant watchfulness at the kiln. A neglected fire, the grain allowed to overheat, perhaps while a race was on to bring in the harvest before a shower or to assist a cow in calf, could only too readily result in an outbreak of fire. Insurance companies were not always too ready to provide cover for mills, the risk being so high, and could insist on awkward conditions, or premiums so far beyond the purse of the small country miller as to tempt him to operate without insurance. As late as 1899 the large and important Port Elphinstone Mills were having some trouble with their insurance company and were forced by them to build a new bypass 'so that you may get water direct from the large cistern to your mills in the event of fire', although the mill owners thought the 'cistern would be useless in the case of fire'.[55] Probably about the beginning of the nineteenth century, that is coincidentally with the introduction of kilns, those mills which could afford to do so were taking out insurance policies. Lanark Town Council took out a policy with Glasgow Fire Office in 1808 for £250 for the mill and an extra £50 for the kiln. In 1810 the whole building was destroyed by fire and its rebuilding cost much more than the amount provided by the insurance company.[56]

The extreme likelihood that insurance cover would not meet the cost of rebuilding may have been one reason, along with a decreased profitability, for mills which had burnt down being deserted and left derelict. Kinross Mill was burnt down in 1844 and there was said to be 'no intention of erecting a new mill', although for the next thirteen years the tenants of the estate continued to pay mill multures to its owner.[57]

Apart from the extra risk from the new kilns, it was the abolition of thirlage which made the insuring of mills necessary. Previously, even if the mill should burn down, it could be cheaply renewed by the tenants' mill services. After the 1799 Act estate owners who had freed their tenants of mill multures and services were no longer obliged to maintain the mills, and, of course, few of them did, there being no longer any great advantage to the landowner in having an estate mill on his land. The advantage was now the farmer's or the miller's, and the responsibility for rebuilding and fire insurance followed suit. The case of

Spottiswoode v. Pringle in 1849 settled the issue by ruling that 'after commutation a proprietor was not bound to maintain the mill.'[58]

So, through fire and neglect, most of the hundreds of mills which used to add interest to the Scottish landscape have crumbled away, only the embanking of a lade or the traceable foundations of walls remaining to indicate the departure of the country craft of meal milling.

NOTES

1. Bennett and Elton, *History of Corn Milling*, 1, 193; Gray, *The Experienced Millwright*, 44-5
2. Scott, *Engineer and Machinist's Assistant*, 85
3. S.R.O. GD 1/1 187
4. Jones, 'Water powered corn mills', 311-2
5. Gray, *The Experienced Millwright*, 44-5
6. Hamlyn/Angus Co. records: Instrument of Sasine in favour of John Inglis, 2 February 1792
7. Gray, *The Experienced Millwright*, 44-5
8. Smith, *Foods*, 161
9. Bennett and Elton, *History of Corn Milling*, 193-6
10. M'Dougall's Trustees, Copy Report by Mr John Duncan, Minutes, 12 June 1837 (NRA[S] 1510)
11. Jones, 'Water powered corn mills', 329
12. Jamieson, *Dictionary*
13. Fenton, *Northern Isles*, 124-9; Fenton, *Scottish Country Life*, 94-7
14. Robertson, *General View of the Agriculture of the County of Perth*, 199
15. Chambers, *Domestic Annals*, 374
16. Lenman, B. P. and Gauldie, Enid, 'Pitfour Brickworks, Glencarse, Perth', *Ind. Arch.* 1969, 340; *O.S.A.*, 16, 472
17. Buchan-Hepburn, *General View of the Agriculture and Rural Economy of East Lothian*, 106-110
18. Smith, *General View of the Agriculture of the County of Argyll*, 60
19. Keith, *General View of the Agriculture of the County of Aberdeen*, 138
20. Headrick, *General View of the Agriculture of the County of Angus*, 266
21. Anderson, *General View of the Agriculture of the County of Aberdeen*, 45
22. *N.S.A.*, XIII, 138
23. S.R.O. GD 46/17/591
24. Gunn, *Stitchill*, 29; S.R.O. GD 135/39
25. Findlater, *General View of the Agriculture of the County of Peebles*, 90
26. Stoyel, 'The art of drying oats in Scottish kilns'

27. Gibb, *A Farmer's Fifty Years in Lauderdale*, 79
28. Stoyel, *op. cit.*, 41; Findlay, *Oats*, 72
29. Stoyel, *op. cit.*, 42
30. *N.S.A.*, XII, 157
31. Henderson, *General View of the Agriculture of the County of Sutherland*, 138
32. *N.S.A.*, XII, 157
33. *Agricultural Labourer*, I, 162
34. On the various measures used for grain in Scotland, *Farmers Magazine*, 1818, 432; Zupko, 'Weights and measures in Scotland', 119-145; Cramond, *Annals of Fordoun*, 56; *Scots Farmer*, 1773, 287-8; Levitt and Smout, 'Some weights and measures in Scotland', 146; Smith, *Gordon's Mills*, 60
35. M'Dougall's Trustees, *loc. cit*; Jones, 'Water powered corn mills', 334
36. See also p. 205
37. Souter, *General View of the Agriculture of the County of Banff*, Appendix, 9; Walker, Bruce, 'Clay Buildings in North East Scotland', Scottish Vernacular Buildings Working Group Newsletter, Dundee, 1977; Fenton, Alexander, 'Clay Building and Clay Thatch in Scotland', *Ulster Folklife*, 1970
38. *N.S.A.*, VI, 833
39. S.R.O. GD 25/8/1056
40. Gunn, *Stitchill*, 169
41. Commissioners of the Annexed Estates in Scotland, *Rules and Articles for the Improvement of Lowland/Highland Farms*
42. Wills, *Annexed Estates*, 39
43. S.R.O. GD 45/18/1983
44. *N.S.A.*, XII, 265
45. *O.S.A.*, 8, 598
46. Marwick and Renwick, *Extracts from the Records of the Burgh of Glasgow*, August 1800, 197
47. Hume, *Industrial Archaeology of Glasgow*, 273
48. Dundee Libraries, Lamb Collection, 279 (10) 15
49. Macadam, *Baxter Books of St Andrews*, 276
50. Wills, *Annexed Estates*, 83
51. Hamilton, *Monymusk*, 197
52. S.R.O. GD 45/18/1983
53. *N.S.A.*, XII, 269
54. *Ibid.*, XII, 985
55. North of Scotland Milling Co. records, letter
56. Robertson, *Lanark*, 274
57. Court of Session, Porteous v. Haig, 1901
58. Court of Session, Spottiswoode v. Pringle, 1849

10

The Unpopular Miller—The Isolation of the Mill

History, literature and folktale provide us with two separate pictures of the miller of the past, equally familiar but quite conflicting. There is the 'jolly miller', a jovial prosperous fellow, floury, smiling, efficient, welcoming customers to his mill. And there is the shifty rogue, cheat and liar, grasping and mean, who would trick a poor cottar out of his hard-won grain. Both are well documented and neither bears much resemblance to the miller known to this century and the memory of our grandfathers, who was a decent hard-working man, differentiated from his fellow countrymen perhaps by an extra independence of spirit and a more enquiring cast of mind but not separated from them in any important way. It is interesting, then, to ask what caused the very strong feelings about millers which produced the two opposite stereotypes of history, and then to consider what were the causes of the change from these two extremes to the moderate character of the country meal miller of Victorian times and after.

Whether the miller was looked upon as enemy or friend, of course, depended very much upon the position of the raconteur. A generally accepted theory is that the feudal imposition of multures and mill services made the miller inevitably a 'master's man' and hated for it. Certainly thirlage affected the miller's position in the community of tenants. But it is interesting that the harshest criticisms of millers come at the very end of the eighteenth century when the least tolerable hardships of thirlage had already disappeared in many places, and that these criticisms come, not from the tenants, who might be supposed to suffer most from the millers' least endearing habits, but from the parish ministers who wrote the statistical accounts of their parishes for Sir John Sinclair, and from the agricultural writers bent upon effecting change in country practices. This, of course, fits very well the theory that tyranny is most resented in the period when it is beginning to be mitigated and when an end to it is in sight. But in this case one suspects that the parish ministers and the agricultural scientists had both been affected by that theoretical enthusiasm for liberty which so inflamed the end of the eighteenth century and that they were as ready to find feudal tyranny in the granary as McCarthyites to find reds under the beds. Their tone is very high-flown and does not always derive too nicely from the facts, even as represented by themselves.

The system of thirlage, then, put the miller in a rather special position, but contemporary intellectuals' not very closely argued dislike of the system led them to blacken the character of millers in general who were, in fact, its victims, or at most its tools, rather than its instigators. If the criticisms of the late eighteenth century, when the Spirit of Liberty was fanning hatred of any semblance of feudalism, are removed from the body of unfavourable descriptions of millers, there is a very much diminished volume of denigration. Strictures like James Anderson's on millers who 'exercised their powers with the most wanton insolence'[1] and the parish ministers' constant blaming of the millers for being 'careless and saucy'[2] and for causing 'the meagre look, the tattered garment, the wretched hovel with the other miserable effects of feudal tyranny'[3] were, unfortunately, taken up with too much alacrity by some later writers. Graham, for instance, echoes the ministers in describing the 'insolence and negligence of the millers, against whom popular dislike and suspicion were inveterate'.[4]

There is less evidence of a genuinely popular dislike and suspicion than might be supposed from such accounts. For a period at the end of the eighteenth century popular feeling was aroused against the millers. After the very bad harvests of the early 1780s and late 1790s millers were blamed, along with 'forestallers, monopolisers, engrossers and regraters'[5] for high prices, and there were 'acts of open violence against bakers, millers, farmers and other dealers in provisions'.[6] But the meal mobs were, for the most part, townsmen, suffering from high grain prices and supposing farmers and millers in league with corn dealers to keep prices artificially high. In the countryside, where the effects of the bad seasons were only too well known, millers were not so often blamed for the ravages of frost and caterpillar plague. Millers were not universally popular, and the reasons for that are worth considering, but it is hard to find any of the savagely critical descriptions of them, which were so common in the late eighteenth century, in any earlier period. Those individual millers who emerge with names and characteristics from the blur of history are not significantly different as a group from any other class of Scotsmen of their period, and differences within the group are those which would emerge in any category. Because of the one-sided criticism they have had, it is perhaps not too self-evident to stress that there were honest and respectable millers as well as cheating and shiftless ones, just as there were clever and stupid millers, hard-working and lazy ones, and toadying and independent ones.

Their place in society was firm but not perhaps too easily understood. They were not members of any craft organisation. There was not traditionally an incorporated trade of millers, which is interesting when it is considered that the other food trades — the baxters, the fleshers and the maltsters — and the other mechanical crafts — the masons, the wrights and the hammermen — all had their incorporations, with strict rules for entry qualifications and conduct. Millers were governed by no such body and entry to their craft was not controlled by anything other than local expediencies. An attempt to form a miller craft union with secrets and mysteries like those of the horsemen had some success in the North-East in the nineteenth century but was never widespread in its influence. It had no roots in strong mediaeval crafts like the other trades. There was, in fact, no real need for early millers to incorporate themselves in self-protecting organisations. The nature of their trade and the need for water power placed them outside the cities where the craft guilds thrived. Their isolation and the patronage of landowners made competition unlikely and co-operation unnecessary, and restrictive practices could be said to have been built into their conditions of lease without being instigated by themselves.

There were, then, no formal qualifications insisted upon by millers for new entrants to the trade, and, until the nineteenth century, there was no set period of apprenticeship. This is not, however, to say that the job was seen as requiring no skills. Baron courts forbade people 'without any kynd of knowleg' to touch mill machinery because they might 'mistemper the mylne'.[7] It was recognised that mills needed some understanding and some practice, and only men known to have the requisite knowledge were employed in them. The safeguard against the employment of men ignorant of mill work was written into Scots law. The earliest statute on the subject required that 'the servants in the king's mylne, or they wha hes ane miln set to them for ferme, or maill, sall have na servants bot be the consideration of the gude men of the burgh', and these servants were to be 'faithfull and of gude fame'.[8] In other words, the miller had to be proficient enough, and known to be so, to satisfy those who were to be his customers. The act was later reiterated to make it clear that the rule applied not only to the king's mills: 'any one who has a miln in their lands shall have ane maister and twa servands like as he that hais the king's milns'.[9]

There was, then, a limit set on the number of servants to be employed in mills, and, as each servant expected to be paid separately by each customer, this was a necessary provision in the interests of the customers. The quality and skill of the servants could be maintained by the right of the gudemen who were the mill's customers to approve the choice of men employed there. In the earliest baronial courts the tenants were told to choose two good men from among their own number and satisfactory to them all to serve the mill. Most communities had then a number of small horizontal mills not of the landlord's ownership where they were accustomed to grind grain as it suited each family's own requirements. The use of these simplest of mills was, therefore, fairly generally understood. At the time when barons were first attempting to enforce astriction to their own vertical mills it would already be known within each community which men were best able to manage the mills and which of them had the necessary skills to keep them in repair. So both the democratic principles of Scots law, which gave the right of approval to tenants, and the landlord's interest to attract tenants to his own mill, dictated that the miller and his servants should be known to the tenants for their skill and their honesty.

Although these considerations still applied in the eighteenth century, in practice the mills were in fact let to whoever made the highest bid for the tack, in exactly the same way as farms and other land holdings were let, except that mills almost invariably had properly drawn up written contracts even in the periods when lease agreements were more usually verbal.[10] It was the custom for landlords to expect the payment of *grassum,* that is, a sum of money paid for the renewing or granting of a lease, by the entering tenant before taking possession of a mill or farm. When a miller's lease was up it was possible for someone else, offering a higher sum, to usurp him even when he had worked the mill to the satisfaction of all the tenants for a large number of years. This was far from the spirit of the act which had intended millers to be chosen to suit the tenants, but it suited the pockets of landlords who could by these means acquire some of the ready money which they were, after the Union, beginning to be so anxious to acquire. Even the improving landlords, like Grant of Monymusk, were tempted by the offer of a higher grassum to evict a long-standing tenant miller. Grant's factor wrote in 1735 advising him against such a course: 'Here is a great talk about this grasum *(sic)* money; your the best judg whether you gaine anything by it or no. My oppinion is that as long as it is alowed to be taken you will have none but poore tenants, for I observe the way is as soon as they find a man lives very well in the farm he has there is another presently enveys his hapiness and coms and bids so much grasum. Then the old tenant must turn out that perhaps hath paid 10 or 20 years rent.'[11] In this case the tenant was the miller, Alexander Norvell, who had for a long time held the tack of Ordmill and the Mill of Monymusk and was being put out because a grassum of 100 marks had been offered for his holdings.

In another case, in spite of the tenant farmers, who had been his satisfied customers for four years, banding together to present a certificate of his 'faithfully and honestly discharging his duties' and of 'his qualifications and moral character', John Bowack was evicted from Arbirlot Mill by the Panmure estate in favour of the much more prosperous Andrew Paterson who had offered 'one full year's rent by way of grassum', which amounted to 31 bolls of meal and £17 sterling compared with the '54 bolls of bere, 1 boll 4 pecks meal and 10 shillings sterling of money' which had been the former rent.[12]

So the old considerations about skill and honesty had been, in the eighteenth century, replaced by the financial needs of the landowners. In the general anxiety to increase the rentals of estates in the name of improvement, the ancient safeguards about the qualifications of millers were forgotten. Those millers whose profits had accumulated sufficiently to allow the higher rents now required as well as the extra money for grassum were preferred by landlords without regard to their acceptability to the tenants. Those profits might have been made by a greater efficiency than that exercised by the outgoing tenant, but they might more easily have been made by straightforward dishonesty. The transformation of grain into meal, especially where the measures which governed payment for it belonged, as they always did, to the miller, made the abstraction of a part of a client's property very hard to detect. The miller's dues, and his servants', were paid as a proportion of the quantity ground, and the quantity was measured by boll measure, a measure not of weight but of volume. A boll was originally 'a vessell capable of holding 164 pounds of the clear water of the Tay'.[13] In fact the quantity meant by a boll varied very much from region to region in spite of a number of acts of parliament attempting to standardise weights and measures. In particular for the purposes of our present argument, a boll was as much as the miller said it was, and there was very little his customers could do about that. As James Thomson complained: 'their measures are heaped and hand-waved'.[14] The tub holding a boll of meal could be piled high with meal, making both the quantity to be paid for by the customer and the proportion retained by the miller greater than if the meal had been levelled off as it properly should have been.[15] Because grain is bulkier than the meal derived from it a customer had no way of being sure that he was receiving back from the miller in meal the full quantity ground from the grain he had brought to the mill. Of course it would have been simpler if a standard amount of meal could always be depended upon from a given amount of grain. But with the best will in the world the miller could not prevent the quantity of meal obtained being dependent upon the quality of grain supplied. Good seed and a good harvest might just make possible the achievement of 'meal for corn', that is, a boll of meal for a boll of corn, as in 'Some oats . . . yielded not much less than meal for corn at the mill'.[16] But poor seed and late harvests might result in only seven or eight pecks from a boll.[17] So customers could not be certain how much to expect and a confident miller could easily, if he chose, deceive.

Even where a customer stood and watched his grain being processed, as customers usually did in the eighteenth century, a miller had the means to cheat him. For instance, in the space between the millstones and the wooden frame which enclosed them, which was called the *mill-ring,* a certain amount of meal was bound to accumulate at the end of a day. By enlarging the space to allow a greater quantity to escape, the miller could increase the amount of this perquisite. From this practice derived the expression *to ring the mill,* meaning to cheat.[18]

Another habit of the dishonest miller was to keep a *mill-bitch,* a bag hung up close to the stones into which he could easily slip a handful of meal now and then. In the Lothians it was even customary to talk of *milling* someone out of something, meaning cheating. Scott has Rob Roy exclaim, 'Fie upon you, Thornie, would you trust to a miller's word?'[19] However, these doubtful habits should be balanced against the custom, common in many parishes, of keeping the poor bag at the mill. A poke, or little sack, was hung up near the stones and a small portion from each customer's meal put into it for distribution to the needy: 'If at any time one or more are bed-rid it is customary to hang up a bag in the mill for them, into which the tenants put a handful of meal, when they grind their corn.'[20] And again: 'Many of the poor also have bags in the mills into which every one puts as he can spare or as charity disposes him.' This must imply some general trust in the local miller's honesty, and in many places hungry children certainly knew where to turn: 'At most of the old country mills there was a gathering of orphans and other poor children on "grunnin'" (grinding) days and the miller took a cog of meal out of each "aught", or lot, for them.'[21] As Charles Murray's *In the Country Places* (1920) illustrates, the increased prosperity of country children was shown in that the handful of meal begged from the miller by a little boy like Murray himself was to feed his pigeons and not himself!

Where a miller was a long-standing member of a small community and where most likely his father and grandfather before him had been accepted by his fellow tenants on the old pre-improvement terms which required his honesty and skill to be known to them, it was unlikely that he would cheat his neighbours. Part of the miller's reputation for dishonesty and trickery comes from this period in which millers of long standing in a community and well known to it were replaced by strangers with more money at their disposal, to the greater profit of the landlord instead of to the satisfaction of the customers. It would be foolish to make too much of this. In a trade where opportunities for cheating were, as we have seen, so many, there must always have been a good many less than honest tradesmen.

Where the tenants felt they had had some part in choosing a miller they were less likely to feel resentful towards him and less ready to suspect him of cheating. But, as well as offering the mill to the highest bidder, the improving landowners of the eighteenth century also seem, in very many cases, to have been more exacting in their enforcement of thirlage. Although tenants had been astricted to mills for a very long time, it would seem that astriction was more strictly enforced in the eighteenth century than it had previously been, for a variety of reasons discussed in Chapter 3, and that landowners were more often prepared to go to law to assert their rights to astrict tenants to certain mills and to exact heavy dues from them. At the same time the greater efficiency of farming methods ensured that a greater quantity of grain was going to the mill. The miller, exacting the same proportion of the total as he had done when the crop was poor, was seen to be deriving a much greater profit as the result of the tenant farmers' work and it was natural for them to resent this. So a certain traditional suspicion of the miller based on the known ease with which he could cheat his customers, whether he did so or not, was reinforced during the eighteenth century by resentment, sometimes against a newcomer foisted upon an unwilling neighbourhood, sometimes against the increased prosperity millers now enjoyed as a result of farm improvements.

Had the miller suffered with the tenants in times of dearth as he prospered with them in times of plenty he might more easily have been forgiven. But in those periods of harvest failure when crops barely provided next year's seed and landowners were impelled to import corn to help their tenants through the hungry season, millers were cushioned against hardship. The corn was invariably imported as whole grain, which stores more safely than meal, and it had still to be ground at the local mills, providing thereby an income to the miller. Towards the end of the eighteenth century, too, when Scotland suffered a series of disappointing harvests, the greater frequency of the miller's dealings in corn and in some areas his developing skill as a speculator in corn prices, caused him to be lumped with the forestallers and speculators as an object of hatred.

There was another reason for the unpopularity of the miller. Because the economy of Scotland at the beginning of the eighteenth century was not money-based and money only gradually and partially replaced goods during the century as the form of payment for services and purchases, the mill had the importance of bank, rent collector, tax office and police station rolled into one. Victual rents were set on an assessment of what grain passed through the mill and were deducted from tenants' meal by the miller and stored by him for collection by the estate factor. So dislike of rent increases was directed against the miller, who did not benefit from them and was, in fact, a fellow sufferer, instead of against the proprietor who had raised the rents and who derived benefit from the increase. The proprietor was often not resident, not within reach of protest, so the man who did the rent collecting came in for the abuse. The miller was the butt for the resentment of countrymen just as the house factor became for town dwellers. Sometimes he even had the thankless task of calculating what the increase in rents should be, both for himself and his customers, and of then exacting it. Thus he earned reproof from his landlord for not getting more and hatred from his fellow tenants for increasing it at all. It could be a distressing situation, as John Davidson found in 1770:

Ogilvie Miln. Dec 20th 1769

I received yours and in obedience thereto have done all in my power with the tennents to settle with the multures at the rate ye propos. I have likeways gotten John Monteath in Cockplay to join with me and he hath drawn up proposals to them which I have enclosed. Ye will see how very few of them have subscribed altho one went from House to House to settle with them. I allso proposed to some of them that we that had subscribed should take the Multars for one year as a trayel but they refuse except some more of the Tennants would Subscribe. There is non of all the Tennants that is averse from settling with the Multars. But all of them says they will be a good deal dearer by this settlement than when they payed at the Miln; — I supose Mr Matland aquented with the offer I made to him which is more than any man shall stand with except the prices of Meall run nine or ten pounds per Boll. The last tack I had of my possession was £34.10 of yearly rent and by this offer I have made it comes to £35.20 of Agmentation which is more than duble Rent,

I am, sir, your very obedient humble ser[t].
John Davidson

P.S. I am credably informed that I have several ill-wishers here in this place which I never knew of till of late, I am bleamed for giving your Honour perverse advise in reasing your Tennants' rents so high. In revenge of which severalls of them at Mercats and other meeting have made it their business to inform Strangers and others that my possession would bear double rent on purpose that it might come to your ears. But all I would demand is to mesure every mans farm by itself and then ye would be the more able to judge whether my possession or theirs were dearest.

Farewll [22]

Poor John Davidson! He was caught between the millstones of two systems. Under the traditional system of agriculture the tenant farmers had paid a certain proportion of all their crop as multure as well as a victual rent and a payment in kind to the miller for grinding, all of these deducted from their crop at grinding by the miller. That in itself was enough, as we have seen, to make him an unloved figure. Under the new system the victual rent, the multures and eventually also the payment for grinding were transmuted into money sums. This would have been hard enough in some districts, although in others the change was welcomed as being more just and rational, even if the proprietors had not chosen the same time to raise rents. To give the miller the responsibility of deciding on a fair amount and persuading the others to agree with it was to put him in an invidious position. And at the same time he had to face the doubling of his own rent without being certain that the mill dues would in future bring in enough income to cover it.

The miller of the baronies also took part to some extent in the administration of the estate and his mill was used as premises for meetings between landlord and tenant or, sometimes, between proprietors and the Commissioners of Supply for the purpose of assessing land values. Although the baron-baillie was the chief administrative officer the miller or his man was, for a number of different purposes, often 'constitut officier'. For instance, when the sheep farmers of Monymusk were troubled by a plague of foxes and stray dogs who were worrying their flocks and killing their lambs the baronial court ordered that each sheep farmer should pay a tax, in proportion to the number of animals kept, to be used for the protection of the farms. They were to pay for this protection in meal and seeds (probably sids) and 'it is to be collected by the miller who is to deduct it and detain it at grinding and for doing so is to be paid two huddishes[23] for each boll he shall so account for his trouble in collecting'.[24] Thus once again the miller had to be tax collector, to do the calculations on which the tax was to be collected, to enforce its collection, and to make himself more unpopular by paying himself for doing so. Where tenants attempted to escape paying their dues at the mill by grinding their own corn at home the miller had the right not only to report them for their failure to bring their corn to him but even to force entry to their homes and to break the querns they were using.[25]

But most resented of all, more even than the payments of meal due to him, were the services exacted by the miller. In the baronies mill and kirk were built and maintained by tenants, all of them bound by their leases to perform such services as were required to keep mill, kirk and manse in good repair. But where the kirk, once built, would need only minor repairs over a long period, and the manse would require only rethatching as a regular task, the mill demanded constant labour for its upkeep. The cleaning of dam and lade was in itself a laborious and endlessly repeated piece of work. The water wall of the mill, subjected to the vibration of the wheel and the constant torrent of water past it, often needed repairs to its stonework. The whole structure of the mill, subjected to the strain of the shaking and rattling machinery, was prone to cracks that needed constant mortaring. All this, as well as the usual needs of a house for rethatching and lime washing!

It would have occasioned grievance enough if it had been left to the estate factor to demand the necessary services for the mill. But instead the miller himself, or his servant, was responsible for announcing the requirement for mill services, for enforcing its performance and for overseeing the work. As the work at the mill could be needed just when a man's own fields needed most attention it is hardly surprising that the miller had often cause to complain to the courts about lack of co-operation and equally unsurprising that he who demanded these unwelcome tasks from his fellow tenants should find himself often miscalled. The frequency of records of repairs in the second half of the eighteenth century and the paucity of records in the first half do not prove that mills were not being kept in good repair before the rebellions, but there is an impression, however hard to prove, that more repair work was being demanded for mills later in the century, that many more mills were being completely renovated, and a number of new ones built. Certainly there are constant references to the state of disrepair of mills in the later eighteenth century, which would suggest that they had been allowed to run down and that mill services had been less stringently insisted upon for some time. If, therefore, mill services were being more often demanded and perhaps a higher standard of workmanship required from those who were forced to do the rebuilding, this would help to account for what seems to be a growing crescendo of dislike for millers culminating in the outburst of criticism at the end of the eighteenth century.

Again, millers were caught between the nether and upper millstones of old and new social systems. Before improvements, when labour and materials were found locally and standards of building amateurish and lackadaisical, mill services might be resented but could be perfunctorily and infrequently performed. After estate improvements, when estate offices had money rents from better farming at their disposal, building tradesmen and millwrights could be employed and paid for, and even if tenant farmers resented the amount exacted from them in money, they minded it less than the time they had once been forced to spend in performing services. But in the transition period between these two systems — and a date can hardly be set upon it because the time of improvement varied so much from one estate to another — greater efficiency might be demanded of the mills to keep pace with improved cropping, while only the old system of tenant services existed to keep the mills in the necessary state of repair. This was not universally the case. There were estates which began to employ and pay for proper tradesmen for the mills fairly early in the century just as there were some estates far ahead of the others in improving their land. But there were enough left which were attempting to create a new and improved agriculture with only the old feudal means of achieving it and it was in these areas that millers found themselves unpopular.

Another reason for the traditional 'bad press' for millers was clearly envy directed at a member of the community both isolated from and slightly more prosperous than the majority.

The mill was most usually physically isolated from the rest of the village community or ferm toun, being sited where the best force of water could be brought to its wheel rather than in neighbourly proximity to its customers. The mill house was often of a slightly more substantial structure than most rural houses. This was partly because, as we have seen, the miller could command help for its building and repair.

Also, because the house often adjoined the mill, which was usually itself of at least two storeys, it was simple enough to give it a top storey with the additional bedrooms lacking in most eighteenth century cottages, which were invariably single-storeyed and of only two apartments. The proximity of the mill and kiln ensured a warmth and dryness not then common in rural homes. In one case at least a house for the miller was made inside the mill itself. At Mill of Ennets, Tornaveen, a chimney was added to warm a living room on the ground floor with a bedroom above inset on the stone floor. Set against the advantage of the mill's warmth, however, could be the damp from the situation close to the stream and the rattling and noise from the mill machinery when in action.

In poor districts the miller's house might not be greatly superior to his neighbours'. Linkwood Mill House was described as 'fitter for the dunghill than offices . . . the walls as well as the roofs are ruinous . . . and the house a hampered hole'.[26] At Wandell Mill, in Lanark, 'the buildings are wretched and little suited to a farm of its extent at the present day. The same remark applies to the dwelling house at Wandell Mill, to which, indeed, a small addition of one room was made last summer, though put down with the least attention to good taste.'[27] But this latter was a nineteenth century stricture on eighteenth century housing, and Victorians were no less harsh in their scorn for eighteenth century housing standards than we have been of theirs. Some existing mill houses show both charm and good taste in the sense that the previous writer meant it, that is in being commodious enough for the rearing of a family in some comfort. Garrel Mill House, a late seventeenth century structure, is a two-storeyed building which originally contained four rooms, and has a pleasantly bowed facade.[28] The picturesque creeper-clad house of Benvie Mill has been built with two rooms downstairs and two dormer-windowed bedrooms upstairs. But at Benholm Mill, where the present miller's house is nineteenth century, the original mill house is a single-storey cottage now housing pigs, cattle and hens. The Scottish Development Department's lists of buildings of architectural amd historic interest show that one-storey cottages were most common in the north-east but that houses built for millers after 1800 were commonly of two storeys and that some of the older houses had dormer windows added later. On the whole, if the machinery in the mill was up to date and efficient, the miller's living quarters were usually tidy and snug. If one was neglected, so was the other.

Within the house the eighteenth century miller's family enjoyed some advantages over their contemporaries. They were, in the first place, unlikely to go hungry. At the mill the supply of corn stuffs would not run out even when cottage kists were empty. Because there was always meal enough, there was also a plentiful supply of husks and bruised corn for livestock, so that, even in communities where the keeping of pigs and poultry was unusual, both were to be found at the mill. It is even claimed that pigs might have become extinct in Scotland if it had not been for those kept at mills. Their rarity was occasioned partly by the scarcity of food in some areas, so that pigs did not survive famine periods, and partly by a very widespread superstition against pigs as unclean animals. 'The aversion to them was so great and their flesh was so much undervalued that, but for those reared at mills, the breed, it is said, would have become extinct.'[29] By the end of the eighteenth century this 'Jewish antipathy against swine'[30] or 'superstitious prejudice against swine'[31] was abating. Mackenzie of Gairloch wrote to his tenants: 'It gives me very sincere pleasure to observe that you are gradually overcoming that absurd prejudice which has hitherto prevented their (pigs) being extensively used.'[32] The diet of the poorer tenants was immeasurably improved by the introduction of pig-keeping on many small farms and cottar lands. But it had not been only their superstition which had prevented pig-breeding by cottars in the earlier period. Not only their own poverty but the embargo of their landlords had in some districts prevented it. On the estate of Craigievar, in Aberdeenshire, only millers were allowed to keep swine in the eighteenth century and they had to keep them chained while the corn was in the fields.[33] It has to be remembered, in this respect, that when fields were still unfenced, wandering pigs could do great damage to crops. Cottages were not then provided with the bottom-of-the-garden pig stye which later became so common. Some of the eighteenth century millers overcame the problem, as some twentieth century Portuguese millers do, by keeping pigs inside the mill, in spite of their detrimental effect on the mill's orderliness and cleanliness.[34] At Monymusk the corn mill had, at one end, 'a kennell for all doggs, with devisions for different ones; at tother end a hogg sty for winter at least, as they will goe in proper fields in summer'.[35]

Even at the end of the nineteenth century some farm servants were forbidden the liberty of pig-keeping 'On the score of temptation to dishonesty',[36] presumably because they might have been tempted to feed the pigs on their master's milk and corn. Even in those areas where pig-keeping was encouraged, the breeding stocks were maintained at the corn mills.[37] The cottars bought young pigs from the miller and fattened them for the bacon curers, bringing thereby a comfortable extra income both to themselves and to the mill. But the miller's pigs were still preferred to those reared elsewhere: 'The large mill swine are most sought after from the great size they grow to.'[38] Some millers had to pay one of their fat pigs as yearly rent to the landlord.[39]

The vast corn-fed pigs in the millers' styes, providing both extra food for the miller's table and extra money for the miller's pocket, must also have been a source of envy to the subsistence farmers who were his customers and whose fields supplied the corn to rear them. 'I ken that the miller's swine's aye fat, but I dinna ken whose meal they're fed oot o'' was a common saying.

The 'Account of swine at Inverarity Mill'[40] shows, in 1834:

	£	s	d
To pigs sold at 11/- a piece	£3	6s	0d
To one fat pig bought at	2	5	
To seven pigs sold at 10/-	3	10	
paid for the boar		5	
To four fat pigs sold	5	15	
Account of swine sold			
August 12 to James Potter 1 pig at 10/-		10	
Sep. 4 to George Smith 2 pigs at 11/-	1	2	

It is interesting to compare this with an entry in the Gilmour estate factor's book for 1828:

1 spoted (*sic*) pig		19s 6d
1 white	do	19s 6d
3 mill swine		£4 5s 10d [41]

Presumably Gaudy, while at Inverarity, was breeding from a sow kept at the mill, selling some of the young pigs to cottars and fattening others. Later he has an entry for 15 stone of pork meat.

Another benefit to the eighteenth century miller's kitchen was the supply of fish from the mill dam. In England at the time of Domesday the value of the eels fished from the dam was taken into consideration in assessing the value of the mill.[42] In Scotland mediaeval law ordered that 'millars take not the fry of smolts of salmon in the mylle dam or lead, contrair to ordinaunce of the law'.[43] Eighteenth century landlords sometimes came to disagreement with their millers because the millers were not letting the salmon up river from their dams.[44] Danish water mills were often equipped with a trout house in which young fry were reared.[45] Fresh trout for the table must have been a welcome change and Scottish millers found them abundant in their dams: 'Many fish (trout) are also caught at the dam dykes belonging to the small mills up the stream; indeed whole sackfuls are taken out of this place in a single night.'[46] An eel trap survives at Milldens Mill, near Arbroath.

Millers were, in most cases, also farmers, baronial lands being let out in parcels supposedly capable of supporting a family. During the period of estate improvement tradesmen of all kinds were encouraged to settle by the grant of a piece of land, it being recognised that the income from the practice of a trade was unlikely to be steady enough to make a man self-sufficient. 'A mechanic, it is true, makes more by his art than by husbandry work, but if he have no farm to depend on, he must go to market for provisions and will be ill provided after all. At any rate he must have a small farm for maintaining a horse and two cows; the former for carrying timber, iron, coals, etc., the latter for milk . . . the quantity of land necessary for supplying all his wants cannot be less than six acres where the soil is good and more where it is indifferent.'[47] From the very large number of farms still bearing the prefix 'Mill of' to their names, it can be seen how very general was the award of some land to the miller. The acreage and quality of the land feued along with the mill varied, of course, very much. It seems possible that, after the break-up of the baronial system, those millers fortunate enough to hold good agricultural land of sufficient extent improved their farms without giving similar attention to the mill up to the point where the farm was providing an income which encouraged the complete abandonment of the mill. Robert Anderson, who had a tack of Lunan Mill in the early eighteenth century, was, for instance, soon in a position to increase his acreage. In 1728 he took a tack of the outfield of Inverkeillor and in 1737 took in yet more land nearby.[48] The quality and extent of land available to the original miller may in fact have been so important a factor among those governing the survival or disappearance of mills as to make those mills which have survived into modern times even more atypical of the early mills than has hitherto been supposed. It was the miller of Benvie who suggested to me that mills like his, which has only a small field adjoining it, survived because of their lack of land, not in spite of it. A miller who had enough land to give him the choice of being either a farmer or miller would have dropped milling in the profitable years of farming. Those mills remaining in use in the twentieth century were either those where some special characteristic of the neighbourhood's economy, such as the survival of payment in meal, ensured their continuing prosperity, or those whose holdings of land were so small as not to provide them with any alternative source of livelihood.

In the eighteenth century at any rate, the lands usually provided upkeep for a few animals as well as for the miller's family. In the earliest period and in the poorer districts until much later[49] there were few, if any, horses and no carts. Sacks of corn were carried on the backs of men to and from the mill. But when carts and cart horses were first introduced into a parish the miller was among the first to equip himself, and the miller on his sheltie became a familiar sight at market. Thus equipped, he was in a position not only to carry his own goods but to earn money by carting for customers. Many a miller's ultimate prosperity had its roots in a flourishing carrier trade. Robertson, the Crieff miller and millwright, was the first to keep a hearse for hire in that town.[50] In the beginning the miller would simply oblige a farmer on whom he was already calling with meal by delivering a sack of potatoes or a bale of hay for him and in many cases the business stopped there. But it was a potential source of money income and some millers built it up into a useful asset. This happened at the end of the history of meal milling as well as during its heyday. The Alcorns of Baledgarno Mill found their income from their contracting business (begun simply as deliveries on behalf of a few farmer customers) overtaking their milling income and eventually gave up the mill which had operated in their hands for fifty years and on the same site for two hundred years.[51]

Particularly after the cessation of thirlage, when millers found it necessary to collect and deliver customers' grain and meal, it became necessary for them to keep a horse and cart and, as a result, to build stables and cart sheds, and to grow more feed corn and hay. The size and prosperity of their property increased, both in relation to their own past and to the present standing of their customers.

The feeling that the miller's skill was 'no' canny' was an additional cause for some reserve in his neighbour's treatment of him. The suspicion that his ability to control natural elements, fire in the kiln and water in the burn, and to set machinery mysteriously a-whirring led superstitious communities to believe him in league with the fairies. In Scotland the fairies were never pretty, gossamer-winged or kindly disposed to the human race. They were mischievous and to be feared. It was certainly in the miller's interest that no one dared set foot in mill or kiln at night because the fairies were known to bring their oats to be ground after dark. So long as his neighbours feared the fairies he could sleep in the knowledge that his girnal would not be robbed. So millers encouraged belief in fairies by their own claims to have seen them about the mill. John Fraser, the miller of Whitehill in New Deer, told his neighbours how he had deliberately put off the mill and hidden behind some straw to watch the fairies arrive one night. 'At midnight the fairies came to the mill and proceeded to grind their grain. The water was let on. It only broke over the wheel and the machinery would not move. The fairy men and women examined every wheel and pinion, but there was nothing wanting or out of gear. When they were on the eve of leaving the miller came from his hiding place and set on the mill. The fairies ground their corn. When they were going away one of the women, in gratitude for what had been done, gave the miller a "goupenfou" of the meal and told him to pack a little of it into the four corners of the empty girnall, saying, at the same time, that he would not see it empty for a long time.'

It was because of this alliance with the fairies that millers were sometimes considered to have powers of healing those afflicted through witchcraft. The miller of Laggan was consulted when a neighbour was stricken with paralysis. He tempted the witch into his mill and there wrestled with her until he caught her between the millstones and forced her to return her victim's power of speech.[52]

A miller coming to a new district would be preceded by rumours of such powers. Add, then, to some varying degree of affluence greater than his neighbour's the fact that the miller was not always a local man and there is reason enough for distrust. We have seen that entry to the trade of miller bore no formal restrictions and that mills in the eighteenth century were most often let to the tenant offering the highest financial inducement to their proprietors. In spite of that, mills were usually let to the sons of millers, in practice the best training in mill work being gained at a father's side by a child growing up in the mill. It would seem that even when a miller was displaced from a mill he had occupied for some years he was likely to find another without too much difficulty, although he might have to move some distance to do so. There does seem to be some evidence for considerable mobility among millers. Not only did they move with some frequency from one mill to another, but their sons, in setting up for themselves, might very well move to another district quite far removed from the father's mill. It is, however, as easy to find examples of millers who stayed at one mill from one generation to another as of those who moved at fairly regular intervals. Alexander Maxwell, for instance, who was miller at Craigoch in Leswalt parish in 1719, was still there in 1741, a spell of 22 years. We know this because Maxwell, who seems to have been one of the more educated and respected of the miller trade, signed his name and designation yearly to a survey of mills in the parish, he being one of three men chosen to judge whether the mills were in good repair when left by an outgoing tenant. It might seem, in fact, from these documents that Maxwell was unusual both in staying so long in one mill and in having a degree of education, because whereas the outgoing tacksman of the mill simply made his mark, Maxwell signed with a confident and literate hand.[53] At the end of the century the same mill was being let on 19-year leases and was held by a miller named Stevenson from 1781 until 1800.[54]

It is unlikely that written records can give anything more than a basis for intelligent guesswork about the proportion of millers remaining for long in one mill. It was the convention, backed by law, that only leases of longer than one year's duration should be given in writing.[55] So that those written leases surviving out of the many thousands which must once have existed, necessarily tell us nothing about the millers who moved most frequently. We know that Robert Henry had made a number of moves before settling at Mill of Ussie, because he wrote that 'my wife and family enjoys better health here than they did in any former place I was residing'.[56] It seems likely that those millers who, because their mills were well situated, were able to attain a certain prosperity and some education for their families, stayed in one place, while those either less fortunate or less able to take advantage of their fortunate situation, moved frequently in hope of betterment. If the eighteenth century pattern did not differ too much from that we know to have prevailed during the nineteenth, young men could expect to have to make a number of moves about the country, working as assistant millers, before they found a place of their own, unless their father's business prospered sufficiently to provide employment for them.

What is fairly clear is that milling stayed in the family. The name Boyack, or Boysack, for instance, appears a number of times and is sufficiently distinctive to make it reasonable to suppose that it refers each time to a member of the same family. James Boyack was tacksman of the Haugh Mylne of Brechin in 1684.[57] Robert Boyack offered for the tack of the West Mill of Brechin in 1695.[58] John, we have already seen, was at Arbirlot Mill until 1767[59] and there is, to this day, a Boysack Mill near Arbroath. The Fairbairn family occur as millers throughout the Stitchill papers, although at different mills at different times.[60]

Of even more interest is the frequent occurrence of the name Miller or Miln among the millers of the eighteenth century, a fact which suggests that the family had been milling as far back as the first giving of surnames in Scotland. We can find, for instance, John Miller, miller of Millheugh, Blantyre, in 1760,[61] John Milne, of Carmyllie Mill in 1757,[62] George Milln of Lethem Milln,[63] James Milne of Buchanstone Mills, Oyne,[64] William Millar, who renounced the corn mills of the burgh of Crail in which his father stood infeft,[65] John Miln, of Miln of Montqueiche in 1618,[66] George Miller of Stitchill,[67] and James Miller, tacksman of the Mill of Provan.[68] Perhaps William Hopper, who was fined £16 by the baron court 'for fyring of his kylle in his drunkennesse', should also be included, the miller being the man who tended the hopper.[69] Of course there can be no scientific assessment of the frequency of the name's occurrence among millers because there is no way of producing a list of all millers' surnames against which to measure the 'Millers'. But it seems of some little interest that the name should pop up so often among eighteenth century records.

It was not, of course, only in Scotland that millers were most usually millers' sons.[70] Where the only way to learn the skills of a miller was to work under a miller at his mill, millers' sons were best placed to learn and most able to graduate from helper at their fathers' mills to mills of their own. The Caw family, for instance, were millers near Crieff for at least a century. John Caw is mentioned in the Reports of the Commissioners for the Annexed Estates as being in some doubt about what rent he is to pay for his mill as there has been so much change in the management of the estate since the Rebellion.[71] He is mentioned again in a *History of Crieff* which also lists a David Caw at Milnab in 1837.[72] William Findlay, who eventually became a lecturer in the North of Scotland College of Agriculture, was born at Mill of Fintray, Aberdeenshire, in 1874, the eldest son of a crofter/miller. His father took a tack of a larger mill at Hatton of Cruden and died shortly after. William left school at thirteen to help his mother work the mill and croft. When he, after twelve years of working all day and studying in the evenings, left the mill to go to College the work of his mill was handed over to a younger brother, although William continued to cycle twenty-five miles home each evening to help with the work.[73]

The miller now living at Benvie Mill is the son of the miller who worked there before him and the grandson of a miller who worked at Benholm Mill, fifty miles north, at the beginning of the century. Because his name is relatively uncommon it is reasonable to wonder whether he is also descended from the miller called Dallas who left a mill in Inverness-shire in the eighteenth century.[74]

In the South-West, the McDowall family bought Milldriggan Mill in Wigtownshire in about 1840 and it was still being worked by the same family in 1971. What is more, the McDowalls were already long-established millers in Galloway when they first came to Milldriggan.[75]

The Coutts family worked Kildrummy Mill in Aberdeenshire for many generations. Of two sons born there at the end of the nineteenth century, one stayed to work that mill, and eventually to buy it, while the other took over the tenancy of Auchendoir Mill first, then, later, of Wardhouse of Insch Mill, Glanderstone Mill and Auchreddie Mill.[76]

The grandfather of the present miller of Benholm was a ploughman who married the daughter of the miller at Arbuthnott and so got taken on at the mill. He moved from there to Craigie Mill where his son learned the trade of milling before moving on to Benholm. The grandfather of William Gavin of Peterculter worked Mill of Ennets, Tornaveen, and his father worked Mill of Leslie before coming to Upper Kennerty.

Miss Alcorn, who now lives at Baledgarno Mill on the estate of the the Lords of Kinnaird, although the mill has ceased working, is daughter, sister and granddaughter to millers. Her father had worked as a miller's assistant first at Alyth, then at Glenisla and Insch, before coming back again to Alyth and, having married there, taking the tack of Baledgarno in Perthshire on his own account.[77]

To come back to the eighteenth century, another interesting pointer to the fact that millers often moved from mill to mill over a fairly wide-spread area occurs in the papers of the Forfeited Estates. The Commissioners drew up a list of holdings of land with the names and particulars of those then resident. One of the things which interested them was the number of people in the Highland districts who spoke only Gaelic. They noted, therefore, against the name of each household, whether the head could speak English. At only one mill out of some eighteen listed in 1755/56 did they draw a blank. Even in districts where the population was exclusively Gaelic-speaking the miller's family spoke English.[78] This suggests either that the millers had more school education than most of their neighbours or that they had come to settle in these Highland districts from other, lowland and English-speaking parts of Scotland. Possibly each is true.

Millers, for a variety of reasons, found it necessary or expedient, for at least part of their lives, to move around the country from mill to mill, sometimes over quite large areas of the country, gaining experience of different practices and seeking always the mill in which they could settle and bring up sons to follow their calling. They were, therefore, often not of long-standing residence in a neighbourhood, a factor which made them the more likely to be treated with suspicion and distrust.

NOTES

1. Anderson, *General View of the Agriculture of the County of Aberdeen*, 48
2. *O.S.A.*, 1, 132
3. *Ibid.*, 2, 499
4. Graham, *Social Life*, 163
5. *Farmers Magazine*, 1, 1800, 446, 473
6. See also Lythe, 'Tayside Meal Mobs', 26-33
7. Barron, *Urie*, 4
8. Skene, *Regiam Majestatem*, 126-7, 'Of Millars'
9. Balfour, *Practicks*, 493, 1209, 'anent milnis, multuris and pertinentis belonging thairto'

10. Hunter, *Law of Landlord and Tenant*, 365
11. Hamilton, *Monymusk*, 115
12. S.R.O. GD 45/18/2272; GD 45/18/1983
13. Zupko, 'Weights and measures in Scotland', 119
14. Thomson, *General View of the Agriculture of the County of Fife*, 337
15. There was an implement kept in the mill especially for the purpose of levelling off the boll measure. See also Jones, 'Water powered corn mills', 306
16. *Farmers Magazine*, 1, 1800, 452
17. *Ibid.*, 217
18. Jamieson, *Dictionary*
19. Scott, Sir Walter, *Rob Roy*, Chapter 7
20. *O.S.A.*, 5, 361; *ibid.*, 9, 160, 578
21. *John o' Groat Journal*, 14 April 1916
22. S.R.O. GD 24/1/639
23. *Huddish* means a measure of grain
24. Hamilton, *Monymusk*, 236. See also Extract Division of . . . the lands of Invergowrie, Clayhills — Henderson Papers, 1767 (NRA(S) 1511)
25. Hunter, *Law of Landlord and Tenant*, 510
26. Adams, Ian H., *Papers of Peter May, Land Surveyor, 1749-1793*, S.H.S. Edinburgh, 1979, 156
27. *N.S.A.*, VI, 833
28. Royal Commission on Ancient and Historical Monuments of Scotland, 1963, 386
29. Murray, David, *The York Buildings Company, a chapter in Scotch History*, Edinburgh, 1973, 41, quoting Dalziel, *Darker Superstitions of Scotland*
30. *N.S.A.*, VI, 36
31. *O.S.A.*, 7, 426
32. Mackenzie, *Hints for the use of Highland tenants and cottagers*, 162
33. *N.S.A.*, XII, 1124 n.
34. Jespersen, 'Portuguese Mills', *Transactions of the 2nd Intl Symposium on Molinology*, 80
35. Hamilton, *Life and Labour*, 143
36. Stuart, Harry, *The Agricultural Labourers, as they were, are, and should be*, Edinburgh, 1854, 309-14
37. *N.S.A.*, XIII, 371
38. *Ibid.*, X, 679
39. Rental Book of Edzell and Lethnott for 1672 and 1699, in Jervise, Andrew, *Land of the Lindsays*, Edinburgh, 1853, Appendix
40. Gaudy's book, in my possession
41. Gilmour MSS, S.R.O. GD 1/335/2
42. Syson, *British Water Mills*, 39
43. Bennett and Elton, *History of Corn Milling*, 112 n.

44. S.R.O. GD 45/18/2254-2275
45. Jespersen, *loc. cit.*, 96
46. *N.S.A.*, IX, 54
47. *The Gentleman Farmer*, 300
48. S.R.O. GD 45/1194
49. E.g. *O.S.A.*, 8, 536-7
50. Porteous, *Crieff*, 181
51. Private information from Miss Alcorn
52. Grigor, 'Kilns, mills, millers, meal and bread', 128
53. S.R.O. GD 154/460
54. S.R.O. GD 135/39
55. Hunter, *Law of Landlord and Tenant*, 365
56. S.R.O. GD 46/17/59
57. S.R.O. GD 45/1609
58. S.R.O. GD 45/1981
59. S.R.O. GD 45/18/2272
60. Gunn, *Stitchill*, *passim*
61. Morison, *Decisions of Court of Session*, 16049; *Minutes of J.P.s of Lanarkshire*, S.H.S. 3rd ser., 127
62. S.R.O. GD 45/18/1864
63. S.R.O. GD 45/21/61
64. North of Scotland Milling Co. records
65. Hamlyn/Angus Milling Co. records, 9 October 1734
66. Barron, *Urie*, 29
67. Gunn, *Stitchill*, 89
68. Court of Session, Magistrates of Glasgow v. Miller, 11 February 1813
69. Gunn, *Stitchill*, 8. Scott has a miller called Hob Happer in *The Monastery*, Chapter 7
70. Cf Syson, *British Water Mills*, 42
71. Wills, *Annexed Estates*, 78
72. Porteous, *Crieff*, 186
73. Findlay, *Oats*, preface
74. Court of Session, Peter Dallas v. James Baillie Fraser, 26 May 1849
75. Donnachie, *Galloway*, 37
76. Private information
77. Private information
78. S.R.O., *Statistics of the Annexed Estates, 1755-56, from the records of the Forfeited Estates preserved in the Scottish Record Office*, Edinburgh 1973, 24, 25, 28, 31, 41, 68

11
The 18th Century Miller's Life — Routine at the Mill

The miller of the first half of the eighteenth century was, like other small tenant farmers, a poor man, having no security of tenure over his mill or his land and utterly dependent upon the goodwill and, even more, the prosperity of his landlord. However, because the other tenants were bound to bring their corn to his mill to be ground he had some little measure of prosperity over and above theirs, increased by the fact that he had his own piece of land, as well as his income from the mill, to live on. He had also a degree of position and authority inside the bounds of estate or barony not accorded to other tenants and he enjoyed, to at least a limited extent, the protection and trust of his landlord. Where that protection was not given it was difficult for a landlord to find a tenant for his mill, as Alexander M'Donald wrote with some irritation to his nephew in 1757: 'your Father and Brothers men having made so many demands on the millar that he would not answeur and thretning his life, has made him leave the mill as he would not serve so many masters . . . you had no concern with ye mill no further than to receive the half of the meal produced. Your meddling with it has I am afraid put it out of my power to get a millar for it this year and if there should be one got he will not be such a good one as the former.'[1] The number of mills was then so large and the surrendering and taking of new leases so frequent that it was not too difficult for a miller to change his place if it was not to his liking.

His work at the mill was, of course, affected by the prosperity of his neighbours. If their crops were good, he was busy. If they failed he had less to do unless, in times of extreme dearth, the landowner imported grain from other districts to prevent the tenants from eating their seed corn. Then it had to be ground at the mill and the miller was busy in spite of the district's crop failure.

His day began early when he rose to 'set the mill on', that is to open the dam, having first made sure that the leads were clear of any refuse that could damage the wheel, allowing the water to run where it would turn the wheel. Either then, or perhaps beforehand, at first light, he must kindle the fire in the mill kiln so that it would be hot enough for use before the first sacks of grain arrived for drying. As well as these early morning tasks he would have beasts to feed and send to pasture, and styes and byres to clean. After breakfast he might have some leisure while he waited for his first customers. They would themselves have been up early to thresh the day's corn in the barn so that there was straw for the beasts, and they had now to carry to the mill such grain as they wanted ground. There might, in the slack time of the year, be a slow trickle of men to the mill with small parcels of oats, beans, peas or barley, stored in quantity in their own barns and brought to the mill for grinding only when meal or malt was immediately required. At harvest time there would be a press of customers. The brewers, with their first purchases of barley, were anxious for quick malting and grinding so that they could hurry on the new season's ale. Farmers came in with larger quantities of grain than those they sent throughout the year. Landowners sometimes pressed for the victual rents to be ground and delivered so that they could be sold at the most profitable time. The miller had then to work all the hours of daylight to keep his machinery in trim and the meal flowing steadily from the stones.

He had also to ensure that each man's grain was dealt with in turn, first comers first served, and that no one usurped another's 'rowm' at the mill. There could be a fair number of people all jostling for attention at one time and a certain amount of ill feeling between customers which sometimes rubbed off on the miller as he tried to keep account of the sacks awaiting free space in the hopper. The sacks had to be kept separate so that one man's crop was not mixed with another's. It might at first seem reasonable that, if quantities of grain were measured before grinding and divided afterwards into proportionate quantities of meal, all customers' lots should be ground together. But it was less simple than that. One man's crop might be poorer in quality than another's, containing a high proportion of weed seeds, imperfectly threshed, or having a small flat grain, while another might bring to the mill a load of clean, well filled, well rounded grain. Barley or oats could be said to 'meal well, or ill', that is, to be easily made into a good or poor quality meal.[2] Some oats were so bad 'as not to be worth mealing',[3] while others reached the desirable standard of 'meal for corn'.[4] Not only the quality but also the quantity of meal produced from each would be different and it was natural that the man with high quality grain would not want his mixed with the poorer quality. So each had to be ground separately and each had to wait until his predecessor at the mill saw his grain through the stones and sieves.

The miller had also to answer individual requirements about the fineness or coarseness of the meal required. One customer might be looking for volume — he would ask for the finest possible grinding. Another, putting flavour first, would require a coarser-ground meal. An early customer might bring in a mixed load of peas, beans and barley, requiring a different setting of the stones from a second customer's oats. Added to all this was the farmer's long-established suspicion of the miller which made customers prefer each to watch his own load through the processes of the mill, anxious lest too much of it disappear in the mill-ring.[5] In fact it seems to have been usual in the earliest times for customers to put each his own grain through the mill, the miller and his men merely supervising rather than helping, their main concern being to ensure that the mill machinery was not in any way tampered with while the farmers used it. They did not allow a customer, for instance, to interfere with the setting of the stones, which was a delicate business and could easily set the mill off balance. If he wanted an adjustment a customer had to await the miller's attention.

So the first job when a customer arrived was to measure his load. Before weights and measures were regularised they differed very much from region to region, but for the purposes of milling a boll was a measure of volume, not of weight and, in practice, within his own mill a boll was just as much as the miller said it was.[6] He owned a skip or measure which held exactly either a 'boll' or a firlot, in which case the vessel itself was known as a firlot, into which the customer emptied his sack. Beside it the miller kept a special stick or rule called a *strike* with which he was supposed to level off the grain in his measure. Rumour had it that he was less than scrupulous in his measurements, the grain or meal being packed down hard in the boll measure and piled up on top, or else allowed to lie loosely and barely to the top just as it suited him. Farmers certainly felt that the amount they brought in was diminished by the miller and the amount they had to pay for exaggerated.

After measuring, the grain then went 'through the mill', was measured again as meal and put back into the customers' own sacks. At this point the miller was required to do some fairly complicated calculations. He had to keep note of the whole quantity each tenant brought to the mill so that, first, he could keep track of it for the estate and allow no dodging of the payment of 'victual rent'. He had to extract from each load the 'multure' due by each tenant according to the conditions of his lease. It might be one seventeenth, one twenty-second, or as much, for some unfortunates, as one tenth. It was up to the miller to measure and deduct it. And after that he took another quantity, in a proportion again laid down by the estate but measured by himself, as payment for services at grinding. This quantity, the miller's own payment, was known as the *lock* or the *lick of goodwill* although its payment was attended with anything but goodwill on the customer's part because of the generous hand with which the miller measured his own payment in contrast to his niceness in measuring what the customer brought.

Even then the payments were not at an end, because the miller's servant felt entitled to his share, a small quantity of meal called the *knaveship* which was usually recognised as being as much as he could hold heaped up in his two cupped hands. In most areas this due was not legally required but was paid by long tradition and common usage, and there was no way a customer could emerge from the mill past the waiting under-miller without paying it. Even further, the payment of *bannock*, an extra handful of meal to another servant, might be demanded. In 1610 a test case decided that 'bannock is rather a voluntary gratuity of the persons bringing their corns to the servants of the mill for their thankful service, not a right of the heritor of the miln.'[7] But in 1622 it was decided otherwise when tenants who had been forced by a court order to pay multures at the mill were also ordered to pay both knaveship and bannock. The matter was left in sufficient doubt at law to allow continual wrangling between customers and mill servants unless a high degree of goodwill existed between them.

While all this measuring and accounting was being attended to, the miller, or his servant, had to keep an eye on the kiln if he had one. In many cases in this early period customers dried their grain in their own farm kilns before bringing it to the mill, but the better organised estates preferred to have the drying done at the mill kiln. The more processes that were carried out under the miller's eye, the better chance there was of having rents and multures paid in full. So the kiln had to be got to the right heat and maintained there, the husks for stoking its fire had to be carried from the mill as they became available, and the grain had to be turned and shifted, turned and shifted so that it dried evenly and not too much. When it was dry it had to be carried again to the position near the mill hoppers where it could cool before entering the stones.

At the end of the day, the last customers gone, the fire raked out, the water diverted again away from the wheel, and the account books drawn up ready for the baron-baillie's examination, the miller would gather his extra perquisites from the day's grinding, the good meal which had escaped the millstone eye and now lay in the mill-ring surrounding the stones, and even the dusty flying meal which lay over everything at the end of the day and could be swept up and mixed with the good meal for sale at market.

There were variations on this 'daily grind'. There were the days — for some millers all too frequent — of attendance at the baron-baillie court, or before the kirk session, sometimes to answer for their own sins, sometimes to report on the sins of others. Millers, for instance, were not, apparently, willing churchgoers, and were often rebuked for working on Sundays: 'David Philip, mouterer of Shyres milne, was ordered to be cited before the next session for grinding on the Sabbath day' and, a month afterwards, on 21st February, 1699, 'Thomas Philip and Patrick Jack compearing and being dsired to confess it they had their milne going on the Sabbath day, went about to cover it, denying that at any time, to their knowledge, their mill was sett on before the Sabbath was over, but would not fully deny the going of their mill sometimes on Sabbath dayes mornings, pretending necessity for it.'[8]

This was a common complaint against the miller, who was sometimes forced to use water when it was available, even if that were the Sabbath, but he was more often in court to give evidence against some one else. Sometimes he reported on fighting within the mill premises, where violence often broke out either between customers impatient of waiting, or against the miller and his servants in exasperation at the severity of the mill dues. Very often he was a witness for the estate about the abstraction of multures. Not all millers were bosses' men. Of those who habitually interpreted the laws of the estate to the advantage of their fellow tenants we naturally have little evidence, for the whole weight of the tenants' silence would defend their generosity from detection. But we know that there were kindly millers if only from the united clamour of tenants against their successors. In 1730, when Alexander Gibbon, tacksman of the Mill of Cowie, summoned all the tenants of the barony for the abstraction of multure, it turned out that 'the haill sucken', that is, all the tenants, were protesting against the claims of this new miller because the former 'gudeman of the mill' had been lenient with them.[9] With one thing and another attendance at court could easily be a monthly occasion.

Another outing, at least for the more respected and efficient of millers, was occasioned by the need to make an inventory or survey of another man's mill at the end of the tenancy. When a miller left his mill the landowner called in another miller to help the estate factor judge whether it had been left in the same condition in which it had been found, whether repairs were needed, or whether compensation was due to the outgoing tenant. In some districts it was not easy to find a miller knowledgeable enough and sufficiently trustworthy to act as 'birlie-man' and so a trusted man might be called upon to travel often and at some distance from home to make a survey on his landlord's behalf. Peter May wrote, in 1769:

> Friday next is the term day and upon that day our mills must be appreciate. I am at a loss to know where to get proper people for birlie men. There are flour millers at Forres and Kilravock; shall I apply to them or will you send the General's miller?[10]

Market day provided another escape from routine. In England millers had been forbidden by law to deal in meal and a separate trade of mealman arose, although the practice of dealing by millers was in fact condoned and had become common by the eighteenth century.[11] In Scotland there was no such statutory provision against millers buying grain, processing it and selling it as meal. There does seem to be some evidence that the habit was on the increase at the beginning of the eighteenth century and that it was not popular with town buyers because of a notion that millers thus unfairly kept up prices. But an increase in meal dealing by millers during the early eighteenth century would be easily accounted for, first by an extra supply of corn to the mills as farm efficiency began slowly to improve, and secondly by the large number of new markets instituted at the end of the seventeenth century.[12]

These new markets, most of them begun by landlords in the hope — not, of course, always realised — of attracting new trade to their lands, created an opportunity for dealing in meal which millers, when they had a surplus to sell, were not slow to take. This was, of course, especially so in the environs of the larger towns. In the remoter country areas there was often neither a buying public nor much of a surplus for sale. Too many of the miller's customers were like Alexander Kennedy, of whom the factor at Ballachneil wrote, 'little can be counted upon his possession because in ordinary years he will with more profit dispose of his corns at stable than make it into meal.'[13] But near the towns not only was there more improved land yielding a surplus for sale, but there was also a population eager to buy and less knowledgeable about the ways in which a miller could stretch his meal for sale. Town customers were not able to attend the mill to make sure that *sids* were not mixed with *groats* at the grinding, that is that husks and clean grain were not ground together. It was said that 'half of the seeds is ground with the meall undiscovered by the Buyers, so it passes for good round meall and to add further to the weight its but bowsing the milners and they'll swip in the Sands which was saved for that use when the Stones were pick'd.'[14] This diatribe accuses the miller of including with the meal for sale even the loose sandstone rubbed off his millstones when they were being dressed or 'picked'. In Lowland Scotland the dealer in meal was known in the eighteenth century as a *meal maker*, a reference to the fact that he was often also a miller.

Some regions saw the emergence of a middle man between farmer and miller and between miller and buying public. His character varied very much from region to region. He might be a reputable and prosperous corn dealer or corn factor who purchased large quantities of grain from farmers for export to other regions. This class of dealer emerged from the farming class as a result of increased output from agriculture, increased demand for food from the towns and the resultant opportunities for entrepreneurship. Eventually the repeal of the Corn Laws, by easing dealings in imported grain, allowed the expansion of this class of corn merchant, but ensured his development away from those quarters of the country most dependent upon home-grown oats.

A smaller-scale, less heavily capitalised form of dealing in grain and grain products was undertaken by the meal-monger, a dealer who emerged rather from the millers than from the farmers, and a descendant of the earlier *meal maker.* He purchased small quantities of corn which he himself processed for retail to small-town tradespeople and labourers. This, of course, was an activity pursued to some extent by most millers, and the question of whether an individual was known principally as meal-monger or miller seems to have been chiefly one of emphasis, decided by whether his income was derived chiefly from selling meal or chiefly from payments for grinding. There were also meal dealers who neither grew nor processed grain but merely bought and sold it at premises owned by them. Such a firm was that of John Allan of Ayr, who found themselves in court over 45 loads of meal which they had bought from a tenant farmer knowing it to be owed for rent.[15] There were dealers quick to buy at the lowest possible prices from farmers reduced to desperation by bad harvests and driven to sell the oats which should have paid their rent or been kept for seed.

Because of their dealing activities millers came in for a proportion of the hatred worked up in the towns against those who made profits out of the hardship of others. The bad harvests of the late eighteenth century gave rise to shortages of meal and high prices in the town markets, and in some places 'meal mobs' rampaged into the countryside clamouring for someone — farmer, corn-dealer or miller — against whom to direct their anger. Farmers considered that the newspapers, numbers of which began to appear in the Scottish regions during the last decades of the eighteenth century, misrepresented the truth and led readers to believe that crops were good and prices kept artificially high by sharp-dealing profiteers when in fact the shortages were real and directly due to widespread if not universal crop failures.[16] The papers contained 'grievous imprecations, warm from the heart, against corn factors and all dealers in grain, with many a side glance also at farmers and meal-men'.[17] Prices during the second half of the century had risen only very slowly and people had become accustomed to only modest increases. The sharp rise of 1782 and the record price levels of 1798/1800 came as an unpleasant shock.[18] Although they were, for the most part, directly attributable to the early frosts and caterpillar infestations which had destroyed crops, townspeople, out of touch with countrymen's realities, were moved to 'acts of open violence and outrage against bakers, millers, farmers and other dealers in provisions'.[19] For a time attendance at market became a dangerous enterprise for millers and less of a pleasant break. But for most of the century market day was a day for meeting the neighbours in friendly companionship, a happy excuse for celebrating bargains in a drop of good liquor after much rubbing of meal between thumb and finger to judge its quality.

Even the small country miller, without the resources of the large-scale meal dealer, attended his local market both to buy what he needed and to sell meal surplus to his own household's requirements, and the produce of his land, especially the fat mill pigs.

Court and market provided, then, variations in the seasons' round. The overseeing and performance of mill services also took up the miller's time. Tenants clearing dams and lades, or fetching and carrying materials for mill repairs, had to be sought from their fields, cajoled and threatened into service, and watched grimly throughout for dodging and for slipshod work. The only exception was the winning home of the millstones from the quarry, which seems to have been usually a happy occasion attended willingly by a large number of tenant-neighbours. At the end of the long day's work involved, it was customary for the miller to give a party for those who had helped. Trestle tables were put up in the mill, ale was provided and the special mill bannocks put before the guests. A mill bannock was a huge oat-cake, as much as a foot round and an inch thick and made with a hole in its centre so that it looked like a small version of the stone they had spent the day rolling home. It was baked on the burning *sids* of shelled oats so that it became 'as brittle as if it had been baked with butter'.[20]

One might guess that the mill was not infrequently the setting for festivity from the number of the other 'treats' for special occasions which are described as being oatmeal products 'baked at the mill'. The *dry-goose* was one of these — a ball of extra finely ground meal, wetted until it could be patted and rolled into a round shape, then roasted in the hot ashes from the kiln. In Strathmore a similar procedure produced a *festy-cock,* a corruption of *fastyn cock,*[21] the substitute for a cockerel eaten at Shrovetide. Obvious imitations of the delicacies of the laird's table, these various oatmeal cakes were the festive fare of people who lived for the most part on bere meal and kept oats for best. The mill was warm, dry and spacious compared to the cot houses of the period and it was natural that it should be the meeting place for such fun and frolic as could not take place out of doors. The fact that dry oatmeal cakes cannot be eaten in any quantity without drink presupposes the intake of some quantity of ale on these occasions, no doubt adding to the good humour of the gathered neighbours.

What does seem to emerge is that, during the first half of the eighteenth century not only is the whole rural population of Scotland beginning slowly to awaken from a long hibernation of subsistence farming but that millers are improving their condition slightly more effectively. There is not a sufficient number of records to prove the point conclusively but it is often noticeable in estate letter books, for instance, how well a miller's handwriting and use of English compares with that of other subscribers, including the factor's, and where a number of tenants have signed their names the miller among them sometimes signs with a more literate hand. It was necessary for a miller, because he was one of the early users of mechanical aids to his craft, to stretch his mind, to use his ingenuity in a way other country workers often did not. It was necessary also for him to learn to keep accurate records and to do fairly complicated sums. At the end of the century, similarly, it was to the millers that the writers to the new *Farmers Magazine* turned for their 'Agricultural Intelligence', a regular report on the quantity and quality of crops harvested in the different regions. Millers were accustomed to keeping records, presenting figures and making comparative judgments.[22] Some degree of schooling, then, had to be acquired, perhaps only at a father's hand, but, in the early eighteenth century particularly, to have some education as well as the improved diet and perhaps improved housing of the miller's family already put a man in a position to better himself.

Because there was wide variation in farming efficiency between the well-run estates of the improving lairds and the backward mosses of the non-resident or feckless landed gentry there was a chance of betterment for an enterprising miller who chose to move from a mill with poor land attached to it and an impoverished *sucken* to another mill, perhaps already better equipped, with land in better heart and with more prosperous customers.

It was not impossible, in short, for a miller to acquire, from judicious dealings in meal and from efficient marketing of his fattened swine and other livestock, a small stock of capital. It would not be enough to make him rich but it could be enough to raise him to a degree of prosperity and comfort above his neighbours. By mid-eighteenth century millers were counted among the 'wadsetters and lesser gentlemen' on some estates.[23]

For millers, as for the rest of the country, the Rebellions brought an interruption to progress. Like other tenants their fortunes fluctuated with those of their landlords. Some were sufficiently singed with the Jacobite flame to leave their mills and follow to the wars. Among a list of attested rebels appear the names of Thomas Kemlar, miller, and Alexander Kemlar, his son, of the Mill of Mondynes, a mill which still stands, although empty and derelict. They 'went in arms to Stonehaven to assist the French ship against the British man o' war'.[24] Millers on the estates of landowners who joined the Prince and were forced to flee their lands were more affected by the removal of that paternal protection which had hitherto enforced attendance at the mill. With the baron absent and his courts in abeyance, tenants seized the opportunity to avoid the payment of mill multures. It is some evidence of the measure of prosperity attained before the Rebellions that millers on attested estates were able to survive this. The miller of Strathgaeth, for instance, had just finished building a new house and mill at his own expense and was occupied with hedging and dyking his property when 'his sucken was broke' and he found himself in some difficulty about payment for labour and materials. John Caw at Millnab found himself 'very much at a loss with regard to paying his rent for his mills'.[25]

For some the banishment of their protectors from the estate meant exile for themselves. Perhaps they were among the less efficient millers. The family of George Caird, for instance, had fallen into arrears of rent during six years of bad harvests at the end of the seventeenth century but had been tolerated by the Panmure estate. They found the York Building Company less forbearing and the mill, under its management of the estate, was given in tack to another. With the reinstatement of the estate George Caird wrote of 'a time which he has long looked for having arrived in which the lands which were formerly the property of your noble predecessor are now again under your management and your honour having it in your power to fulfil the promise of your late noble Countess . . . to procure him a lease of Carmylie milne how soon the death of the possessor at that time an old man, should happen'.[26] The Panmure estate had already been forfeit during the 1715 Rebellion and the mills on its lands had consequently suffered neglect over a long period. The Commissioners of Forfeited Estates reported in 1723 that £674 was required to put Balmossie Mill back into trim, the Earl of Panmure having been 'obliged to have kept the foresaid miln, bridge, pier and coble in sufficient repair and the samen not having been so kept but neglected whereby they are become ruinous'.[27]

After the 1745 Rebellion, in spite of the consequent neglect of property and fall-off in custom, millers were often among the first to lift their heads and begin work, showing 'an uncommon spirit for this part of the country',[28] building in stone, liming their ground, slating their roofs, trying out new crops like lint and potatoes. Alexander Robertson, for instance, of Mill of Brunty in central Perthshire, although 'quite a common country man . . . does more service in the neighbourhood and creates an emulation beyond any improvement that can be made by a gentleman'.[29]

Some estates handled during the period immediately after the Rebellions by the Forfeited Estates Commissioners or by the York Building Company experienced a degree of concerned and intelligent management they had not hitherto known so that millers, among other tenants, were encouraged both by good factoring and by estate expenditure on repairs and improvements to increase their own efficiency. The shake-up of the old feudal estates induced a spread of information about the latest scientific methods of land improvement which gradually brought about a measure of prosperity to Scottish farming from which millers could not fail to benefit. The period after the Rebellions and before the end of the Napoleonic Wars brought millers to the height of their prosperity. After that they sank back in status and in financial standing relative to the farming community in which they lived. During the late eighteenth century those millers who had the enterprise were able to acquire the capital to emerge as small-scale entrepreneurs within the food industry, and even those who confined their activities to the running of one mill enjoyed within it a comfortable living for themselves and their families.

Gradually, throughout the country, better farming produced better crops which brought more work to the mill. While tenants were still thirled to the local mill this could not fail to fill the miller's girnal better than it had ever been filled. For the period between the settling down of the country after the Rebellions, say about 1760, and the end of the Napoleonic Wars, some millers did very well indeed.

Not only did the meal in their girnals improve in quality and increase in volume, but the market for it increased as well. Population changes had so far resulted in some increase of people living in towns without as yet too marked a decrease in rural population. Those mills within reach of towns, or, like the Inverurie mills, well placed for transport to the towns, found a ready market for their meal among the new industrial workers.

It began to be necessary to provide some storage at mills. Where the earlier millers' customers had brought their sacks to the mill, attended the grinding, and carried the meal away immediately thereafter, the new system was more likely to involve the leaving of grain at the mill for delivery after grinding. Storage space was never provided on the scale of the southern English flour mills, with their imposing four-storey waterside palaces, their lucams, their piers and their granaries. The oatmeal mills of the North of England are not unlike those of Scotland but even they are more likely than the Scots mills to have the additional storey to accommodate a sack loft and sack-hoisting machinery. The difference in need for storage was occasioned chiefly by the different system of supplying the bakery trade. London, for instance, was chiefly supplied with corn by dealers who sold to millers in the public markets. The millers carried it to their countryside mills, manufactured it and brought it back to the London market again where it was sold to the bakers. In Edinburgh the bakers bought direct from the farmers who carried the grain to the mill and deposited it in the 'bakers' loft' there. The miller delivered the bakers' sacks, after grinding, directly to the bakehouse.[30] Thus the miller was providing the service of grinding for grain which he at no time owned. He had not, therefore, the need for storage space which would have been occasioned had he been speculating in grain, buying at low prices and storing until prices rose. Some millers did speculate in this way, but the scale of their operations was not large and the consequent need for storage not great. It was resolved chiefly by the provision of a new slated roof to replace the old turfs. Thus the sacks he stored beneath it could be kept free of the damp and deterioration to which anything stored under the old rotting thatch had been subject.

Not only was better farming increasing grain production and therefore increasing the business of the mill, but the improvement of transport allowed the movement of the surplus to the most profitable markets. The more settled state of the country after the putting down of the Rebellions made travel and the carriage of goods less hazardous. The money spent on road-building opened up to wheeled traffic areas that had been virtually closed to loads bigger than could be carried on horseback. To show how bad some roads had been one has only to quote a description of a much appreciated improvement: of Little Mill of Torr it was said 'the roads around this mill are so good and level that a horse can with ease carry an extra load.'[31] In areas where only the little Highland ponies had been known, much stronger cart horses began to be seen and properly constructed wheeled carts replaced the sleds that had once been dragged along the rutted tracks. Millers, partly because they had always the means of feeding a horse, partly because of their increasing need for sack carriage, were among the first to equip themselves with horse and cart.

Especially during the period before landlords began to interest themselves in manufacturing industry, a period whose beginning and end is ill defined and varied very much from region to region, mills benefited to a considerable extent from landowners' investment. The repair of the old estate mill or the building of a new one, better sited, was seen as part of the plan of agricultural improvement of the estate. On many estates millers found themselves, during the period when harvests were improving, better equipped to process them. By the time the protection of thirlage was removed from them, many millers were in a position to do very well without it. Some, indeed, were not at all averse to seeing the end of the system. Although they might make money through their neighbour's efficiency, they might equally lose it through his laziness. Although customers might lose through a miller's dishonesty, he as easily lost by their constant attempts to abstract the multures or to dodge payment. Above all, under the multure system, a miller could neither be certain of his income nor do anything in the way of attracting more custom to increase it. And landlords sometimes set the mill's rent on an unrealistic assessment of what the miller might take in multures. Robert Henry, for instance, wrote, 'When I took this mill I had still hopes that the mill dues would pay the rent, or nearly so, but I find myself greatly disappointed in my ideas, for the mill dues as yet has not paid me more than one half the rent.'[32] If complaints against the millers increased during the period when the abolition of thirlage was being pressed for, so too did millers' complaints against abstracted multures. Whatever the justice of the matter, it was becoming harder and harder to force tenants to pay up. So for many millers the change to a system of fixed money payments for grinding at the mill was a relief, even although it might mean facing competition from other mills in the neighbourhood when tenants ceased to be astricted.

NOTES

1. S.R.O. GD 201/4/82
2. Jamieson, *Dictionary*
3. *Farmers Magazine*, 1800, 476
4. *Scottish Journal of Agriculture*, 1918, 1, 13
5. See p. 176
6. See p. 176
7. Morison, *Decisions of Court of Session*, 15962, 15965
8. Beveridge, *Culross and Tulliallan*, 1, 27
9. Barron, *Urie*, 134-6
10. Adams, Ian H., *Papers of Peter May, Land Surveyor, 1749-1793*, S.H.S. Edinburgh, 1979, 155; also S.R.O. GD 135/39
11. Jones, 'Water powered corn mills', 309
12. Alexander, William, ed., *Acts of the Parliaments of Scotland*, Edinburgh, 1841, e.g. Act in favour of the Earle of Lothian for a fair and weekly mercat at Newbotle; Act in favour of John Lennox of Woodhead for three yearly fairs and a weekly mercat at the toun of Barorach; etc., etc.

13. S.R.O. GD 25/8/1339

14. A discourse or dialogue between an old meal maker and a Young One as they were on their way home from Dalkeith Mercat, National Library of Scotland 1938, 10(43)7

15. Court of Session, Barns v. Allan & Co., 1864

16. *Farmers Magazine*, 1800, 447-8

17. *Ibid.*, 473

18. Mitchison, Rosalind, 'Movements of Scottish Corn Prices in the 17th and 18th Centuries', 289-90

19. *Farmers Magazine*, 1800, 446

20. Mactaggart, *The Scottish Gallovidian Encyclopaedia*, 132/10

21. Jamieson, *Dictionary*

22. E.g. *Farmers Magazine*, 1800, 217: 'I should suppose from some enquiries which I have made at different mills that the quantity will not exceed two fifths of the preceding year.' *P.P.* XXVIII, 1799/1800, Appendix 8, Experiments by millers

23. Wills, *Annexed Estates*, 46

24. Cramond, *Annals of Fordoun*, 75

25. Wills, *Annexed Estates*, 78

26. S.R.O. GD 45/18/1271

27. S.R.O. GD 45/18/1864

28. Wills, *Annexed Estates*, 78

29. *Ibid.*, 19

30. *Farmers Magazine*, 1800, 217

31. *N.S.A.*, X, 1276-7

32. S.R.O. GD 46/17/591

12
Rents and Repairs for the Mill

In the eighteenth century rents were set in relation to an estimate of what the miller might expect from his multures. Landlords, or their factors, when deciding what rent could be expected from a particular mill, would make an estimate of the multures which could be expected of the lands in thirl. Such an estimate survives in an 'Account of grain to be milled at Ballochneil Mill from various farms to be annexed in thirlage to the said miln at the usual multure of half a peck of shillin out of the boll of shillin'. It was reckoned that the eleven farms would yield 70 bolls yearly which would give the miller in multures two bolls and three pecks of shilling, that is, the grain from which the husks had already been removed.[1]

Interestingly enough the account then goes on to estimate that the miller could make four bolls, one firlot and two pecks of meal out of this amount of shilling, which is almost certainly a gross over-estimate. *Meal for corn* was the expression used to describe the ideal extraction rate, attained only under exceptional circumstances, of one boll of meal for one boll of oats. Even at Findlay's time of writing, that is the middle years of the present century, oats were reckoned to be of good quality if they could produce one boll of meal from one quarter of oats.[2] At Barry Mill they reckon to get six or seven bolls from 15 cwts at the present day, very much what Findlay reckoned satisfactory. To make matters more complicated *meal for corn,* like the vessels which measured it, has meant different things at different times. A report of milling tests on different varieties of oats in 1918 stated, 'All the returns were up to the "meal for corn" standard of 140 lbs meal from 240 lbs oats.'[3] These tests, of course, were being carried out under ideal conditions with the best quality oats. The quality of the oats affected the extraction rate more than the quality of the milling. Some years, like

1800, produced reports that the best varieties of oats 'yielded not much less than meal for corn at the Mill'.[4] Whereas a bad year like 1818 brought reports that oats were producing only 8 to 12 pecks (a peck was 8 lbs when a lb was 17½ oz) from a boll and that some were so bad 'as not to be worth mealing'.[5] In the 1830s William Gaudy's books at Lunan Mill show that he got something like a boll of meal from a boll of oats, perhaps an indication of the quality of the oats grown around the Red Head. Certainly the Ballochneil factor's estimate that the miller could get double the quantity of meal from his two bolls of oats seems unlikely if not impossible by any standard of measurement.

But it was on the landlord's notion of what he could make from the mill that the miller had to pay his rent. The theory was that the multures should bring in enough to pay the rent and give a comfortable living to the miller, his 'lick of goodwill', the payment for grinding, providing merely the extra jam on his bread, not the bread itself. In fact the multures did not always cover the rent and some millers would have known hard times if their land and their beasts had not made them something near self-sufficient without the multures. Where the rent was subject to regular and open-minded review it is likely that millers did reasonably well. But where the pattern of farming had changed very much since a miller's lease was drawn up, where, for instance, the thirled farms had turned to dairying or to crops not subject to multures, he could find himself without the income to pay his rent. On the other hand, where farm leases had been so drawn up as to subject all grindable corns to multures, the miller could find himself growing prosperous in good arable country. Multures were, however, designed in the first place to bring in a high income to the landowner, not to the miller. The whole purpose of allowing the miller to extract multures was to make it possible for the estate to extract higher rents from the mills than would otherwise have been possible.

The income from mills was an important and valuable part of an estate's whole income, as can be seen from the frequency with which 'half the mill' was granted to favoured relatives or as marriage settlements. So mill rents were set higher than rents of the lands round about them. On Portsoy estate in 1814, for instance, there are 83 tenants. Of these 23 are 'on improvements', that is on marginal land newly in cultivation, and they pay only from £1 to £3 annually. Of the other 60 only one pays a higher rent than John Taylor on the mill lands. Taylor, the miller, is paying the same rent for his two acres as James Imlach, farmer, pays for a farm of nine acres. At £15.10s, however, Taylor was still paying a small amount for a year's rent.[6]

In the county of Kirkcudbright at the end of the eighteenth century the usual rent for the largest farms was from £40 to £70 and the rent of the mill £45.[7] John Davidson at Ogilvy Mill was paying £34.10 up to 1769 but had to suffer its being doubled in 1770.[8] Craigoch Mill paid £33 in 1781 and £79.5.1 in 1800. Dinduff went up even more in the same period, from £24 in 1771 to £112 in 1799, while Balwhirrie went down from £30.6.8 in 1771 to £25.6.8. William Baird at Galdenoch paid £30 annually from 1786 to 1800.[9] William Leggat at Kirkchrist Mill paid only £23.4.4 in 1786 but paid a further £18.8 rent for his kiln, whereas Baird at Galdenoch was paying only interest of £1.10 yearly on the loan of capital to him for the kiln he had built himself.[10] Pinclunty Mill, where Edward Hutchinson was miller in 1820, had its rent set at £25 for the next 19 years. He paid also 6 stones of meal, 12 hens and 12 chickens, but was allowed £4 yearly from the estate towards the upkeep of the dam.[11]

The change in some mills from a victual rent to a money rent makes comparison of one period with another difficult. At Arbirlot Mill, for instance, the rent in 1766 had been only ten shillings sterling in money with 54 bolls of bear and one boll four pecks of meal. When Andrew Paterson was given a 45-year lease of the same mill the year afterwards, his rent was set at 31 bolls of meal and £15 sterling yearly for the first 15 years, 31 bolls of meal and £16 yearly for the next 15 years, and 31 bolls of meal and £17 for the third 15 years, 'the meall being for the mill Eye'.[12] Taking meal at 15 shillings a boll, that would make his rent, in 1811, £40.

Where former meal rents were converted into money, rents were set by fiars' prices, that is the fair prices struck for meal by the courts. These prices, and the manner of striking them, varied from region to region as well as from period to period.[13] A few established grain merchants sent to the Sheriff an account of the quantity of grain bought and the prices paid for it by them while a similar group of millers sent in a statement of the quantity of oatmeal sold and prices reached for it. The average prices, those that would then be considered fair prices for the region during the forthcoming season and on which rents and wages would be set, were struck by a committee of jurymen who had listened to millers' and dealers' evidence. The matter was complicated by the need to set prices for different qualities of oats and the question of which category individual loads of grain fell under could lead to some dispute. It all made more bookwork for the miller and more cause for discontent between landlord and tenant. In the North-East it was not until 1918 that the fixing of prices became the business of the Sheriff rather than the jurymen.[14]

Thus rents which now seem small in comparison with others of the same period might perhaps have been explained by the low prices for grain fetched in that neighbourhood at that particular time. William Gaudy paid £36 at Lunan Mill in Angus in 1840. In 1835 mills in Perthshire were paying rents as low as £2, for the Mill of Fortune at Comrie, and as high as £207, for the Newmill of Scone.[15] This wide variation was caused by differences in the extent and quality of the land attached to the mill (a factor hard to assess at this distance of time) as well as by the prosperity of the surrounding farmland. If there can be said to have been an 'ordinary' rent for an average mill with an average amount of land in Perthshire in the 1830s it was probably about £60 or £70 yearly. Such discrepancies explain to some extent — even if there had been no other reasons — the miller's willingness to change his situation. He must always have been on the lookout for a place with a lower rent than his own and with equal opportunities or for one with the same rent and a better clientele.

Even at the end of the seventeenth century a distinction can be seen between lands described as 'with the mill thereof' and mills named 'with the mill lands'. The first were of larger acreage, and the mill merely an appendage, and they paid higher rents. There were farms on which, most probably, the mill would eventually be allowed to become ruinous as agricultural improvements increased the land's prosperity, or perhaps from which the mill would be detached and let separately. The second were smaller holdings, some of them no more than crofts, on which the mill was the prime source of income and the rent gauged accordingly.

By the nineteenth century the distinction had hardened. The larger farms, while retaining their 'Mill of' names, had ceased to have any connection with milling and were now entirely farm lands. The usual mill was a *country* mill, with a small piece of land, producing an income and owing a rent higher than that of the crofters and the smallest farms but very much smaller than that of the large farms.

In common with all tenants, mills experienced a sharp rise in rents in the period between 1760 and 1815 when landlords, bent on expensive improvements, were attempting to raise the income from their lands. For most tenants the rise in rents was justified by the granting of longer leases which made it worthwhile for them to spend time and money on manuring and liming their soil and so eventually increasing their incomes. But millers had already been accustomed to tenure of reasonable duration and to properly drawn up leases, the law of Scotland having decreed that mills should be separately described and given written contracts,[16] so there was for them little compensation to balance the higher rents. The abolition of thirlage, which might indeed have made millers feel that their rents should be lowered rather than increased, came in most cases after this period of rising rents. The miller's problem, then, was to set his dues for grinding at rates which would comfortably cover his rent without tempting his one-time suckeners and now his customers to wander away to a competitor's mill.

To sum up, eighteenth century mill rents had been considerably higher than the rents paid by the majority of the miller's customers. To match this economic fact, the miller's position in society was superior to that of most of his customers. He was a man of more education, more authority and with better hopes of prosperity than his neighbours. After the rise in rents between 1760 and 1815, although the miller's rent rose like that of the others and his actual standard of living probably did not change materially, his relative position in society changed quite considerably.

The absorption of many small farms and cot towns into a much smaller number of better-run farms meant that the poorest of the cultivators of the land, except in the Highlands, disappeared from the land or lost their self-employed status, becoming labourers on the larger farms. The remaining smaller number of farmers, now cultivating a larger acreage, living very often in a new-built and superior farmhouse, improved both their financial and their social position to a marked extent. They became men of some standing in their parishes, their long leases making them much less cowed by the proprietors of the estate, their new buildings distinguishing them from the rut of the country dwellers, and good prices for corn and cattle making them into solid and respected citizens, elders of the kirk and trustees of the parochial schools, removed from the squalid subservience their grandfathers had known. Relative to them the miller, still an independent and respected figure, had little standing in the community. He was much less likely to become an elder or to be looked up to as the more important farmers were. On the other hand he was self-employed and self-sufficient, dependent on no-one and beholden to no-one. He did not fall into the category of the crofters, whose land barely supported them and whose traditional extra income from hand weaving or stocking knitting disappeared with the introduction of the factory system. The miller came somewhere in the middle of the rural hierarchy, below minister, teacher and farmer, and above cottar and ploughman. He was aligned more with the independent craftsmen, the blacksmith and the millwright, than with anyone else but, because his trade was a source of food as well as of income his material prosperity was perhaps greater than theirs. He aspired to education rather than to gentility and, if he had no fortune to pass on to his children, he left them something of greater potential than the farmer's acres, an enquiring mind.

The social change was emphasised by the effect of the abolition of thirlage on farm rents. Towards the end of the eighteenth century it came gradually to be recognised that thirlage, although having its roots in a more ancient feudal system, had become merely a hidden means of extracting higher rents. By allowing the miller to exact multures the landlord had justified charging him a higher rent than would otherwise have been possible; and for the tenant farmers who paid the multures, especially on estates where they had to pay 'dry multures', the amount involved was simply an inevitable extra charge upon their income in addition to their rent. In abolishing the system the landlords rationalised the rents, raising the farmers' rents to cover whatever diminution of mill rents the estate might suffer. Thus the miller's rent, and eventually his position in society, diminished relatively as a direct result of the abolition of thirlage. On some estates, the process by which thirlage was commuted resulted in millers becoming, instead of direct tenants or tacksmen of the estate as they had traditionally been, sub-tenants of farmers. This happened because tenant farmers, wishing to be freed of astriction to the estate mills, sometimes made an agreement with the factor that they would take over the payment of the mill rents in compensation for their freedom.[17] This made them, in practice, landlords of the mills, which they could then sub-let, if they chose, to the millers at rents which allowed for the cessation of multure payments. Where there was no real local need for the mill it would not be re-let at the end of the resident miller's lease. The building would then be used as barn or shed at the farmer's convenience. If there was continuing custom the mill would be let and kept going. But the relative position of the miller and farmer had been, by such a transaction, radically changed. The miller, for instance, could find himself evicted from his mill because of the principal tenant's, the farmer's, bankruptcy.[18] He had become dependent upon the farmer in a way quite new to both of them.

Eighteenth century millers, we have seen, were more likely than most tenant farmers to have been granted properly drawn up leases. By his lease the miller was given certain rights and some authority over the other tenants, the right to extract multures, to sue for abstraction, to exact services and even to enter houses within the sucken for the purpose of breaking querns.[19] To enter into possession of these rights and of the mill he had to pay entry money or grassum, a sum amounting to more than a year's rent. Thereby he purchased his right to the mill 'in the faith that no other mill of the same kind could lawfully be erected within the thirle to interfere with him'.[20] The machinery within the mill was likely to have been installed by his landlord rather than by himself and he could expect some repairs at the estate's expense, although by the end of the century he often paid interest on the cost of new installations paid for by the landlord.

In the next phase the miller's lease gave him duties rather than rights, restrictions rather than authority. Although his fellow tenants were not now forced to give him custom he, however, could be bound not to alter the price of his grinding without the consent of his landlord. While both eighteenth and nineteenth century leases bound miller/tenants to leave the mill in at least as good a state as they found it, the nineteenth century miller could not depend on having either repairs or improvements at his landlord's expense. In a test case in 1849 Peter Dallas, miller of Easter Moniack, sued the landowner, James Baillie Fraser, for not complying with the terms of a lease drawn up by his agent in which Dallas had persuaded the agent to insert a clause containing an obligation on Fraser to keep house and mill wind and watertight and to keep the mill dam and lade in good repair. Dallas lost his case, Lord Mackenzie saying in his conclusion that 'It would be better for a landlord to give up his property altogether than to agree to such a clause.'[21] This may have seemed just enough to both law lords and landowners. To the millers it seemed less obviously fair. While eighteenth century landowners had not been bound to uphold mills on their property, the better managed estates had usually done so and, at the worst, had made, by the terms of mill leases, the services of other tenants available to the miller for his repairs. Now the miller was left with neither patronage nor services. Repairs and extensions were his own problem, the cost of them having somehow to be found from income. To increase his costs and his responsibilities his lease now often held an obligation upon him to spend a certain amount of money on machinery, this being a new way of improving the value of an estate, and — an additional expense — he was now expected to pay insurance adequate to cover damage to the mill by fire.

The first generation of millers after the abolition of thirlage, which was general if far from complete in the first quarter of the nineteenth century, faced, then, some new difficulties not experienced by eighteenth century millers. No longer the favoured beneficiaries of a feudal system, they now had to face the market unprotected. Their income became dependent on their ability to provide a genuinely wanted service and to perform it efficiently. And there were new claims upon that income. Nevertheless there were benefits, especially at first. If they now had to attract customers instead of taking them for granted, at least their customers had moved away from the familiar pattern of dearth and famine. Thirled customers whose crops had failed brought little comfort to the miller, whose own prosperity was necessarily bound up with, if not entirely dependent upon, the efficiency of his neighbour's farming methods. During the period of the Napoleonic Wars, which coincided with the period in which commutation of thirlage rights was most generally sought, high prices for corn brought plenty of custom to the mill. In the first place landowners, encouraged by the profits to be made, spent money on the improvement of their land. In the second place tenant farmers chose to plant corn in preference to other crops because of the encouragement they received from the estate factors and the prices won at market. So, while the blockades kept out imported corn, while the armies' need for food and fodder lasted, while the growing industrial towns cried out for home-produced supplies and until the Corn Laws were abolished, mills were kept busy and prosperous.

Another benefit to compensate millers for the end of feudal astriction was their new ability to organise their businesses in their own way. Not all feudal patronage had been helpful and some of it had been better termed interference. The generally accepted view that thirlage protected the miller from competition and that its abolition made him face competition for the first time is indeed in some doubt. For one thing, astriction was never complete. All the watchfulness of estate factor and miller's men could not, in fact, prevent tenants from constantly slipping away to the mill of their choice, whether because it was nearer to them than the one to which they were thirled or simply because they preferred the manners of the miller there. The large number of cases of suing for abstraction of multures shows how common was the habit.

The strictest enforcement could not entirely prevent it. In fact it could be fairly suggested that the reasonably efficient miller was likely to suffer less rather than more from competition after the end of thirlage. Many badly placed, run down or otherwise unsatisfactory mills were kept in existence during the eighteenth century only by the estate's insistence on astricting their tenants to them. With the end of astriction they quickly found themselves without tenant or custom and the remaining mills in the district benefited from their disappearance, their millers finding in the succeeding period not more but less competition for the existing customers in the neighbourhood. Assessment is difficult, but it would seem that there was no large surplus of millers at the end of the eighteenth century, and no queue of millers looking for mills. Glasgow Town Council had difficulty finding tenants for their mills, and Perth city mills could find managers but not miller/tacksmen for theirs. It seems to have been possible for millers to choose, at least to some extent, in which mills they would accept a tenancy. In these circumstances, the run down, badly situated mills simply failed to find tenants, leaving more customers in the new free market for those mills which best satisfied their needs. There was, in fact, a quick and fairly painless shake-out of the inefficient, resulting in the number of mills being reduced to the point where each served a neighbourhood large enough to support it. The competition which country millers had to fear came not from rival meal millers but from steam-powered mills grinding imported wheat into white flour for the new town bakeries. But this came later in the century. For the first quarter of the nineteenth century the miller, bursting forth from his cocoon of feudalism, spread his wings in the warm sunshine of prosperity. Farmers needed his services, a growing population needed his products, and he had the technical knowledge and the equipment to supply them.

NOTES

1. S.R.O. GD 25/8/1339
2. Findlay, *Oats*, 193
3. *Scottish Journal of Agriculture*, 1, 1918, 13
4. *Farmers Magazine*, 1800, 453
5. *Ibid.*, 1818, 117-8
6. S.R.O. GD 248/3109
7. *O.S.A.*, 2, 131

8. S.R.O. GD 24/1/1639
9. S.R.O. GD 135/39
10. See p. 82
11. S.R.O. GD 142/46 35
12. S.R.O. GD 45/18/1983
13. Mitchison, 'Movements of Scottish Corn Prices', 280
14. Findlay, *Oats*, 15-7
15. Gloag, William, deputy collector of cess, *Rental of the County of Perth*, Perth, 1835
16. Hunter, *Law of Landlord and Tenant*, 383
17. *O.S.A.*, 3, 473
18. Court of Session, Robt. Wilson v. Walter F. Campbell of Shawfut, 12 December 1839
19. Hunter, *Law of Landlord and Tenant*, 394
20. S.R.O. GD 135/39; 45/18/1983; Morison, *Decisions of Court of Session*, 10050
21. Court of Session, Peter Dallas v. James Baillie Fraser, 26 May 1849

13
The 19th Century Miller

After the commutation of multures the miller's daily life did see a change. Many mills simply disappeared; the number of mills operating within a parish was everywhere reported as having diminished between the first and second Statistical Accounts, that is between the 1790s and the 1840s. Of these, some had been ill placed at the time of their first building, either with an inefficient supply of water or, sometimes, on the wrong side of the river for the bulk of the customers. Some had been built in areas which were corn producers at the time of their building but had since switched to pasture. Some had been neglected so much by uninterested landlords that only continual bullying by the estate factor had ever driven the tenants to use them and, with the removal of the astrictive clauses in their leases, the custom was withdrawn and the mill allowed to crumble. Such a one was Drummore where 'the miln is so every way insufficient that the Barony have deserted her.'[1] Some, situated on good farm land, were tenanted by millers who found their income from their fields outstripping the mill's takings and therefore concentrated on farming, allowing the mill to fall into disuse. Some others, placed within reach of the towns' industrial influence, or on the estates of landlords hopeful of profits from the new industries, ceased to operate as meal mills and turned their wheels for manufacturing industry, often as flax-spinning mills or as washing mills for the bleachfields. Of those that were left some, well placed for sales to the towns' populations, grew into large concerns, switched to white flour production, installed steam power and passed out of our present sphere of interest.

What the miller had most feared as a consequence of the removal of astriction was that competition among the very large number of mills would be cut-throat. In fact, for this variety of reasons, the number of mills was naturally reduced so that, in general, each served a neighbourhood sufficiently wide to give the miller not a large but a reasonable income.

The water-powered meal mills of the nineteenth century, for the most part small mills serving the farmers of a not very extensive area, were operated by a new kind of miller, thrown on his own resources, without the protection of a feudal landlord, and quite able to survive in that condition. His mill was now equipped with some new pieces of machinery, much of it his own property, paid for with his own profits, and so treasured and understood by him throughout its long life. Instead of summoning the tenant farmers and crofters to help him when he needed new parts, he ordered them from the millwright's shop, itself now better capitalised and equipped, or direct from the wholesale suppliers. This, of course, had to be paid for with money but, although the farm servants he supplied with meal were still paid largely in kind, the farmers paid the miller in cash and his own dealings in meal had increased, so he had money at his disposal.

If he had less responsibility and status within the community now that he no longer enjoyed so much paternal protection from the estate, he had the compensation of not being required to attend the baron-baillie's court with its endless squabbles over multures and mill services. However, the miller's reputation for litigiousness grew, if anything, during this period when the very keen competition for water power meant in some districts that rights over every inch of river bank were fought over in the courts. This competition, of course, for the most part, affected those mills situated closest to the towns which were, in any case, to be swallowed up by industrial spread during the immediately following period. The miller surviving into the nineteenth century, and barely changed in his ways until the Second World War, is the country miller, a peaceable fellow, with little business outside his own immediate area, either for court or customers.

The markets which once gave him cause for absences from his mill were reduced in numbers and changed in character. In parts of Scotland the period between the early nineteenth century revival of the old corn markets which had earlier fallen into disuse and their permanent replacement by the newly organised wholesale and retail grocery trade was very short. Most districts in Victorian times had two 'feein' markets' a year which operated chiefly as employment exchanges, their chief purpose being not so much the buying or selling of goods (although that did take place) as the hiring of farm servants. They became a much looked forward to social occasion, a break in the year's round which the miller enjoyed as much as other country folk:

Week in and week oot, when I'm millin,
The sids seem to stick in my throat,
Nae wonder at markets I'm willin'
To spend wi a crony a groat.

An if I've a shaltie to niffer (trade)
Or maybe some barley to sell
An onslockened bargain's aye stiffer —
Ye ken that fu' brawly yersel'.[2]

The nineteenth century miller had two main sources of income. He ground grain sent to him by the farmer to the farmer's requirements and was paid for his services. The grain remained the farmer's property and was simply processed for him at the mill. This was known as 'customer work'. Mills near enough to the towns to attract custom there would also do a certain amount of work for the bakeries and grocers, unless the towns' mills were already owned or tenanted by the bakers' corporations. William Gaudy of Lunan Mill supplied oatmeal to the Arbroath Cooperative Association in the 1840s.

As well as this customer work the miller also bought grain from the farms which he ground into meal and sold to the grocery trade or to private customers who chose to buy their meal straight from the mill. These were, for the most part, small transactions, taking place steadily throughout the year. David Lindsay, the farmer at Courthill, sent oats to the mill in January, July, August and October each year, the quantity in 1840 amounting in all to 70 bolls.[3]

As long as threshing, whether by flail or machine, was a farm operation it was carried on at intervals throughout winter and spring and the resultant grain sent regularly in small quantities to the mill. Only when threshing began to be let out to contractors who treated the whole harvest in one yearly operation did the system change.

The mill was kept steadily at work through winter and spring with perhaps a slack time at sowing time when farmers were too busy in the fields to waste men on barn work. But then the miller was glad of the opportunity to get on with his own field work.

He remained almost always a tenant and he did not often increase his land holdings. While some farms amalgamated and increased very much in size, he remained among the small-scale tenant farmers, in status within the community one of them, although he was by the isolation of his craft a more independent and multi-skilled character. He worked his fields, but he was not entirely dependent upon their produce, so his life was not entirely comparable to that of the crofter and farmer. The blacksmith, who prepared ironwork for him, and the millwright who carried out repairs which needed parts he and the blacksmith could not improvise, were his nearest counterparts, his craft skills and his self-employment allying him with these independent country tradesmen. But his life differed from theirs in many ways. He had a product to sell as well as a service to render, and his roots within the community went back much further than the other tradesmen's. Even when he and his family were incomers, his mill had stood in its place since beyond the memory of the most ancient farm dwellers, a part of the countryside almost as much as the water that turned it. But the small tenant farmers and country tradesmen were his neighbours, friends and customers and it was their community the meal miller served.

He set his mill on in the morning and lit his kiln just as did his eighteenth century predecessor. Like Tammas the miller in Charles Murray's poem, he:

> Ran to the mill and pu'd the tow
> That set the water on;
> Syne busy banged the girnal lids,
> An' tossed the sacks about,
> Or steered again the bleezin' sids.[4]

But he did not then wait about for his customers. He would have already arranged the round of collections and deliveries his horse and cart would make that day, for one of the consequences of the end of thirlage was that millers now had to do their own fetching and carrying. A farmer might sometimes send grain to the mill and sometimes ask for it to be collected by the miller, but the deliveries of meal were the miller's job. Each mill kept a list of farm servants to whose cottages regular deliveries were to be made, with the amounts due to them from their employer as wages and their own preference in quality of meal. The miller of Lunan, William Gaudy, sent meal ground from Courthill's oats to the cattleman, the blacksmith, the forester, and three cot houses as well as two pecks to the beadle and two bolls to Lindsay's own household — the 'House'. He had to be careful that each got only the amount due to him and on one occasion, in 1840, he wrote in his meal book, 'I consider that the cattleman has got more meal than I have heard of.'

For many mills production of this meal for 'boll wages' made the most important because the steadiest part of their custom. The bothy men, or the married men's wives, would leave instructions with the miller about how much they wanted at a time and he would either keep a record of the quantity still due or, if they chose, buy from them what they did not require. Thus some cash reached the ploughmen's pockets and the miller was left with meal to sell at the mill or at market to those country customers who were neither producers of grain nor farm employees.

From the time when farm cottages were improved by the installation of good iron kitchen ranges, some cottar wives were accustomed to ask for a part of their boll wages in wheat flour, although the majority still took it all in meal. The miller was not, after the middle of the nineteenth century, usually called upon to grind quite such a variety of grains as his eighteenth century counterpart. Barley was by now not normally used as flour, except in the Northern Isles, and peas and beans were ground for human consumption in only a few places. The chief trade was now in oatmeal for porridge and bannocks and for thickening kail, and in animal feedstuffs, which were crushed rather than ground. These included a fairly wide range of materials including the imported locust bean which little boys loved to steal from the miller's sacks and chew as a modern child chews gum. The miller kept one pair of stones for shelling, one for grinding oats and, if he wanted to grind wheat, he set the meal stones close. Some mills kept three pairs of stones so that one pair, of the harder burr that milled the best flour, was always ready for wheat when required. In addition there was a crusher for the feed corn, usually driven by a belt off the main drive. The miller kept his stones ready for business by 'picking' them himself, and some of those particularly skilled in this work would travel to other mills to dress the stones for fellow millers.[5]

The fact that the miller had to collect and deliver sacks meant that he needed help either at the mill or with the carting. The eighteenth century miller, the *gudeman* or *moulturer* of the mill, had kept *pickieman* and *knave* to help him, each entitled to his own payment from each customer at the mill. The nineteenth century Scots miller employed a *ladester* to help with loading and unloading the carts and moving the sacks from one stance to another about the mill, and a *dryster* to attend the kiln. The installation of *elevators*[6] early in the nineteenth century had diminished the amount of sack handling from storey to storey within the mill very considerably. This invention cannot be said to have been inspired by the removal of thirlage because it originated in the United States of America and arrived in Scotland via Liverpool.[7] But undoubtedly the ending of a system which had allowed the miller to stand by and watch while customers heaved their own sacks between one machine and another must have spurred millers to find the money to install so labour-saving an invention. In the same period, mechanical sack hoisting by rope pulleys or by an endless chain was also introduced. The processes within the mill were beautifully streamlined to allow the grain entering the hoppers to reach the waiting sacks as meal without any need for handling or interruption on the way. But on the way to the hopper and from the mill to the customer there was still occasion for much carrying of sacks and for lifting them on and off carts. It was work heavier than a boy could do and required the employment of a grown man. No wonder the lads were asked at feeing markets, 'Can ye throw a bow o bear ower yer shouther?'[8]

Similarly the much improved kilns installed from the last decades of the eighteenth century, although in every respect superior to the dangerous old farm kilns of the earlier period, meant more work for many millers. Again, the pattern was different in the Northern Isles, but on the mainland of Scotland farmers gradually ceased during the nineteenth century to kiln their mown grain but brought it undried to the mill kiln. There it had to be constantly watched and turned to bring it to the right state of milleability to the point where each grain was exactly as dry, as brittle, as friable as would grind most readily without its flavour being dried out. This was hard labour, and because it required judgment and experience it had to be done either by the miller himself or by an employee dryster of some competence. The 'reekit dryster in the kil' became one of the characters of the countryside, the constant figure firmly allotted his place to whom a small boy could run for a 'news' and ask for an 'oxter pooch filled with shillans for his doos'.[9]

Both dryster and loadster had to be paid for by the miller himself, unless he was blessed with sons grown to the business. Customers would no longer heap the mill servants' cupped hands with meal and, in any case, the mill servants would no longer have been prepared to live on such a pittance. Wages for mill servants did not differ from those of the farmhand. In the second half of the nineteenth century by far the greatest proportion of men working on farms were young unmarried men who,[10] if they failed to get jobs as grieves or foremen before they married, would leave farm work for 'whatever it's my luck tae be — the Bobbies or the trams'.[11] Farmers would take on fairly large numbers of 'loons' and 'halflins' to live in the bothies and work for low wages but would not employ more than a few when they grew old enough to demand a man's wage. Similarly millers employed young men as prentices at a small wage while teaching them the trade, although their chances of bettering themselves by the three years' apprenticeship seem to have been better than those of the farm servants.[12] Conversation with any elderly miller soon elicits the fact that he has knowledge of a great many mills other than the one in which he is presently found. In his youth he had moved quite frequently from one mill to another before finding one in which to settle and, because his father and grandfather very often were millers too, even before he reached working age his childhood home had been moved from mill to mill several times.

There were many reasons for this constant 'flitting'. In the first place, millers' servants were not so very different from other farm servants, whose habit of shifting jobs at the term was notorious. The two classes of worker were in fact, at this age, often interchangeable, millers' sons sometimes taking jobs on the farms until there should be a place in the mill for them, young ploughmen sometimes marrying millers' daughters and getting taken on at the mill in consequence. A miller's servant was given a year's contract, whereas the farm worker had only six months, and towards the end of the year, unless he was both pleased with his situation and certain that his master would offer him another year's work, he would be on the lookout for another mill to go to.

Mill servants did not, however, suffer the indignities of the feeing markets, where ploughmen lined up to have their muscles felt by selecting farmers. They were in a position to make private arrangements with millers who were probably already known to them through family connections. Young millers, partly of course because their conditions of employment were more desirable, were less footloose than farm servants, but they were still inclined to suppose that the wheel turned more smoothly up or down stream from their present situation. It has to be remembered that the move did not necessarily entail a major upheaval. There were still so many mills, especially in the North-East, that moving might be only a question of putting one's kist on a cart and travelling a couple of miles along the same river bank to an environment hardly different from the one he had left.

However, some young mill servants moved, not only because of their discontent with the old place, but because they wanted to widen their experience of mill work. Although most country mills contained almost the same machinery, so that to know one was to know all, there began to emerge some leaders in the industry, more lavishly equipped than the usual 'run of the mill', and with a higher quality product. To gain experience in one of these mills was obviously to the advantage of a young man, whether his ambition was to be taken on as foreman in a large mill or eventually to find a mill of his own. Employment in the larger mills situated in or near the town had both advantages and disadvantages. Better equipped they might be, but some at least of the men who had left country mills to work for the larger concerns returned home to seek their old jobs again, reporting that there was 'a very low class of miller' employed in the town.

It was not only experience of different sets of machinery that a young miller required. He also needed to learn the ways of different neighbourhoods. A mill in a cattle-rearing area had a different kind of customer with different needs from one in an entirely arable area, and the miller had to understand the requirements of the different trades. In one district he might be occupied almost entirely with customer work for farmers. In another his trade might be mostly with retail shops. In yet another he might be dealing with the export market, bagging his products for delivery by rail to the nearest seaport. The young miller had to learn to handle the business side of milling as well as to understand its processes, and he could only learn by observing and comparing.

Another spur to moving from one mill to another was marriage. Some mills had a couple of cottages for mill servants but many more had only a house for the miller himself. Like the young ploughman forced, on marrying, to leave the bothy and look for a place with a cottage, the young married miller had either to find a place where the miller could put a house at his disposal or to look for a mill of his own. This required savings. To get his own mill he had to be able to offer a rent higher than that paid by the existing tenant and he had to have enough business sense to judge whether the income from the mill would be sufficient to justify the higher rent. The landowners' habit of letting to the highest bidder was a major cause of millers' moving. One man, well settled and content in his mill for many years, might find himself ousted by another offering more rent, and so be forced to seek another mill at a rent he could afford. Another, having offered an unjustifiably high rent in his anxiety to get a mill of his own, might afterwards find difficulty in earning enough to pay that high rent, and subsequently have to leave and move to a lower-rented place. Yet another, doing well, making profits and able to offer his landlord a higher rent to prevent him letting to another tenant, might still choose to move, once he had reached such a prosperous position, to another, perhaps better equipped and better situated, mill.

The last step in the series of moves from one mill to another made by a miller during his lifetime's work both as employed man and as tenant was, if he was fortunate, towards ownership of his own mill. Some young millers were lucky. Where the father already owned a mill of his own he was sometimes, particularly if he were blessed with more than one son so that one could stay with him while the other moved on, in a position to buy or perhaps take the tenancy of another mill and put in the boy as manager. More often a miller had to save a lifetime towards the moment when the mill of which he was tenant was put on the market so that he would be able to purchase both the source of his income and his home rather than let it go to a stranger.

Another factor spurring millers towards ownership was the already noticed reluctance of landowners to make repairs and, especially, to introduce improvements. Landowners were, in the words of one old miller, 'awfu sweir to put in new machinery'. If a miller wanted new equipment he had to buy it himself. He was naturally unwilling to restock the mill with machinery at his own expense if he might be evicted or have his rent put up at the next term. So the miller who had capital saved and who wanted to improve was likely to buy a mill when he could.

For one reason and another, then, millers moved fairly often during their lifetimes and with extra frequency during their youth. Though a served apprenticeship was desirable it was not insisted upon. A ploughman who had acquired a bit of experience by helping about the mill, perhaps with an eye to courting the miller's daughter, had a good chance of getting a job in the mill without having served his three years under a miller. And as so many millers were millers' sons they could be said to have served their apprenticeships while hardly out of long frocks. The 'secret mystery of the miller's word' began to have some currency among mill servants during the nineteenth century. The rites accompanying the conferring of the secrets upon the apprentice were similar to those of Freemasonry and of the Horsemen, but the mill as a setting for the ceremony, with its creaking and clacking machinery and its dark cobwebby shadows, added some extra drama to the ritual. The young miller, blindfolded and half undressed, kneeling on one knee among the corn firlots with his leather apron tied round his neck, was made to promise to help his brother millers in adversity and was put through some fairly alarming trials involving a good deal of horseplay and devil raising. Then he was taught 'the word' which was, interestingly enough, 'ART', and was told how to stop a mill by taking three steps backward in the name of the devil and gathering some earth from a grave to scatter in the lade by the mill wheel, no doubt a useful piece of knowledge. How far this 'fe-fa-fumry', as one writer called it, was believed in is hard to say, but it was doubtless the excuse for some intake of alcohol in a dry and thirsty job. Almost certainly those who joined in the ceremonies knew very well that 'the whole art of millery is of no more value, in the estimation of an educated and intelligent man, than the explosion of a quantity of air, when the rectum of an old horse has been the condenser.'[13]

At any rate, most mills were operated by father and son where there was a son, with the help of another man. There were, of course, regional differences, some of the larger, wheat-grinding mills employing larger numbers of men even before they turned to steam power. But in the north a miller could give employment only to a couple of men. Even his sons, if they proved too many, had to find work on the farms round about, or perhaps with millers some distance away who had no sons of their own.

Imperceptibly the country miller's status within the community had changed between the eighteenth and nineteenth centuries. The size of the mill, the number of men employed and the quantity of produce had shown some increase until the first quarter of the nineteenth century but they remained remarkably unchanged thereafter, whereas, during the same period, many very small farms had been absorbed into larger ones and the feudal estates had been broken. Tenant farmers had increased the size of their land holdings, their prosperity and their status. In many cases they had built better houses for themselves and banished their servants from their kitchens. Millers, who had once owed allegiance only to the barony and had enjoyed some superiority over the farmers, now found themselves very often paying rent to farmers who had taken over the land on which the mills stood and so, in both the social and legal sense, the farmers became their 'superiors'. In some cases the farmer, instead of putting a tenant into the mill on his land, chose to put in a miller/employee and to keep the handling of the mill's business to himself. Customers then went to the mill for their meal but to the farm to pay for it. Thus the miller became in these cases merely a paid technician instead of the minor capitalist he had hitherto been.

At the same time the miller's mechanical skills were no longer unique. The eighteenth century miller had enjoyed the awe with which an uneducated community had regarded his ability to make wind and water work on his behalf and his understanding of the mysteries of gearing. But in the nineteenth century these things became matters of common knowledge. Townsmen were accustomed to the wonders of steam power, and on the farms the ubiquitous threshing mill had introduced rural workers to the principles of mechanics. Villages had business enough for country millwrights, and millers became almost as dependent on their services as anyone else. So, although millers retained some skill and ingenuity above those of the common agricultural workers, they were not so much wondered at, nor were they so highly regarded for them. Similarly their perhaps slightly superior education during the eighteenth century was at least caught up with, if hardly overtaken, by the farmers during the nineteenth century.

What millers lost in social status, however, they may perhaps have gained to some extent in the regard of the community. With a properly agreed payment for their services there was much less occasion for contest about their profits and less need for unscrupulous millers to cheat their customers. The constant accusations of dishonesty and extortion died away. Even in the districts where thirlage still prevailed — and there were still quite a number of them — it seems to have been justly applied and equably accepted. Millers began to be trusted as members of rural society in a way they had not been before. They grew to be respected and well liked. In Forglen, in Banffshire, the minister wrote, as if with some surprise: 'There is a smith, an elder of the church, and a miller fit to be one.'[14] That was in the 1790s. By the 1840s a few millers were beginning to be counted among the heritors of the parish although they were always among those of 'smaller property'.[15] Those landowners engaged in the Utopian dream of planning the perfect village settlement included millers among the upright and congenial settlers they hoped to attract. Colonel Dirom's plan for Bridekirk, for instance, proposed that 'on the opposite side of the river a situation is feued for corn mills . . . the great advantage to be derived from such an establishment is the increased value that lands acquire from having a number of industrious people settled in the heart of an estate.'[16]

The nineteenth century miller hoped that his sons might marry into the farming rather than the servant class. John Ross, the miller at Kildonan, courted Eppy Mackay, housekeeper at the manse and therefore a most respectable house servant. But he was a 'cake and pudding wooer', that is, glad enough to come courting while the kitchen provided plenty of feasting — a cupboard lover. When Eppy lost her job he transferred his affections to a farmer's daughter. Their wedding feast, incidentally, lasted throughout two whole days and culminated in the procession of the whole wedding company over the frozen river to a house-warming party at the mill.[17]

The miller was an employer rather than an employee, but only on a very small scale. He was tenant rather than owner of his mill in almost every case. However hard he worked, he could not fail to be dependent upon the agricultural prosperity of his neighbourhood. His trade gave him a little more stability than the farmers had, but he still operated too near the verge of failure. For a clever man — and millers were cleverer than most — the difficulty of making much more than a living was depressing. William Gaudy, the miller of Lunan, wrote one night in black letters across the sums in his meal account book, 'This is near Christmas but its no like to Be a great Christmas wi me in this Clorty Country and I am in a state of hypecondria and nothing can pleasure me.' But William had an illiterate wife and ten children. His chances of rising out of the mud were poor, in spite of his horse and his cow and his well-fed pigs.

The miller of the end of the eighteenth century and the beginning of the nineteenth had enjoyed some prosperity. High prices for corn, occasioned both by the embargo on imports and the increased demand from the growing industrial towns made certain that farmers would continue to plant cereals. The town mills had not yet equipped themselves sufficiently well to cope with the whole demand and the grocery trade was not yet organised. At the same time thirlage astrictions still applied to many estates and millers were protected from competition for customers and helped by estate expenditure of capital on their buildings and machinery.

But it was a short-lived happy period in which the troubles to come could already be seen. Although the growth of industry increased demand for meal, it also increased the clamour for riverbank sites. Millers, just when their customers were on the increase, found themselves competing in a fight for water power with the new capitalists of the textile trade. It was a battle they were not equipped to win, and wherever the spinning and bleaching mills crept along the rivers they displaced the meal mills. Sometimes this was only a temporary setback and, with the advent of steam power, the spinning mills moved into the towns and allowed the old wheels to revert to corn milling.[18] More often the millers, once displaced from a river, did not come back to it. The delay in abolishing the thirlage system meant that water milling emerged from its period of mediaeval restriction so late that it was faced too immediately with competition for water power, involving endless lawsuits, competition from new, steam-powered town flour mills and competition from retail grocers' and bakers' shops. The abolition of the Corn Laws allowing the import of cheap foreign wheat meant that the meal miller had to face up to the new demand for white flour at the same time as the grocery trade was organising itself, with wholesale and retail outlets, to carry the new products into regions which had hitherto been supplied solely by the meal mills. The traditional meal miller had only a short period of possible expansion before imported American wheat flour and the invention of roller milling left water-powered meal milling as a rural relic.

Yet there were whole areas of Scotland in which these developments were by no means apparent, and there the miller flourished. In the North-East, as we have seen, oatmeal played, if anything, a larger part in the ordinary people's diet. For Scotland as a whole the number of people working in industry was slow to overtake the number working in agriculture and the agricultural population remained heavily dependent upon oatmeal for their daily food even where white bread was beginning to be adopted. Some meal mills, like Grant's oat flour mills on the Dighty near Dundee, expanded throughout the nineteenth century, while still using water power, by refining and specialising their product. Others, like Kirriemuir's, in areas where farm wages were paid in bolls of oatmeal until the 1950s, remained prosperous with very little change in their equipment and organisation. Not many millers grew rich but a very large number continued to operate in exactly the same way as their forefathers until the Second World War. Then Government policy demanded a wholesale switch to animal feed milling to replace the very large pre-war quantities of imported feedstuffs for which there was not now room in the merchant shipping convoys. The mills adapted to this wartime need and in many cases did not switch back after the war to meal milling, which required more skill and brought less profit. The jerky working of a tractor engine will suffice to crush animal food, and the water wheel, whose beautifully smooth operation produced the best oatmeal, was often allowed to fall into disuse and disrepair.

The last decades have seen the amalgamation of numbers of small mills into a few large milling companies whose executives, while showing some interest in and concern for the old mills for which they have now become responsible, are necessarily motivated chiefly by economic pressures towards rationalisation and modernisation. There remain a very few independently owned water-powered meal mills, those for instance at Benholm and at Peterculter, cherished now but perhaps unlikely long to outlive their present owners. In England and in Scandinavia public interest in water mills has ensured that numbers of them survive and are preserved either with public funding as museums of traditional craft or with private backing as profit-making tourist attractions. In Scotland, perhaps because it is a relatively short time since water mills were a common enough sight in our countryside, we have been slow to recognise that they have been steadily disappearing since the end of the last war. There has been of recent years some revival of interest in the rural traditions of Scotland. It would be unfortunate if public interest in the traditional meal mill were to be aroused only after the last of them has gone.

NOTES

1. S.R.O. GD 135/39
2. 'The Miller Explains', from *Hamewith*, by Charles Murray, introd. Andrew Lang, London 1911, 18
3. William Gaudy's meal book
4. 'The Miller Explains', from Murray, *Hamewith*
5. Mr Coutts from Kildrummy used to travel to Alford to pick the stones at Montgarrie Mill. Information from his daughter
6. See pp. 156-7
7. See p. 49
8. Gorrie, *Passages in the Life of a Ploughboy*, 43
9. 'It wasna his wyte he was late', by Charles Murray, *In the Country Places*, London 1920, 1
10. Carter, Ian, 'Class and culture among farm servants in the North East, 1840-1914', in MacLaren, A.A., ed., *Social Class in Scotland*, Edinburgh, 1977
11. From 'Nickie Tams', traditional bothy ballad

12. Most of the present-day retired millers had spent a period of their youth working for millers at some distance from their homes

13. Singer, *An Exposition of the Miller and Horseman's Word*, 5

14. *O.S.A.*, 14, 537

15. *N.S.A.*, VIII, 156; *Ibid.*, XII, 278

16. Dirom, Alexander, 'Remarks upon the preceding paper', *Prize Essays and Transactions of the Highland Society of Scotland*, 2, 267-9. For 'the preceding paper' see Rennie, Robert, 'Plan of an inland village', *loc. cit.*, 250-66

17. Sage, *Memorabilia Domestica*, 99

18. Jespersen, 'Watermills on the River Eden', 237

Bibliography

Manuscript Sources

National Register of Archives, Scotland:
Clayhills-Henderson Papers NRA(S) 1511
Hamlyn/Angus Milling Company Records, including Cupar Town Mills, Kirriemuir Mills and North of Scotland Milling Company Mill, NRA(S) 1138
Alex M'Dougall, tacksman of the Perth Meal and Barley Mills, sederunt books, 1826-1846, NRA(S) 1510
Maltmen Incorporation of Dundee, NRA(S) 1795

Scottish Record Office:
Abercairney Estate Papers GD 24
Airlie Estate Papers GD 16
Benholm Estate Papers GD 4
Cassillis Estate Papers GD 25/8
Gilmour Estate Papers GD 1
Seaforth Estate Papers GD 46
Broughton Estate Papers GD 10
Dalhousie Estate Papers GD 45
Registers of Sasines

Privately held:
William Gaudy's Meal Book and other papers

Books and Articles

Adam, James, 'On the construction of reservoirs of water for agricultural purposes', *T.H.A.S.S.* 1833, 2nd ser. VI, 308-14

Adam, R. J., *Sutherland Estate Management, 1802-16*, S.H.S., Edinburgh, 1972

Adams, Ian H., *Descriptive List of Plans in the Scottish Record Office*, H.M.S.O., Edinburgh, 1966

Agricultural Labourer — see Report of the Royal Commission on Labour

Anderson, James, *General View of the Agriculture of the County of Aberdeen*, Edinburgh, 1794

Arbuthnot, James, of Rora, 'A true method of treating light, hazelly ground', Buchan Farmers Society, 1835

Ayrshire and Galloway Archaeological Society, *Charters of the Abbey of Crosraguel*, Edinburgh, 1886

Balfour, Sir James, of Pittendreich, *Practicks of Scots Law*, ed. Peter McNeill, Edinburgh, Stair Society, 1962-3

Barron, D. G., *Court Book of the Barony of Urie, 1604-1747*, S.H.S., Edinburgh, 1892

Baxter, T. C. et al, *Dietary Surveys of Dr Edward Smith, 1862-3*, London, 1970

Beatson, Robert, of Pitteadie, *General View of the Agriculture of the County of Fife*, Edinburgh, 1794

Bennett, R. and Elton, J., *History of Corn Milling*, 4 vols, London, 1898-1904

Berg, Gosta, 'The introduction of the winnowing machine in Europe in the 18th century', *Tools and Tillage*, 1, 1976

Beveridge, David, *Culross and Tulliallan*, Edinburgh, 1885

Boucher, C. T. C., *John Rennie, 1761-1821*, Manchester, 1963

Brunskill, R. W., *Illustrated Handbook of Vernacular Architecture*, London, 1970

Buchan-Hepburn, George, *General View of the Agriculture and Rural Economy of East Lothian*, Edinburgh, 1794

Buchanan, Mungo, 'Notice of a pair of quern stones found at Highland Dykes near Falkirk', *P.S.A.S.* XLVI, 1911/12, 367

Burnett, John, *Plenty and Want*, London, 1966

Butt, John, *The Industrial Archaeology of Scotland*, Newton Abbot, 1967

Butt, John, Donnachie, Ian L. and Hume, John R., *Industrial History in Pictures*, Newton Abbot, 1968

Butt, John and Lythe, S.G.E., *An Economic History of Scotland, 1100-1939*, London, 1979

Cadell, Patrick, *The Iron Mills at Cramond*, Edinburgh, 1973

Caird, J. B., 'The Making of the Scottish Rural Landscape', *Scot. Geog. Mag.* 80, 1964, 72-80

Caird, J. B., 'Land of the Scots: Revolution on the Farm', *Geographical Magazine*, LI, 12, 1979, 832-7

Cameron, Archibald C., *The History of Fettercairn*, Paisley, 1899

Cameron, Donald Kerr, *The Ballad and the Plough: a Portrait of the Old Scottish Farm Touns*, London, 1978

Carlisle, Nicholas, *Topographical Dictionary of Scotland*, London, 1813

Carter, Ian, *Farm Life in Northeast Scotland, 1840-1914: The Poor Man's Country*, Edinburgh, 1979

Census of Production, 1907, *P.P.* Cd. 6320 Final Report, Parts II-VII, Section VII, *Food, Drink and Tobacco Trades*

Chalmers, George, *Caledonia*, London, 1807

Chambers, Robert, *Domestic Annals of Scotland*, Edinburgh, 1885

Collins, E. J. T., 'Dietary change and cereal consumption in Britain in the 19th century', *Ag. Hist. Rev.* 23, 1975

Colville, J., 'Lowland Scotland in the 18th century', *Blackwoods Magazine*, Edinburgh, 1892

Commissioners of the Annexed Estates in Scotland, *Rules and Articles for the Improvement of Lowland/Highland Farms*, Edinburgh, 1773-4

Cramond, W., *Annals of Fordoun*, Montrose, 1831

Cregeen, Eric, *Argyll Estate Instructions, 1771-1805*, S.H.S. Edinburgh, 1964

Cruden, Stewart H., 'The horizontal water mill at Dounby', *P.S.A.S.* LXXXI 1948/9, 43

Curwen, E. C., *Plough and Pasture: the Early History of Farming*, New York, 1953

Devine, T. M., ed., *Lairds and Improvement in the Scotland of the Enlightenment*, Edinburgh, 1979

Donnachie, Ian L., *The Industrial Archaeology of Galloway*, Newton Abbot, 1971

Donnachie, Ian L., 'Sources of capital in the Scottish brewing industry, 1750-1830', *E.H.R.* 2nd ser. XXX, 2, 1977

Donnachie, Ian L. and Stewart, Norma K., 'Scottish windmills: an outline and survey', *P.S.A.S.* XCVIII 1964/5, 276

Edward, Robert, *A Description of the County of Angus*, Dundee, 1793

Evans, Oliver, *Young Millwright and Miller's Guide*, Philadelphia, 1826

Fairbairn, Sir William, *Treatise on Mills and Millwork*, London, 1861

Fairlie, S., 'The corn laws and British wheat production, 1829-76', *E.H.R.* 2nd ser. XXII, 1969, 109-16

Farmers Magazine, Edinburgh, 1800-30 (especially 'Agricultural Intelligence')

Fay, C. R., 'The miller and the baker: a note on commercial transactions', *Cambridge Historical Journal* I, 1923-5, 89

Fenton, Alexander, 'The place of oatmeal in the diet of Scottish farm servants in the 18th and 19th centuries', *Studia Ethnographica et Folkloristica in Honorem Bela Gunda*, Debrecen, 1971

Fenton, Alexander, 'Farm servant life in the 17th-19th centuries', *Scottish Agriculture*, 1964-5, LXIV, rep. Scottish Country Life Museums Trust, 1975

Fenton, Alexander, 'Traditional elements in the diet of the Northern Isles of Scotland', *Ethnological Food Research*, Helsinki, 1975, 2-16, rep. Scottish Country Life Museums Trust, Edinburgh, 1976

Fenton, Alexander, *Scottish Country Life*, Edinburgh, 1976

Fenton, Alexander, *The Northern Isles: Orkney and Shetland*, Edinburgh, 1978

Findlater, Charles, *General View of the Agriculture of the County of Peebles*, Edinburgh, 1802

Findlay, William, *Oats*, Edinburgh, 1956

Forrester, David Marshall, *Logiealmond*, Edinburgh, 1944

Franklin, T. Bedford, *A History of Scottish Farming*, London, 1952

Fraser, James, 'On the extended application of water and other power to farm purposes', *T.H.A.S.S.* 2nd ser. 7, 1832, 61

Fraser, W. R., *A History of Laurencekirk*, Edinburgh, 1880

Freeman, M. D., 'Milling capacity in Portsmouth', *Ind. Arch.* II, 2, 1974

Gentleman Farmer, The, being an Attempt to improve Agriculture, 4th ed. Anon., Edinburgh, 1798

Gibb, D. Robert Shirra, *A Farmer's Fifty Years in Lauderdale*, Edinburgh, 1927

Gilly, W. S., *The Peasantry of the Border*, Edinburgh, 1842

Gorrie, David, *Passages in the Life of a Ploughboy*, Dundee, 1857

Gourvish, T. R., 'Cost of Living in Glasgow in the early 19th century', *E.H.R.* 2nd ser. XXV, 1972, 73

Graham, Henry Grey, *The Social Life of Scotland in the 18th Century*, London, 1909

Grant, James, *Old and New Edinburgh*, London n.d.

Gray, Andrew, *The Experienced Millwright*, Edinburgh, 1804

Gray, Andrew, *Explanation of the engravings of the most important implements of husbandry used in Scotland*, Edinburgh, 1814

Gray, W. Forbes and Jamieson, J., *East Lothian Biographies*, Haddington, 1941

Grigor, Rev. Walter, 'Kilns, mills, millers, meal and bread', *Buchan Farmers Club*, 3, 1892-5, 126-159

Gunn, Clement B., *Records of the Baron Court of Stitchill, 1655-1807*, S.H.S. Edinburgh, 1905

Hall, Rev. James, *Travels in Scotland by an Unusual Route*, London, 1807

Hamilton, Henry, *Selections from the Monymusk Papers, 1713-1755*, S.H.S. Edinburgh, 1945

Hamilton, Henry, *Life and Labour on an Aberdeenshire Estate, 1735-1755*, Third Spalding Club, Aberdeen, 1946

Hamilton, Henry, *An Economic History of Scotland in the 18th Century*, Oxford, 1963

Handley, James E., *Scottish Farming in the 18th Century*, London, 1953

Hay, Geoffrey D., 'The work of the Royal Commission', *Scot. Arch. Forum*, 8, 1977

Hay, T. T., 'Watermills in Japan', *Ind. Arch.* 6, 4, 1969

Headrick, Rev. James, *General View of the Agriculture of the County of Angus*, Edinburgh, 1813

Henderson, John, *General View of the Agriculture of the County of Caithness*,

London, 1812

Henderson, John, *General View of the Agriculture of the County of Sutherland*, London, 1812

H.M.S.O., Ministry of Public Building and Works, *Click Mill, Dounby, Orkney*, Edinburgh, 1966

Hobsbawm, E. J., 'The British standard of living, 1790-1850', in Hobsbawm, ed., *Labouring Men*, London, 1968

Holderness, B. A., 'Credit in English rural society before the 19th century', *Ag. Hist. Rev.* 24, 2, 1976

Horn, Barbara L. H., *Letters of John Ramsay of Ochtertyre, 1799-1812*, S.H.S. Edinburgh, 1966

Houston, James M., 'Village planning in Scotland, 1745-1845', *Advancement of Science*, 1948, 18, 129-32

Hume, John R., *The Industrial Archaeology of Glasgow*, Glasgow and London, 1974

Hume, John R., *The Industrial Archaeology of Scotland: the Lowlands and Borders*, London, 1976

Hume, John R., *The Industrial Archaeology of Scotland: the Highlands and Islands*, London, 1977

Hunter, Robert, Advocate, *A Treatise on the Law of Landlord and Tenant*, 4th ed., Edinburgh, 1876

Hutchison, Robert, 'Dietaries of Scotch agricultural labourers', *T.H.A.S.S.* 4th ser. II, 1-29, 1869

Hutton, Kenneth, 'Distribution of wheel-houses in the British Isles', *Ag. Hist. Rev.* 24, 1, 1976

Jamieson, John, *A Dictionary of the Scottish Language*, Edinburgh, 1846

Jespersen, Anders, *Nationalmuseets Molleudvalg, Annual Reports*, Copenhagen, 1966

Jespersen, Anders, *Reports on Watermills*, 1-15, 1955-66, Copenhagen

Jespersen, Anders, 'Watermills on the River Eden', *P.S.A.S.* XCVII 1963/4, 237

Jespersen, Anders, *Standard Proposals for Mill Survey Work*, Copenhagen, 1965

Jespersen, Anders, *Danish Mill Preservation Board: Problems of Preservation*, Copenhagen, 1966

Jones, David, 'Water powered corn mills in England, Wales and the Isle of Man', *Transactions of the 2nd International Symposium on Molinology*, 1969, 303

Journal of Agriculture, 'Report by a Committee of the Synod of Angus and Mearns as to Agricultural Labourers, 1856', March 1861, 729

Juridical Society of Edinburgh, *Complete System of Conveyancing*, Edinburgh, 1907-8

Juridical Styles — see Juridical Society of Edinburgh

Keith, George Skene, *General View of the Agriculture of the County of Aberdeen*, Aberdeen, 1811

Knowles, L. C. A., *The Industrial and Commercial Revolutions in Great Britain during the 19th Century*, London, 1946

Levitt, Ian and Smout, T. C., 'Some weights and measures in Scotland', *S.H.R.* LVI, 2, 162, 1977

Levitt, Ian and Smout, T. C., *The State of the Scottish Working Class in 1843*, Edinburgh, 1979

Lythe, S. G. E., *The Economy of Scotland*, Edinburgh, 1960

Lythe, S. G .E., 'The Tayside meal mobs, 1772-3', *S.H.R.* XLVI, 1967, 28

Macadam, J. H., ed., *The Baxter Books of St Andrews*, Leith, 1903

Macgrigor, A., *Reports on the State of Certain Parishes in Scotland, 1627*, Maitland Club, Edinburgh, 1835

Mackenzie, Sir George Stuart, *General View of the Agriculture of the Counties of Ross and Cromarty*, London, 1813

Mackenzie, Sir J., Bart., of Gairloch, *Hints for the use of Highland tenants and cottagers, by a proprietor*, Inverness, 1838

MacLaren, A. Allan, ed., *Social Class in Scotland*, Edinburgh, 1976

McNeill, F. Marian, *The Scots Kitchen*, London, 1971

MacPhail, J. R. N., *Papers from the collection of Sir William Fraser*, S.H.S. Edinburgh, 1924

Mactaggart, John, *The Scottish Gallovidian Encyclopaedia*, London, 1824

Marwick, Sir J. D. and Renwick, R., *Extracts from the Records of the Burgh of Glasgow, IX, 1796-1806*, Scottish Burgh Record Society, Glasgow, 1916

Maxwell, Robert, *Select Transactions of the Honourable Society of Improvers*, Edinburgh, 1743

Melville, Lawrence, *Errol: its Legends, Lands and People*, Perth, 1935

Millar, A. H., *A Selection of Scottish Forfeited Estates Papers*, S.H.S. Edinburgh, 1909

Mitchison, Rosalind, *Agricultural Sir John*, London, 1962

Mitchison, Rosalind, 'Movements of Scottish corn prices in the 17th and 18th centuries', *E.H.R.* 2nd ser. XVIII, 1965, 289-90

Morison, William Maxwell, ed., *Decisions of the Court of Session*, vols 1-21, Edinburgh, 1801

Morton, J. C., *Cyclopedia of Agriculture*, London, 1855

Murray, R. W., 'A brief survey of the history and nature of millwrighting', *Journal of the Institute of Electrical Engineers*, 1944, 91, 1, 41

Musson, A. E. and Robinson, Eric, *Science and Technology in the Industrial Revolution*, Manchester, 1969

Pole, William, *The Life of Sir William Fairbairn, Bart.*, London, 1877

Porteous, Alex., *History of Crieff*, Edinburgh, 1912

Quinault, R. E., Review of E. J. T. Collins, 'Dietary change' (q.v.), *Ag. Hist. Rev.* XXIII, 2, 1975

Report from the Committee to consider present high prices of Provisions, *P.P.* XXVIII, 1799/1800

Report of the Royal Commission on Labour, *The Agricultural Labourer, P.P.* III Scotland, 1893, C 6894 xv, XXXVI

Reynolds, John, *Windmills and Watermills*, London, 1970

Robertson, A. D., *Lanark: the Burgh and its Councils, 1469-1880*, Lanark, 1974

Robertson, George, *General View of the Agriculture of Kincardineshire*, London, 1813

Robertson, George, *General View of the Agriculture of Mid-Lothian*, Edinburgh, 1793

Robertson, George, *The Progress of Improvements in the Lothians*, London, 1829

Robertson, James, *General View of the Agriculture of the County of Perth*, Perth, 1799

Roger, James, *General View of the Agriculture of Angus or Forfar*, Edinburgh, 1794

Sage, Rev. Donald, *Memorabilia Domestica: or Parish Life in the North of Scotland*, 1st ed. Wick, 1889; rep. Edinburgh, 1975

Sanderson, Margaret H. B., 'The feuing of Strathisla: a study in 16th century social history', *Northern Scotland*, 1979, 2, 1, 3

Scots Law Times Reports, Edinburgh, 1893-1901

Scott, David, *Engineer and Machinist's Assistant*, 2 vols, Glasgow, 1847

Shaw, Patrick, ed., *Principles of the Law of Scotland contained in Lord Stair's Institutions*, Edinburgh, 1863

Sinclair, Sir John, ed., *Statistical Account of Scotland*, 21 vols, Edinburgh, 1791-9 (*O.S.A.*)

Sinclair, Sir John, *General Report on the Agricultural State and Political Circumstances of Scotland*, 2 vols, Edinburgh, 1814

Singer, William, *An Exposition of the Miller and Horseman's Word*, Aberdeen, 1865

Skene, Sir John, of Curriehill, *Regiam Majestatem*, Edinburgh, 1609, Chapter 68, 'Burrow Lawes, of Millars', 126-7

Smiles, Samuel, *Lives of the Engineers*, London, 1861-2

Smith, Edward, *Fifth and Sixth Reports of the Medical Officer of the Privy Council*, London, 1863

Smith, Edward, *Foods*, London, 1883

Smith, J. H., *The Gordon's Mills Farming Club, 1758-1764*, Edinburgh, 1962

Smith, John, *General View of the Agriculture of the County of Argyll*, London, 1813

Smith, W. G., 'The improvement of cereals', *T.H.A.S.S.*, 5th ser. XXII, 1883, 106

Smout, T. C., *Scottish Trade on the Eve of Union, 1660-1707*, Edinburgh, 1963

Smout, T. C., 'Scottish landowners and economic growth, 1650-1850', *Scottish Journal of Political Economy*, XI, 1964, 218-234

Smout, T. C. and Fenton, Alexander, 'Scottish agriculture before the Improvers: an exploration', *Ag. Hist. Rev.* XIII, 1965, 73-93

Smout, T. C., *A History of the Scottish People, 1560-1830*, London, 1969

Souter, David, *General View of the Agriculture of the County of Banff*, Edinburgh, 1812

Stephen, Henry, *The Book of the Farm*, 5th ed., Edinburgh, 1908, vol 1, Land and its Equipment

Stoyel, Alan, 'The art of drying oats in Scottish kilns', *Scottish Industrial History*, Autumn 1976

Symon, J. A., *Scottish Farming Past and Present*, Edinburgh, 1959

Syson, Leslie, *British Water Mills*, London, 1965

Taylor, William, *Glen Fincastle, 1841-1901: a Study of a Perthshire Glen*, Edinburgh, 1968

Telford, Thomas, *On Mills*, London, 1796-8

Thomson, John, *General View of the Agriculture of the County of Fife*, Edinburgh, 1800

Transactions of the International Symposia on Molinology, Brede, 1965, 1969, 1971, 1977

Turner, W. H. K., 'The evolution of the pattern of the textile industry within Dundee', Inst. Brit. Geog. 18, 1952, 107-119

Turner, W. H. K., 'The significance of water power in industrial location: some Perthshire examples', *Scot. Geog. Mag.* 74, 1, 1958

Tytler, Alex. Fraser, ed., *Memoirs of the Life and Writings of the Hon. Henry Home of Kames*, Edinburgh, 1807

Ure, Andrew, *The Philosophy of Manufacture*, London, 1835

Ure, Andrew, *Dictionary of Arts, Manufactures and Mines*, London, 1859

Usher, Abbott Payson, *A History of Mechanical Inventions*, Harvard, 1974

Wailes, Rex, *The English Windmill*, London, 1954

Walker, Bruce, 'Notes on fieldwork', Scottish Vernacular Buildings Working Group Newsletters, 1-4, Dundee and Edinburgh, 1974-78

Walker, Bruce, 'Influence of fixed farm machinery on farm building design', *Scot. Arch. Forum* 8, 1977

Walker, Bruce, 'Vernacular buildings of N. E. Scotland: an exploration', Roy. Scot. Geog. Soc. 95, 1979, 45-60

Walker, N. M. L., ed., *Digest of Sheriff Court Cases, 1893-1943*, Edinburgh, 1944

Warden, Alexander J., *The Burgh Laws of Dundee*, London, 1872

Watt, James Crabb, *The Mearns of Old*, Edinburgh, 1914

Watts, R. G., 'Water power and the Industrial Revolution', *Transactions of the Cumbrian and Westmorland Antiquarian and Archaeological Society*, N. S., 67, 1967

Wight, Andrew, *Present State of Husbandry in Scotland*, Edinburgh, 1778-83

Wills, Virginia, ed., *Reports on the Annexed Estates, 1755-1769*, S.R.O. Edinburgh, 1973

Willsher, Betty and Hunter, Doreen, *Stones: 18th Century Scottish Gravestones*, Edinburgh, 1978

Wood, J. D., 'Regulating the settlers and establishing industry', *Scottish Studies*, 15, 1971

Young, David, *Farmers Account Book*, Edinburgh, 1768

Zupko, Ronald, 'Weights and measures in Scotland', *S.H.R.* LVI, 2, 1977, 162

Index